~~UN~~MUSICAL?

Redefining Musicality in a Disconnected World

Sara Stevens Zur, Ed.D.

Praise for *Unmusical*

Shining through this brilliant volume is the joyful essence of the musical experience, and the realization that we are all humanly wired to make music, to revel in the music that surrounds us, to know music as a part of our daily lives. Because of her own musical story, her interactions with musical children, her journeys into a wide expanse of cultural communities—in Israel, Arnhem Land (Australia), South Africa, and elsewhere, Sara Stevens Zur is persuasive in her pronouncement of the innate human capacity there is to sing, to dance, to play, and to value music as an indispensable part of our lives. This is an important read for those who wonder about their own musical inclinations and involvements, how musical we all are, and how fostering human musicality may be the way forward to a more balanced and joyful world.

— Patricia Shehan Campbell, University of Washington

Sara Stevens Zur's book offers a powerful reimagining of what it means to be musical, weaving together vignettes, cultural practices, and personal stories that challenge narrow definitions of talent. With insight and warmth, she demonstrates how music permeates many aspects of human life—from healing and activism to identity and everyday rituals— reminding us that we are all, in fact, musical beings.

—André de Quadros, Professor of Music, Boston University

Zur reframes what it means to be musical, reminding us that music is the timeless "human thread" that has bound people together, long before notes were written on a page. She challenges us to see musicality not as a skill reserved for the few but as a birthright we each carry. By inviting us to take ownership of our unique musical identities, in whatever form they take, she makes music feel personal, communal, and alive.

—Kimberly Monzón, Associate Professor of voice, Baylor University

In this daring book, Zur digs deep and asks important questions. She confronts conventional ways of thinking and challenges the reader to reconsider how they've been conditioned to listen to and play music.

—Joe Deninzon, violinist/rhythm guitarist in the band Kansas;
Lead singer and electric violinist of the band Stratospheerius

At 16, I was on American Idol — a moment that both highlighted my talent and revealed how media, as a cultural channel, can distort and diminish artistry by reducing it to age, image, or marketability. Instead of inspiring me, it left me questioning my place in music. Zur's reframing/shift reminds us that musicality is not defined by industry standards, or competition with others, and to reconcile this once and for all in this harsh/critical modern era. This book reclaims music as something for everyone with passion for music — not just the "chosen few."

—Melissa Karger, jazz singer

Sara Stevens Zur has been listening and watching children make music for decades. Her curiosity and enchantment has led her to fascinating conclusions about why children play with music and what we as adults can learn from them — both about how to teach them and how to grow ourselves musically. Telling stories collected over a lifetime, she advocates for a curriculum based in JOY — a truly novel and exciting concept. Recommended reading for all who have had or aspire to have musical experiences!

—Lori A. Custodero, Professor of Music Education,
Teachers College, Colombia University

Music isn't reserved for experts; it's a language we all share. This book helps make it joyful and deeply rewarding to bring music into your life, even if you don't have the "right" background or experience.

—Brian Karzen, singer and performance coach

Contents

Introduction

Vignette: The Subway Singer

"You better shut your mouth and sit back down! You're making a fool of yourself!" A girl, who looks about six years old, stops and glares at her older sister, who chides her with these harsh words. Up until a moment ago, she was dancing joyfully around the subway pole, her braided hair jangling with beads, as her song grew louder and bolder. The New York City subway is filled with sound. From the high-pitched tones of the trains accelerating out of the station, to the rhythmic *clatta-clack* of the wheels on the tracks, to the crowds of people going about their lives, it is a highly stimulating environment for the ears. Some riders open a book, read the paper, close their eyes, or adjust their earbuds, tuning out. Yet as a music teacher and music education researcher, I tune in to this subway song incident, waiting to see what will happen next. Will the young girl cry? Sit down with a huff? Shout back?

No. She takes a big breath and carries right on singing and dancing. As an experienced observer of young children's spontaneous singing, this girl's particular song and her will to sing do not strike me as unusual. What stops me cold in my tracks is her decisive action to ignore her sister—resiliency, rather than dejection. An inner knowing that superseded the force of judgment. What is happening inside her in that single moment? What inner musical knowledge or confidence does she possess that allows her to keep doing what feels good and right to her?

Children instinctively dance and sing throughout their day. It is both necessary and natural for them to express their lived experiences through song. As infants and babies, our caregivers used music to help soothe and regulate us throughout each transition in our day. Humans of all ages all over the world have made music since ancient times. Yet most adults lament that they are "not musical." At some point, most of us stop believing in our natural music-making capabilities. Children stop feeling free enough to sing and dance on the subway, in public places, or even in their own homes, and start responding to judgment of their musical abilities. Reclaiming our musical selves is not about skill, talent, or performative abilities. It is about connecting with a deep and precious part of our hearts.

An Urgent Call for Connection

As children, almost all of us sang and danced freely—we had that connection to music, but somewhere along the way, we lost it. We were told to sit down quietly, to mouth the words, or tone it down. Many of us have come to believe that we aren't musical at all. Before diving into how to reclaim our musicality and rewrite the score on our abilities, I want to explain why it is so important to do so.

We are at a unique moment in time that futurist Amy Webb describes as a "Technology Supercycle"—an extended period of change where the confluence of generative AI, biotechnology, and our very ecosystem is creating immense uncertainty[1]. These changes are happening so quickly that everything feels new and hurried all the time. We find ourselves questioning what it means to be human and figuring out how to feel at home in our shifting surroundings. Music (in its many forms) helps to regulate us. It stretches time and creates space for connecting with ourselves and others. Music offers us both a way to fit in through collective experiences, as well as a way of standing out through personal expression.[2] Music acts as a placeholder for specific times and

---

[1] "30 Takeaways from Futurist Amy Webb's Talk at SXSW." Https://Www.Siliconhillsnews.Com/2024/03/28/30-takeaways-from-fut Urist-amy-webbs-talk-at-sxsw-2024/. March 28, 2024.

[2] Lori A. Custodero, *Before We Teach Music: The Resonant Legacies of Childhoods and Children.* (Oxford University Press, 2024).

events in our lives and can transport us to those grounding places in an instant. Simply speaking, being in touch with our musicality gives us a sense of home within ourselves and helps us to understand our humanness in the face of change and uncertainty. Recognizing and believing in our musicality puts us in touch with what is most meaningful in our hearts. Our resumés and Instagram updates might be flashy and impressive, but we are simply saturated by societal crises from climate change to racial equity and political turmoil. Boston University professor André de Quadros says that we are experiencing an epidemic of loneliness. Humans have always turned to the arts, and most especially music, as they reach for hope, connection, and community.

The young girl on the subway instinctively knew that her musical outpouring should not be stopped. Her inner need to sing and dance superseded social norms. Yet so very many people in our culture are socially embarrassed by what they feel is an utter lack of musicality. What do people mean when they shyly state, "Oh, I'm not musical at all!"? Or when they say, "I can't sing to save my life!"? As our lives feel more and more fragmented, researchers Parker and Hutton state, "The human voice—specifically the singing voice—represents an important way for individuals to care for one another in the world, a care desperately needed as discord appears more prevalent than consonance."[3]

Maybe it's time to understand that singing, or feeling musical, *can* actually save our lives.

Why Me?

I have been a music teacher and music researcher for over 25 years. I have taught music in preschools, home settings, parks, camp settings, and three different elementary schools. In my music classes composed of Palestinians and Jews in Israel, tears would run down my cheeks each time we sang Louis Armstrong's

---

[3] Hutton, J. C., and E. C. Parker. 2023. Review of *Singing and Caring*. In *The Oxford Handbook of Care in Music Education*, edited by Karen S. Hendricks, 268–79. York: Oxford University Press.

"What a Wonderful World." As a Fulbright scholar in Australia, I learned children's songs from an indigenous woman in a dusty one-room schoolhouse in Arnhem Land, and worked with a teenage indigenous rock band in Darwin. In South Africa, I learned Freedom Songs and heard the true story of "The Lion Sleeps Tonight"—a stolen song. Here in America, I have studied many singing cultures from the source, ranging from rural Appalachian Shape Note to Civil Rights songs, and First Nation ceremonial songs.

As a music teacher, I have worked with a widely diverse population of students, including nonverbal and neurodivergent children, newly arrived immigrant children, the children of millionaires, children so anxious that they only speak in whispers, and children who want their voices to be heard nonstop. In my thousands of conversations with parents and caregivers, I frequently hear about musical hopes and dreams, the many challenges of practicing an instrument, as well as the yearning that caregivers have to enrich their child's life through music. In these conversations, I always ask them to tell me about their musical interactions and traditions at home—the joyful and informal music-making experiences, such as family dance parties and invented songs. Over the years, I have come to understand the many ways that families can nourish and celebrate their child's musicality just by integrating the musical worlds that *they already have in place.*

My own musical journey from being a classical violinist to becoming a folk singer, a classroom teacher, and a researcher and scholar in music education included many twists and turns wherein my musical identity was challenged and reshaped. From performing in Carnegie Hall to learning Bulgarian harmonies and Jamaican mountain songs, I have personally experienced music-making in many different arenas across myriad cultural landscapes.

While working towards my doctoral degree in music education, I researched young children's music making in several different countries, seeking to understand how their creativity is connected to surrounding contexts and cultures. I was particularly fascinated with children's invented songs and spontaneous music-making. I wanted to understand the many reasons why children sing spontaneously throughout their day, as well as what makes their singing come to a stop. This is both a fascinating and awkward area of research. Beyond my official research in classrooms, I would frequently hear children singing around me in public and whip out my notebook or stare in fascination. A song-stalker! Staring at singing children in elevators, supermarkets, and parking lots is not socially acceptable. I often found myself having to explain my research to parents or caregivers so that they wouldn't think me odd.

As I analyzed the data from hundreds of incidents of spontaneous singing, I realized that children *have* to sing to get through their day, as they self-regulate, process information, socialize, and express themselves all through the music they create! In many ways, adults use music for the same reasons. We are usually too inhibited to create our own songs, or sing spontaneously as we walk down the street, but we use music to self-regulate, soothe, communicate, and connect, just as people have done for millennia.

All of these experiences, along with my research about children's music-making came to a startling head several years ago, when I was clearing out old emails and found a collection of "Musical Autobiography" homework assignments sent to me by former students at the Aaron Copland School of Music at Queens College in New York. This assignment, inspired by a class I had taken with Lori Custodero at Teachers College, invited students to write about significant musical memories and events that had shaped their lives from birth to the present. It was a required course, designed for undergraduate elementary school majors to learn ways of integrating music into their homeroom classes.

One of the unique aspects of Queens College is that the student body has an incredibly diverse range of cultures, religions, classes, and ages. I once counted up to thirteen different home countries represented in a class of just twenty-three students.

And yet, as I read through these old assignments, I was struck by how many stories had striking commonalities. I remembered how almost every student entered my classroom with what felt like an apology—"I'm sorry, but I'm not musical." Or, "I don't know why I'm here. I don't know anything about music." But in their autobiography assignments, almost all of them described a childhood rich with musical memories—parents or grandparents who sang to them, danced with them, and celebrated life events with music.

So many of these papers contained the sentence, "From that

moment on..." *From that moment on, I stopped playing the piano. From that moment on, I decided I would never audition again. From that moment on, I didn't sing in front of others. From that moment on, I decided to focus on writing instead of music.* For many of these young adults, there was a memorable turning point when they were made to feel unmusical. Music, which had been a powerful and welcoming aspect of their childhood, was closed off in their minds as an element of their adult identities. The idea that someone could be musical without being a performing musician was new to many of these students, and I remembered seeing tears in many of their eyes as they played with the possibility that they were all, at least in my mind, still musical people.

After reading through these old assignments and seeing this common thread, I began vigorously collecting more stories. I asked anyone I could grab hold of: "Did you have any musical turning points in your life?" and "What made you turn towards or away from feeling like a musical person?" I collected hundreds of stories from children, adolescents, and adults who willingly shared significant musical experiences from their lives. I interviewed professional musicians, as well as musicians who have non-musical careers, and also people who do not consider themselves particularly musical in any way.

For a while, I was convinced that a single moment of harsh musical judgment could potentially turn someone away from feeling musical forever. Perhaps this is why the singing girl on the subway and her resilience were so exciting to me. One interview led to another, and I found myself with an opportunity to interview the world-renowned cellist Yo-Yo Ma, who opened up an entirely new perspective for me.

When I first sat down with Yo-Yo, I asked him the same question I had been asking in each interview so far: Tell me about significant musical turning points in your life. Instead, he described how most people have a musical journey from "Rivulets to rivers," where musical identities take shape over the course of many micro-decisions and moments that eventually make it clear that one is on a musical path. There was no singular moment for Yo-Yo. Up until that point, I had heard so many "non-musicians" describe a single experience or moment that turned them away from music, and I had not considered that it could look quite different for professional musicians.

I then looked back through my other interviews with

professional musicians and found that this seemed to be the case for all of them! There seemed to be no single defining moment, but a series of affirming, encouraging musical experiences throughout their childhood and early adult years. For performing musicians, music seems to be a part of their surrounding world in such a way that makes mess-ups and harsh judgmental statements slide off their shoulders more easily.

Looking at these stories with fresh eyes, I began to realize something even more compelling and eye-opening: People who consider themselves "unmusical" are defining musicality in terms of a narrow performative lens (not being able to play the piano well, or sing in tune, for example). Yet for professional musicians, being musical is hardly about being in tune or about the technical aspects of practice. For them, it is mostly about the ability to deeply communicate with listeners and express something authentic that could allow others to feel something in a personal way. It was all about connection—that same vitally human thread of relating to others through the arts that has existed since ancient times, in traditional cultures all over the world. Where have we gone wrong? When did we lose this notion that music is just something that all humans do?

As I share these compelling stories with you throughout this book, I also provide research studies and personal experiences that highlight the importance of music in our lives. The array of stories and studies in this book offers us a chance to ask ourselves not *if* we are musical, but *how* we are musical. Whether someone chooses a career in music is not the point of this book. We know from anthropologists, psychologists, educators, therapists, and social workers that people need music to connect with themselves and with others. We know that music uplifts us, transforms us, heals us, and acts as a time capsule for the important moments in our lives. We all long to feel musical, yet very few people dare to call themselves musical people.

How we define musicality matters. This book will transform your thinking about what it means to be musical, as we take a deep dive into this essential question:

How do our society's definitions of "Music" and "Musical" allow or disallow us to live the rich and joyful lives we all long for and deserve access to?

This book is for anyone who has ever felt unmusical, who can't carry a tune. It is also for the hundreds of thousands of musicians and music teachers who hold the power to shape musical identities in others. If you are a parent or teacher, you will find both inspiration and relief as you realize how musical your children already are, and gain a deep understanding of how to easily influence and nourish your child's or student's musicality. Most importantly, this book is for anyone who yearns to feel musically connected.

In Part One, I will begin by showing you how you are biologically wired for musical expression and interaction, and share stories that illuminate why music was and is vital for human survival. Part Two takes you on a journey through your childhood musical development so that you can better recognize the musical parts of yourself that may have been erased or muted over time. Through the stories and research in Part Three, I will critically examine the reasons why our society has come to define musicality in the way that it does. You will learn to rewrite your own musical story, piecing together the reasons why you have come to believe what you do about your ability. Lastly, I will share resources and inspirations for reclaiming music as a natural part of your life.

Whether it's singing in the shower, dancing at a rock concert, soothing your baby, or performing a solo on stage, it is time to allow yourself the pleasure of playful musical exploration. As you read through the unique and sometimes surprising stories and research in this book, I invite you to be bold and brave with your musical experiments and expressions, not only for yourself but for others around you. When that little girl sang her heart out on the subway, she undoubtedly affected others nearby. There may have even been another child listening who was inspired to sing out too—who went on to feel bolder and brighter about being musical too.

Part One:
The Shaping of Our Musical Worlds

1 — Music in Our Bones

Vignette: Oh, Puerto Rico

"What's wrong with him?" asked Nina, one of my second graders, as we passed Omar, our school's Spanish teacher, on the way to my music class. Omar was visibly upset, talking in a hushed voice with another teacher. Students overheard bits and pieces: *completely destroyed... they lost everything...* As we made our way to music class that day, I sensed that my lesson plan was about to change. These students were suddenly worried about Omar and wanted to know what was going on.

In 2017, Puerto Rico was struck by two hurricanes, Maria and Irma, which devastated the island. It was my first year as an elementary school music teacher in Cambridge, MA, and many of my young students were talking about what they had heard on the news. As Nina's class entered the music room, she and her friends were still asking about Omar. I told them that he was from Puerto Rico and that most of his family still lived there—he was probably upset about the powerful hurricanes that had just damaged so many homes on the island. I explained that music helps people feel cared for and connected and asked them to think about a piece of music or a song that might make Omar feel better. What if we gave him a song that made him feel cared about and that could soothe him? What if he gave that song to his family? And what if this lifted their spirits as they shared it with others nearby?

We tossed around some options, but nothing felt quite right. Then Nina raised her hand: "How about if we make up our own song for him?" Though I had never tried to write a song before, and had never led students in a song-writing process, I took a big breath, scrapped my lesson plans for the week, and went for it. "What are some things we could say in our song?" I asked. Students started listing things:

—We love you
—We're here for you
—Have hope
—We're sorry about what happened
—All of that rain and wind was bad
—You can rebuild
—It takes great courage to go through this

Then, I heard a voice from the back of the class singing:

And then another voice:

I took out my guitar and started finding the chords to fit their melody. Little by little, a song was born that day. After a few more lines were in place, we decided to add the sounds of rain sticks, an ocean drum, and other small percussion instruments to round out the expressive feelings of water and storms. We practiced throughout the next three music classes until we felt ready to share, then invited Omar to come hear our song in our community room.

Omar listened with tears in his eyes and a hand on his heart. When the song was done, he thanked us and let us know how much it meant to him.

Omar shared the song with his family in Puerto Rico, and even though I don't know whether it was shared beyond that, I witnessed a few things about the effect of that experience. That second-grade class became passionate about the idea of creating healing music—music as a gift. The energy and time they spent thinking through those lyrics helped them process the event and made them feel connected to each other and to Omar profoundly. I myself felt strongly connected to Omar after sharing that song, and our collegial friendship deepened. I felt more securely connected to my new school community as they began to see me as someone who cared about them and who valued music as a community builder.

My students and I also felt more connected because they saw me as someone who valued and trusted their ideas, and who would journey with them through a creative process.

Creating one song to share with one person changed that person and affected our relationship and our community. As the pop star Bono famously said, "Music can change the world, because it can change people."

Music in Traditional and Ancient Cultures:

Some time after her divorce, my friend Lauren created a dating profile and entered the world of online dating. As a singer-songwriter, she decidedly began each potential connection with a question: "Any musical bones in your body?"

Lauren's potential dates often told her about how vital music was in their lives and how music was a lifesaver for them.

"For some people, it is like a life force that rushes into their very core," she said. "Music is important to everyone, but not everyone allows the music to come inside them and transform them."

Several men Lauren chatted with responded by saying, "Sorry—not a musical bone in my body." What did they mean by that? That they weren't performers or "good" singers, whatever that means?

How about you? What images or sounds are conjured in your mind when you hear the word *music*? Someone playing the guitar? A favorite song you like to listen to as you commute to work each day? A soothing lullaby that lulls your baby to sleep? If you are a person living in a Eurocentric industrialized culture during the 21st century, the concept of music probably makes you think of something you can listen to, dance to, or something that is produced using your voice or an instrument. Our modern English word for music comes from Ancient Greece—the Nine Muses, or goddesses who represented many art forms, including poetry, theater, song, dance, and playing instruments. These art forms were often expressed *together*. In other words, being "Muse-ical" has always meant to include art, poetry, theatre, and dance. Yet many people I have spoken with have said things like "I'm not musical, but I love dancing!"

Throughout the world, there were (and still are) many traditional language groups that did not have a separate term for what we might call "music." There might have been terms for specific rhythms or instruments or terms for songs that were intended to be used for a specific purpose, but the abstract notion of music as a separate art form was not common.

In many cultures, music-dance as a fully integrated concept was more common, and in many traditional cultures, language continues to reflect that integration. The music-dance connection can be found in Sanskrit—*sangīta*, in Thai—*wai khruu*, or the Nigerian Igbo word—*nkwa* (Trehub and Becker, 2015). For the Yolŋu People of Australia, whose traditions have remained largely in place for over 60,000 years, music is so intricately connected with other aspects of life that its meanings and definitions overlap with their cross-hatched bark art, astronomy, landscapes, and even the complex system of how people are named (Zur, 2007).

Traditional and indigenous cultures around the world seem to embody this broader, more inclusive definition of music, but we have largely lost what it truly means to be musical in the face of competition and Eurocentric colonization. I will explain this in greater depth throughout the chapters of this book. To begin to reclaim our musicality, it is vital to understand the essential and central role that music played in our lives in more traditional times, as well as our musical roots in early childhood, which we will explore in Chapter 5. Since music was an essential and natural part of being human, we also need to understand why it no longer feels that way! How did music go from being central to being perceived as something outside of the normal experience of being alive?

Throughout this book, as I write about music, you will probably find yourself thinking, "That's true for art as well!" Or "I feel that same way about dancing!" Yes! This is precisely because all forms of art provide humans with the same basic need for resonant and expressive connection. The focus of this book is music because that is my area of expertise. Music is also the first form of art that influences us, from the rhythms and sounds we hear in the womb to the musical interactions between caregivers and infants, and beyond. Music *is* in our bones from the time we enter the world.

Music, in its many definitions and forms, has been a part of daily life since the beginning of human existence. In pre-modern times, music had a purpose: to call the rain, bless an animal spirit, or assist the soul's passage into the afterlife. Songs and chants were used in indigenous sweat lodges to cleanse the spirit. Algonquin medicine men used songs to heal the sick (Pritchard, 2001). The Lebu people of Senegal have a deep ceremonial tradition called Ndeup, in which music, dance, grain, and animals are intensely incorporated to lift a person from depression (Solomon, 2001).

In Italy, the dancing trance-like music of the Tarantella worked to cure illnesses and heal sexual trauma. Songs could also be communicative, such as the *Dohori* songs of Nepal, used to sustain dialogue between two large groups of people. The powerful battle *Haka* chants of the Maori people made visitors aware of their power and standing.

Music also connected people to their natural surroundings. Singer-songwriter Moira Smiley, who studies global singing traditions, described how the Tuvans of northern Russia harmonized their "throat singing" with the rivers. The *Kulning* songs from Sweden were used to call out to animals across a far distance. Animal spirits were honored in Balinese *Kecak* chants, Scottish *Canntaireachd* songs, indigenous Australian *yidaki* playing, and ceremonial dance. In many cultures across the world, music-making ensured that the harvest would provide food. It defined a person's place within their family or acted as a cultural placeholder for stories, life lessons, or community expectations. Drum rhythms from various West African cultures, for example, were used to pass down cultural traditions and values through generations.

In many traditional cultures, when people gathered to sing as a community, it naturally ensured that commonalities were reinforced, allowing harmony to be established or reestablished in times of quarrel and unease. This is also the reason why music continues to act as a necessary binding force in our lives, connecting us with the feeling of home, both within ourselves and across physical or emotional distances. Yet feeling unmusical—singing as quietly as possible in church or while singing "Happy Birthday" to a friend, for example—can make us feel isolated and less connected to those we care about.

Food, Water, Shelter, the Arts

When my colleague Omar listened to the song we had created for him, he felt a deep sense of connection to our school community. Anthropologist Dissanayake explains that the arts provide humans with a way of experiencing themselves within their community, fulfilling basic needs for belonging, mutuality, meaning-making, and competence. She describes in detail how the arts were as essential as food, water, and shelter for human survival (Dissanayake, 2002). If this seems like a far-fetched notion, consider the fact that among the rudimentary tools, baskets, fishing equipment, and log homes, anthropologists have uncovered art and discovered musical instruments in every pre-modern culture ever examined. This indicates a biological need for artistic expression. The handle of a knife, for example, might have contained an intricately carved design. A clay pot had pictures or patterns around it. People adorned themselves with beautiful necklaces made of seashells, seed pods, feathers, or stones. People rhythmically clapped sticks together, blew into ram horns, danced, and sang. Even predating *homo erectus*, the most ancient instrument ever uncovered was a Neanderthal flute made from the leg bone of a cave bear, over 40,000 years ago (Borish).

If life was so basic and survival so unpredictable, why would humans take time to carve flutes or decorate their everyday objects with beautiful elements? And, as we will read about later in this book, why bother trying to build a music school in the middle of the West Bank during a war? Why would a pediatric oncologist, who spends his days trying to cure cancer in children, play his horn during his free time? In our modern everyday lives, the need for music (and the arts) is especially felt during hard times, when the world around us seems to fall apart.

I recently heard writer Suleika Jaouad describe how art changed how she felt about her life. Speaking with the author-activist Glennon Doyle on the podcast *We Can Do Hard Things* (May 23, 2024), she described her difficult recovery from a bone marrow transplant. Upon being released from the hospital, Suleika described her despondency at having to use a walker to get around. She explained that, being only 34 years old, each time she saw the walker, it seemed to be the very symbol of the weakness she felt. She decided one morning to order a glue gun and a giant bag of plastic rhinestones. She adorned and bedazzled that walker, and it completely changed her outlook, thus "alchemizing" her pain into something beautiful and fun.

On a mural tour in the Roxbury neighborhood of Boston, I met graffiti artist Genaro Ortega (artist name GeO "GoFive"), who said, "I was on the streets getting into all kinds of trouble. Being called to make murals gave me a reason to show up every day and paint. We played music together. We ate food together. It literally saved my life."

After my tour, I contacted GeO to ask if he could tell me more. We met on Zoom along with two other graffiti artists, Pheebz and Luis "TakeOne," who often collaborate with him. I share this conversation because it perfectly highlights how art and music can save lives:

GeO:

In school, I was a really bad student, and I only found out I was dyslexic in my Junior year of college. I was more of a visual-audio learner. So for a long time, I thought I was just stupid, but I could draw. I would literally draw through every single class. That's how I processed everything—visually. That went with music as well, so for a long time I did music. In high school, I was with a male *a cappella* group that toured around churches and did music. So, for me, music and art were the ways I registered/received the world.

I grew up in a rough neighborhood, or neighborhoods, I should say. Being able to go into different neighborhoods and being able to apply my art and apply my music and just feel comfortable where I went was definitely the way I was able to blend in with people and make friends. For me, art and music were my intro to everyone. That's how I made friends. How I started socializing with people. Those things were my voice and are definitely still a big part of my voice now. The neighborhood guys spent their time on the street corners. So some people would hire me to do stuff for them, so I wasn't in that environment. They would see me and know I had too much skill, so they would say, "Go draw this for the shirt business that I'm putting out…" or a barbershop. So they would always get me out of the areas I shouldn't have been in by using my art, by using my music. A lot of people viewed it for what it was before I had a chance to see it.

Me:

I remember on that tour how you mentioned music and how it was such an important part of keeping everyone there while you painted because it brought people together as they made the art.

GeO:

Oh yeah. It's funny because when we're painting, someone will see me and say, "Oh wow, you're not focused," and they'll put on some R&B music to help me refocus myself. And you know we've got these guys hanging around who listen to hip-hop all day long, and then they'll say, "Let's play some really romantic music to get you focused." You know what I mean? So it's kind of funny when it starts to happen, but for them to know me that well and understand, "Yeah—you need this." It's very helpful to me.

Luis:

I was talking with my wife today about when hip-hop became a more essential part of my life experience. I grew up in a mostly Puerto Rican neighborhood in Lower Roxbury—The South End—and graffiti legitimately saved my life. When I started with hip-hop, graffiti art became the main contribution to that culture for me. There was a lot of animosity between neighborhood youth, which created a dangerous environment. Just crossing the street was dangerous. I was stuck within my two to three blocks until people realized that I did art. So I did graffiti, and because of the graffiti, I had access to those other neighborhoods because they knew I was a graffiti writer. That allowed me in a lot of spaces to be safe. I could walk around safely. It wasn't about gangs. It was the neighborhood you were from. You were just as likely to get hurt just for being there. But because I did art and graffiti, I was safe.

Pheebz:

I've always made art. I don't stop. Art keeps me alive. Literally, actually. I have super depression problems, and if my hands aren't busy or my mind's not occupied, I'm in hell, and sometimes just picking up a pen and paper is what I need. But that being said, I have this drive to always make something to survive. I've met other people who feel the same way. If there's anything I've learned from this, it's basically just that we're not all isolated in that feeling. We all have our struggles and things we go through, so to be able to contribute my own voice to that, onto the walls, and to give the kids or whoever else is looking at the walls, the inspiration that they can contribute to something bigger than themselves. It's never easy to get out of your own mind and get out of that isolation hole, and because art saved me, I'm always going to share it, and I'm never going to gatekeep *(leave people out, or try to get ahead of other artists)*. I'd rather everyone gets to experience it in case it's something that they also need.

GeO:

For me, it's definitely a big part of my voice. It's how I truly learned to communicate with people outside of just expressing anger. Anger, I was able to express super easily. For me, it was everything else. I couldn't express what else I was feeling, or how I wanted you to see me, or what I was thinking. It was just about anger. Art and music helped me transition and express other things super smoothly.

On our mural tour, graffiti artist Robb "ProBlack" Gibbs led us to a space in the school where they had painted the very first mural. There had been a lot of violence occurring between gangs, and I remember him describing a body-shaped dent in the wall where the mural now was. I asked GeO, Luis, and Pheebz to tell me more about how art and music can transform a community space:

GeO:

Actually, Luis and I were the ones who painted that wall. It was the intro wall. The kids had been slamming and pushing themselves into that space, destroying that wall. So it had to be repaired every other week, and they got frustrated with having to repair it. Since it was a vocational school, it was part of their lessons (repairing that wall), but they just got tired of fixing that one space. It's a transitional space, so everyone walks through it. So they had to repair it. It couldn't sit like that for long periods of time, so what they did was they asked us to bring what we were doing outside the school inside. And that was the transitional wall that led us to do what we have done at Madison. Luis and I painted that wall, then we had two other artists come down and paint two other walls down the side. That introduced us to the inside of the school, to the teachers, and they decided that they wanted more of it. So we wound up coming back a second time and doing other murals inside the school itself. A lot of those transitional spaces went from being a nasty space, with human waste, drugs, and needles, and all that type of stuff...

We started painting in it, and the community and school started taking care of it. The janitors made it a point to make it part of their route and make sure it was clean because we had so many people visiting the space. So art itself changes spaces, and if you add events with music and art? Please! You'll have a party all the time.

Luis:

Yeah. I always talk about the Broken Windows Theory. You know, if you start with the broken windows and the more unwanted sides of society move in and it's kind of like graffiti was always one of those markers—the broken windows concept. But we, as a crew in the city of Boston, if not the art form, changed that theory. So many spaces we took over, and because of our art, it elevated the spaces.

In their case, creating public art brought people together as they played music, ate food, and worked to change the feeling of their community. The art itself also brought people together who cared about maintaining the new, better feeling of those spaces and continuing to uplift their community in that way. Community-building through the arts is certainly nothing new.

In traditional cultures, one's survival depended heavily on the strength of the community. The arts allowed people to connect with each other, express love, and experience a sense of belonging. These personal and interpersonal connections ensured one's place in society. The stories that Pheebz, Luis, and GeO shared serve as a reminder of how the arts can still be a central and essential part of everyday life. Of all the arts, music is something we can all access and take with us wherever we go. We hum, sing, tap rhythms, respond to a beat by rocking or dancing, or tune into our favorite tracks whenever the mood strikes.

Though many Western societies have lost the community connections that facilitate natural gatherings of informal music making, we can still see evidence of thriving musical communities. I am talking about everyday casual gatherings—not perfectionist performance. In Ireland, for example, music spills from the windows of pubs, where friends gather after a hard day's work. In Mexico, almost every social gathering includes guitars and singing. In other cities, DJs might set up on a street corner on a hot summer night, bringing an entire neighborhood out to dance.

The music that permeates most early childhood centers and elementary schools around the world is also a clear indicator that music is used to communicate and create community with children.

People all around the globe, whether they are corporate lawyers, sanitation workers, preschool teachers, or parrot trainers, regularly engage with music. My aunt Lidia sings Italian partisan songs while hanging laundry. Heather, my librarian friend, plays guitar and sings in a band. I am sure that you yourself can describe many moments when music filled you, changed you, or carried you through a rough time. Even the most industrial, capitalist societies realize that music can bring people together. Dissanayake (2002) describes it like this:

> The arts help us shape and control, thereby reducing anxieties and uncertainties. Describing in words, finding expressive movements, or creating visual images and forms for one's own loves, hates, fears, fantasies, and aspirations can become a way of articulating the inner world and then imagining extensions or alternatives to it. By enabling the searching out and expressing of one's own feelings and the exploration of others', the arts expand awareness of what it means to be human.

Music is especially powerful because it vibrates and resonates within our very cells. The power of music to instantly change a mood, shift a group of people from violence into peace, or heal our wounds makes it indispensable to human life. You don't need me to tell you just how powerful these musical connections are. You feel it within yourself each time you make a musical choice, go to a concert you love, or get jolted back to a specific time and place when you hear a specific piece of music from your past.

What I am hoping to show you through the stories, anecdotes, vignettes, and research in this book is this: there are many reasons why humans need music for survival, connection, and wellbeing, and the ways we interact with music make us, by nature, musical beings. We *do* have musical bones in our body, because music's necessity in our lives, whether we realize it or not, means that we cannot help being musical, each in our own way. We can locate those musical bones and reclaim our musicality as a true and important part of who we each are.

Folk Dancing on Patches of Ice

In our modern-day lives, most people don't speak as much about "needing" the arts. Yet in moments of crisis or during challenging times, music is one of the first things people use to feel better, heal, or connect in solidarity with others.

On a windy and frigid morning in December 2020, I wheeled my clanging metal music cart down a ramp and onto the school's blacktop. Ten bundled-up and masked first graders trailed behind me and stood waiting as I reached my hand under the waterproof tarp I had strapped to the top of my cart and turned on my speaker. I attached my headset under my wool hat and placed my body mic over my mask so that I could be heard over the wind. I felt like a chilled robot as I addressed my class.

"Stop kicking at the ice chips, please! Form a circle. Put down the snowball! Follow my moves for the first part and make up your own moves when we move into the circle."

I led them in a clumsy and noisy Irish folk dance to the tune "Rakes of Mallow." As we stepped in time together, adding claps, kicks, and stomps, my frustration and exhaustion at having to teach under such conditions eased a bit. In those few minutes, I knew we were finding some sense of joy and community.

At the peak of the Covid pandemic, most schools had moved entirely online, yet our school, blessed with a wealth of resources and financial resources, found a way to stay open. Since people were not vaccinated yet at that time, and fears were quite high, the administration did not allow us to sing or dance indoors. As a music teacher that year, I often wondered what would drive me nuts more: not being able to sing or dance with my students, or having to brave the sun, wind, mud, ice, and random playground distractions to do what I knew we needed most.

One day, my outdoor "classroom" had a large sampling of turkey droppings on it. Another day, the rhythm of a car alarm had us tapping and singing an improvised song.

On one particular day, while teaching a group of kindergarten students, my speaker battery died in the middle of a song, and I could not remember the words to be able to continue teaching that particular lesson. Too exhausted to think creatively on the spot, I asked the children for ideas about what to sing. We sat on the pavement, each child separated by individual, Clorox-wiped Hula-Hoops, and sang bits and pieces of suggested songs. At the end of class, feeling quite deflated, little Arya approached me with a smile: "Sara! That was the most fun we had all week! I love music!"

Pandemic aside, I could have hugged him. Yes—it didn't matter what we sang, how we danced, or whether they were "learning." The importance of simply singing together was clear.

My "music cart," which replaced my music classroom during the Covid pandemic.

Many forms of musical bonding and connection happened across the globe during the COVID-19 pandemic, temporarily soothing our loneliness and isolation. Yo-Yo Ma told me about his realization of the influence of music during the pandemic:

> I think the idea of music consists of three basic elements: energy, time, and space. I learned during the pandemic the way that these elements are felt all around us. During the pandemic, there were patients totally isolated in a room dying; people couldn't be there with their loved ones. But music could. Not just as something to listen to. Music is energy that moves air molecules that touch your skin. If you sit next to a big speaker, the floor vibrates. You feel it. There's a physicality to music, and I think there is great comfort in feeling that presence.

Pandemic music reminded us that we were not alone, even though we were physically isolated. Hospitals played celebratory music on the speakers for Covid-19 patients who recovered and could finally go home. Pop stars live-streamed special concerts from their homes as thousands of fans tuned in from their kitchens, bedrooms, and living rooms. Orchestras and bands configured special masks for their tubas, flutes, and other breath-based instruments. The musicians *had* to keep playing. People sought out music to keep their spirits up, like my partner, who went outside to the beach or park every day with dance music playing through her headset, and simply danced herself into an alternate reality. Many found ways of connecting with others through music, from their apartment balconies or in the streets after working from home all day.

The efforts made to connect musically were astounding. SYREN, a New York City-based modern dance company, got to work creating a piece called "Thina" entirely on Zoom, shaped by the conditions of the pandemic. Choreographed by co-founder Kate St. Amand, "Thina" was inspired by the work of South African composers Rueben T. Caluza, Philip Miller, and Ann Masina, whose music related to the Influenza pandemic of 1918.

The six dancers worked together to determine the exact time lapse created by each of their video cameras through Zoom so that they could breathe together and appear to move in sync. As Kate explains, dancers rely on their coordinated breath to communicate their movements along with the music. Without being able to physically breathe together and without being able to hear the same music in the same space together, the dancers still managed to figure out how to appear to move as one, expressing the desperation of disease, death, and community.

After the Thina video was released, I showed my young students, who seemed to understand the complexity and sentimentality quite well. We could all feel what was being expressed: being boxed in; not allowed to touch, we could break through the proverbial ice so beautifully by connecting through music and dance.

Violins, not Violence:
A Barbed Wire Barrier Can't Stop an Orchestra

I could choose from hundreds of stories of common suffering to highlight ways in which music can "save" us from harsh realities or change our life perspective. As someone who has taught Israeli Jews and Palestinians in shared spaces, I found the following story to be particularly striking. I am not here to enter into or trigger any political debate, but to provide a powerful window into how music can transform pain and save lives. It is a moving example of the human need to make music together. You can read the complete and beautifully told story yourself, in Sandy Tolan's *Children of the Stone* (2015).

As a boy living in a Palestinian refugee camp in Ramallah in the 1980s, Ramzi was a stone thrower—a poster child for the intifada against Jewish Israelis, angrily fighting for Palestinian land rights. With the 1995 Oslo Accords, the Israeli army's occupation of Ramallah ended, and tens of thousands of exiled Palestinians were able to return to the West Bank and Gaza. Among those returning was Mohammad Fadel, a violinist who had believed he could be part of a cultural renaissance—a musical and cultural awakening for Palestinians.

Ramzi was invited inside Mohammad's new National Conservatory of music and was handed a viola because of his large hands. With hard work, several international connections, and invitations to keep learning, his life was transformed through music.

Later, Ramzi was invited to play in the West-Eastern Divan Orchestra, an ambitious orchestral workshop made up of Arabs and Jews living in the same region. Co-founder Daniel Barenboim felt that simply playing together in close contact would help them feel closer. Yet for Ramzi, simply being physically close was not enough to ease generations of violence and anger. He wanted and needed dialogue and political action.

Ramzi also realized that he wanted to directly help other Palestinian children rise up from their anger and hopelessness and find beauty and purpose. With international support and years of effort, he eventually established his own music school in Ramallah: The Al Kamandjati School, which transformed the lives of hundreds of young Palestinians. Tolan writes, "Now another generation of children had let the music enter them. It was reconfiguring them, forming a new core; rewiring a new generation." (p. 313).

In a region still rife with conflict, tension, and mistrust, when the Al Kamandjati Orchestra was invited to play a concert in the Old City of Jerusalem in 2013, the logistics were quite problematic. The Qalandia military checkpoint between Ramallah and Jerusalem was (and at the time this book was written still is) a major, seemingly impenetrable concrete barrier guarded by Israeli soldiers holding M16s on their shoulders. At this checkpoint, twenty Palestinian musicians were ordered to leave the bus and cross on foot through the trash-strewn, narrow, cage-like corridor and place their instruments on a conveyor belt for inspection. Five of these musicians, a double bass player, a violinist, a violist, and two timpanists, who did not carry the proper paperwork, were not allowed through. The concert would have been canceled without them. With four hours to go until curtain call, they paid a smuggler in a white van to drive them to a less-guarded section of the 20-foot-high barrier, where the barbed wire at the top had already been cut, leaving a small gap to climb through. A knotted rope allowed them to climb down the other side of the barrier. If they had been spotted, they would have been shot on the spot.

Aside from the incomprehensible image of a double bass player having to surreptitiously hoist his instrument over a barbed wire barrier to play a Beethoven symphony in Jerusalem, why should this story matter to us?

It is time that we stop seeing music, even classical orchestra music, as simply entertainment for those few wealthy and elite patrons of the arts. This story is a testament to the fact that participation in a music ensemble can change lives, change identities, and give those players a reason to be alive that is more powerful than violence—the risk of not playing that concert in Jerusalem seemed greater than the risk of being caught scaling a twenty-foot barbed wire cement barrier.

But here's another thought. We all know how powerful music and the arts can be to our human existence, yet we continue to need reminders that these subjects are more than just a hobby or frill. We know that we have each had powerful musical moments in our own lives that drive us, help us carry on, or give us a new perspective on our circumstances, yet so many of us continue to feel that we are outsiders, incapable of learning an instrument.

What are the barbed-wire barricades that stop some of us from trying? What are the cement barriers that keep some of us from crossing over into allowing ourselves to feel musical, and who put these walls up in the first place?

2 — Everyday Music & Rituals

Vignette: The "Obsessive Music" CD

I was driving to Oyster Bay, Long Island, with the air conditioning blasting on a hot August morning in 2012. My best friend Elissa had passed away suddenly that March, but living overseas with two young children prevented me from being able to attend her funeral. I had barely been able to process the shocking news of her drowning.

While visiting home for the summer, I arranged to meet her mother, Dolores, at Elissa's memorial bench with pizza from their favorite restaurant. I was navigating weekend traffic over the Whitestone Bridge, and as I made my way onto the Cross Island Parkway, I shut off the news. It would be a long drive—I needed music.

Before leaving, I had grabbed a stack of old CDs from my childhood bedroom at my mother's house. As I sat in the car leafing through these CDs, I spotted the "Obsessive Music" mix that Elissa had made for me—a collection of our favorite songs from the late 90s. My heart beat anxiously as I slid the disc into the slot of my mother's car.

The opening chords of "Both Hands" by Ani DiFranco (1990) hit my ears, and my heart lurched with an ache so deep that I needed to pull over to the side of the road. I sobbed into the steering wheel for a good ten minutes, allowing myself, for the first time, to cry about her death. The song brought me instantly back to her poster-clad and glittery pom-pom decorated dorm room in college, where we giggled about our latest crushes and talked about art and politics.

My "Obsessive Music" CD, which allowed me to mourn my dear friend.

I know that if you are reading this, you can remember a time when music opened, pierced, or allowed your heart to soften. That is what music does. The effect of music on our psycho-emotional arena is quite obvious and nothing new. What I would like you to consider is *how are you being "musical"* in those moments? I made a choice to play that CD at that moment, and I made a choice to *keep playing it* even as my tears flowed because I knew subconsciously that I needed to hear that music to help process my feelings, which I was ready to do. The musical choices, rituals, and traditions that we invite into our lives and consciously select are important aspects of being musical in our daily lives. And I have never met anyone who didn't have a musical relationship with some moment or memory in their lives. Elizabeth, one of my former students at Queens College, described it like this:

Depending on my emotions, I pick different types of songs that calm me down and make me realize many things, and make me feel grateful for many things in my life. Music always keeps me going. If I am in a good mood, I listen to happy music and I dance a lot. If I am sad, I listen to sad music like R&B soul music that helps me stay calm and relax, and I pick songs that relate to what I am feeling at that very moment. It lets me know that I am not the only one going through the situation.

Musical Time Capsules

On a Thursday morning in late August, my cousin Aaron, age 46, sat strumming his guitar. A scattering of family had gathered on his enclosed porch. His stepmother stood to the side with a cup of coffee in her hand, his teenage daughter, still in pajamas, sat across from him, and I sat next to him, ready to sing along. After singing some favorite tunes, laughing at words that no one could remember, Aaron was strumming the opening chords of James Taylor's "Rockabye Sweet Baby James" (1970). The group softly began to sing along, but by the chorus, Aaron stopped singing.

"Dad! Why are you crying?" asked his daughter.

"I don't know!" Aaron answered, with tears streaming down his cheeks. "I just...I used to sing this to the kids every night. Then, in the summers when we had groups of people around the campfire, this was always our last song. It just brings back so many memories."

"It's a time-capsule piece," I said.

"What's that?" asks his daughter.

Nicole, an elementary school teacher in training, described the "Time Capsule" effect beautifully:

I know I use music as a timeline for myself. Certain songs remind me of certain times, ages, or just something that happened at that time for me. It could have been important, or it just could have been dumb, but either way, it helps me with memories. I love it when old songs come on, and it brings me back to a good time. I remember when I was little, my favorite song for my mom to sing to me was "You Are My Sunshine." Even to this day, when I hear it sung to someone else in my family, I still remember sitting on my mom's lap, having her rock me back and forth, and her singing that song. I remember when September 11th happened and they had all those on-air concerts to support everything that was going on, and I know that when I hear those songs now, that's exactly what I remember. Everything comes back to me about that day—what I remember. I feel everything. [Also] if I hear a certain song, it's like, "Oh, I was going out with what's his face when this song came out." Music is important to everyone, whether it was because they had a first kiss with that song, or because their mother sang it to them, or because that song helped them to get through a bad relationship. Music does help shape your memory.

Jonathan Kramer, who studied the experience of time in music, explains that how we experience time when we are engaged in music (whether listening or producing it ourselves) is significantly different from how we experience time in other arenas of our daily life. Music, he claims, can create, suspend, or alter our ordinary sense of time (Kramer, 1988).

Perhaps it is precisely this disappearance of time that makes us unaware of just how often we engage with our musicality throughout the day. Custodero reminds us that many of our adult musical experiences go unnoticed by us. She explains how "...music functions as both a signifier of emotional intensity, taking one more deeply *into* the moment, and as a vehicle for transcending the present, taking us out of the moment into the past, as in reminiscences of personal associations or images, or even into an anticipated future." (Custodero, 2024, p. 4).

The time-capsule effect of music can, of course, have very negative or even traumatic connections for us as well. Can you think of a song or piece that, if you were to hear it right now, would cause your finger to stab the "off" button faster than lightning? Maybe it's a song that you danced to with a long-lost love? Perhaps it is a perfectly likable song that some employee selected for their company's on-hold music, and you have been on hold for forty-five minutes, furiously waiting to ask about the mistake in your bill. You will never want to hear that music again! Or maybe there is a piece of music that you played loudly to drown out the sound of ongoing arguments and fights between your parents before they divorced.

What songs or pieces of music exist in *your* personal time capsule? What song brings you back to your childhood or your high school years in an instant? What music did you play obsessively over and over again until you couldn't stand it any longer? Do you have a piece of music that, if you heard it, would make you want to leave the room because of its painful association? Perhaps you've even considered what music you would wish to have played or sung at your funeral? Naming these specific pieces of music means that you have strong musical associations. You are a musical person because music has attached itself in your heart and mind to specific moments in time.

Christmas Carols, Birthday Songs

Imagine your friends and family gathered around your living room. Balloons and party decorations adorn the table, and someone turns down the lights for a birthday cake lit with candles. Now imagine that a choral conductor enters and says, "Okay everyone! This is your starting pitch: Laaaaa. Everyone, match your voices to this note. Let's begin..."

Surely that would be absurd! Singing "Happy Birthday" is one of those times when, for the most part, everyday people allow themselves to sing without worrying about how they sound. In fact, we even expect and enjoy a cacophony of mixed out-of-tune voices.

Today, in our modern lives, rituals such as birthdays, weddings, funerals, and holidays are some of the only spaces where community singing still takes place. The ritual of communal celebration takes precedence over musical ability in those arenas because we are more "in tune" with celebration and community than with perfection. These songs usually begin with eye contact, smiles, and a voice in the group saying, "Ready?"

And just like that, we *are* ready. We are ready to sing together in celebration because that's what we do in that circumstance. There is no stage or spotlight, and no one auditions for a role. Within some families, this celebratory and free relationship with music exists in abundance. Lauren Cregor, a professional singer/songwriter, describes her early childhood like this:

> There was a lot of music and joy within the family—it was their family love language. Unabashed joy! At family gatherings, people would just jump onto the piano and play, and everyone would sing. Playing music was living. A beautifully alive way of living.

Would you say that Lauren's family sounds more musical than yours? Maybe your family had a different "family love language," such as playing games after dinner or kicking around a soccer ball in the yard together. But I am guessing that your family still gathered to sing "Happy Birthday" on occasion. Maybe you all found yourselves dancing to some pop tune in the kitchen from time to time. Maybe someone sang lullabies to you, or sang little tunes while pushing you on a swing when you were little.

The amount of music-making in a family might differ widely, but I would bet you still had *some* family music going on. If you had a less musically abundant upbringing than Lauren, it doesn't mean you came from an unmusical family. It just means music happened in different ways.

Alarm Clocks and Cleanup Songs

If you have spent any time around young children, you have probably found yourself creating a little song or musical signal to give directions, establish a routine, or communicate an expectation. For example, if you take a young child to the park each day, rather than saying, "Hey, it's time to go to the park, let's put our shoes on," you might find yourself saying something like this:

Or even creating a little song:

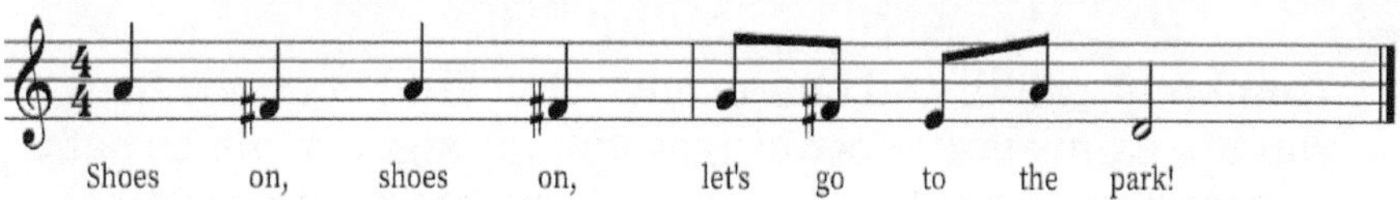

This seems to happen instinctively among adults in many cultures around the globe. Transitional songs help babies and young children understand what is happening around them and what to expect. The power of these musical cues and songs is tremendous and can last a lifetime. If your parents or caregivers are still alive, ask them if they remember creating little songs for you. When I teach baby and toddler music classes, I use a "Cleanup Song" taught to me by Lori Custodero (professor of early childhood music education at Teachers College):

It only takes me two or three rounds of singing this song while holding out a basket for the little ones to start placing things inside it. My own two children heard me sing this song many times, both as participants in my music classes, and as a mother, trying to teach them how to clean up at home. Now, at age sixteen, my son will still occasionally make a joke by whistling or singing this song when I ask him to put things away, which he knows will make me laugh and ease up on the nagging.

Transitional songs are not just for children, of course. What wakes you up in the morning? Is it a favorite song? Something bright and motivational? If you choose one of the prescribed tunes that your phone offers you, do you prefer something energetic, or do you prefer to wake up to the gentle sound of chimes?

Or perhaps you are one of the lucky few whose schedule or body rhythm allows you to wake naturally. Does music accompany you as you get ready for work? As you go for your morning jog? What specific musical choices do you make throughout your day that represent your tastes, preferences, moods, or moments? What is your "cleaning the house" music? Stop and think carefully about the music that has shaped the daily transitions of your everyday life.

> **Your body, mind, and heart *know* what kind of music fires you up, calms you, encourages you, or signals you to act in a certain way. In this sense, you are being musical through the conscious connections you create for yourself.**

Lullabies and Sleep Songs

At the end of a long day, getting into bed and turning out the light to get to sleep seems like it should be the most natural thing in the world. So why is it so hard?!

Music education researcher Meryl Sole explains how, in most Eurocentric cultures, young children are expected to sleep alone in a crib or cot, and that this is often the only place and time when they are left unsupervised. Bedtime becomes a private and solitary affair. Children often face bedtime fears associated with the dark or abandonment, and parents are often encouraged to establish a calming "bedtime routine" that might include bath time, stories, and songs (Sole, 2017).

After noticing how her own young children often sang as they fell asleep, Sole studied the songs that toddlers spontaneously create for themselves while transitioning to sleep in their cribs. As they separate and detach from their caregivers, she explains that young children invent songs as a self-soothing "transitional object" to give themselves a feeling that their caregiver is still with them in the room.

What these songs seemed to have in common was that the content reflected moments of bonding and connection that they had with their caregiver throughout the day. Songs that were shared throughout the day came back at night, reinforcing the social-emotional connection of that musical experience.

Do you also routinely use music to help you fall asleep? A basic search for "Sleep music" on Spotify turns up thousands of suggestions. Maybe you have tried falling asleep to a variety of these sleep tracks before finding one that is most soothing and sleep-inducing to you. A gentle harp? No. A monk's medieval singing tones? No. Tibetan singing bowls? Maybe. When you find that "perfect" sleep track, you probably know it right away. Ahhhh, yes. *This* is the type of music that my body can relax with!

You have an inner physical and musical knowledge based on your life experiences, cultural connections, and probably even your particular cellular makeup that guides your musical choices. You know what kinds of music your body resonates best with for sleep. So yes, as you select music to fall asleep to, you are a musical person, even if you might not be a sleeping person!

Grieving Through Music

Kimberly Monzón, professional opera singer and professor of voice at Baylor University:

> My mother was a church choir director and music teacher, and she also taught private voice lessons in our home. Students would come through the house all the time for lessons, and sometimes they had voice recitals. My mother had season tickets to the opera in Kansas City. Each child in our family would have a turn to go to one of those performances with our mother, which was a special bonding experience. It seemed like a normal part of life, but I realized later on that none of my other friends did this. It was a big event—we would get dressed up and have a fun dinner together afterwards. Another thing about my mother is that she only listened to classical music in the car. It seemed like a normal part of life, and it shaped my childhood.
>
> My mother developed cancer, and she died when I was twenty-five. She was in a coma with a DNR (Do Not Resuscitate). But in her last days, she was kept on life support just until my brother and I could get to the hospital. I held her in my arms and sang her a hymn called "It is Well with My Soul, Peace Like a River." I didn't plan to do that. It just felt like the thing my mother would need to carry her through her transition out of this life that was filled with so much music. I somehow knew I needed to sing to her.

The transition from life to death is perhaps the most elusive and powerful transition that we humans bear witness to. In addition to Kimberly's story, I have heard many other personal accounts of singing a special song or playing a specially selected piece of music for someone during their final moments of life. Because of music's ability to instantly transport us to another place and time, or to alter time, it can feel like music erases someone's old age or can even suspend one's final moments in a place that is simply rhythm and melody. And because we can use music to "alchemize" (Suleika's word again) pain into something else, we can create an alternate reality for the person who is leaving us as well as for ourselves.

Hearing "The Blue Danube" waltz by Strauss (1867), for example, could send my grandmother Lea aglow in an instant—at age eighteen, dancing with her husband Gastone at their wedding in Italy. In her final days, at age 100, she was quite confused about where she was and who was in the room with her. moving in and out of reality, hallucinating, and sometimes quite upset. My mother played "The Blue Danube," some Puccini arias, and piano music by Chopin to calm her. My mother described how she could often see an almost instant transformation in Lea's mood—a smile would spread across her face, or she would briefly hum along. Transporting her to those solid memories through those specific pieces clearly helped. My mother reflected, "I also played those pieces for myself. It was difficult to see her like that, and the music also helped me to feel better."

In his book *Musicophilia*, Oliver Sacks explains that music can be preserved in the brain even when severe dementia is present. "...musical perception, musical sensibility, musical emotion, and musical memory can survive long after other forms of memory have disappeared. Music of the right kind can serve to orient and anchor a patient when almost nothing else can." (Sacks, 2007, p. 337).

Once someone passes away, music or chanting can help the living to share in a collective sadness that helps to process the pain. In traditional and religious communities, it may also serve to release the spirit to the afterlife, ensure the protection of a higher being, or act as a blessing. Sacks explains that people seem to instinctively turn to music to process grief. Many people seek out sad songs to allow themselves to cry, just as I did to grieve my friend Elissa. Music somehow seems to permit them to let the tears flow. Sacks also describes how music can help people feel less alone as they grieve. For example, they might find relief or comfort in the lyrics of a specific song that relates to the situation or context. Or music might allow for collective grieving during a funeral ceremony, so that those who are present find comfort and solidarity among each other.

3 — Powerfully Persuasive Musicality

Vignette: War Song or Caribbean Party Song?

It was my third time teaching "Music in Childhood" for elementary school teachers in training at Queens College when I decided to experiment: "Take out a piece of paper and divide it into four sections," I instructed. I wanted to show them through experience why understanding music is relational and contextual. I wanted to talk about assumptions. "I will be playing four pieces of music that are probably unfamiliar to you. I want you to describe these pieces as best as you can and try to make some guesses about any emotion you feel is being expressed, what meaning the song might have, and, if possible, what culture you might associate the song with." I started with a flute piece called "Wulankuntewakan" which translates as Peace, Lenape (Avery and Devol, 2008), and then played an Irish reel and some slow jazz music.

Finally, I played a song called "Ndodemnyama Verwoerd," by Vuyisile Mini (1965). Students described this song as:

- *Relaxing*
- *Feels like a fun party—I can imagine people dancing*
- *Festive. Maybe a little flirty?*
- *I think it's from the Caribbean*
- *Something from the tropics.*
- *Hawaiian?*

This song, sung by the famous and late singer, Miriam Makeba, was created as a fierce warning to Hendrick Verwoerd, then Prime Minister and prime architect of Apartheid in South Africa: "Watch out, Verwoerd! Here is the Black Man. Your days are over!"

This was one of the most popular and fierce "Freedom Songs," which empowered black South Africans to take to the streets with spears, kicking their feet up as they danced and sang it. The song and its movements acted as a powerful warning to the white supremacists.

Yet many of my students, not knowing its history or understanding the Xhosa language, guessed that this song was a Caribbean party song. The first three pieces they heard were more culturally stereotypical, and many of those students described them in similar words. They recognized what sounded like Irish music, Jazz music, some type of Native American music, even if they didn't know the exact meaning of the words or the symbolism of the melody in the flute music. I did, after all, want them to feel they understood some things about music.

But this last piece was a complete surprise. There was no way that they could have guessed it was an anti-Apartheid South African Freedom Song, because none of the students in that room were culturally connected to that place, language, or musical style.

Misunderstanding the Message—
It's Not a Universal Language

When Mickey Katz sits down in his cello chair at Symphony Hall for this season's first rehearsal of the Boston Symphony, he will open up the score to whatever music is on the program and start to play. Without the need for exchanging words, the cellists around him can look at that music and understand what to play. Cellists in Helsinki, Budapest, Taiwan, Bangkok, France, or Argentina could look at that same score and play the same thing even though they might not be able to communicate with words. When people say that music is a "universal language," I believe this is what they are referring to.

Yet Western classical music is not exactly universal. To be able to understand that particular type of musical "language," one must devote a considerable amount of time to learning to read and produce what is written. And then, of course, there are different ways to interpret that score, which is why some people prefer to listen to Beethoven's Seventh Symphony as conducted by one maestro and not another.

Not everyone has access to this particular classical music learning—in fact, the classical system weeds people out through auditions, judgment, and lack of funding—the "untalented," or the underprivileged.

How can it be universal when such hierarchies, access, and privilege surround it? And are we still only referring to "music" just in terms of this Western classical domain?

When I search online for an image of "music," I see hundreds of pictures of G clefs, eighth notes, and quarter notes colorfully dancing their way up and down a five-line stave. For me, this is *not* music, but notation. European symbols for European sounds.

Imagine if we could depict music as an inner feeling. A magical movement within, guided by a connection to our personal stories and our surrounding culture. I don't think such an image exists. If you would like to paint one for me, I would love to see it!

The act of making or participating in music is relational. My relationship with the violin, which I played from age three until age twenty-one, is unique to me. The people I engage with, my surrounding culture, and the context in which that music occurs are what allow specific music to affect me in a particular way. Musicologists agree that musical traditions are more different than similar across the globe (Cohen, 2015).

I like to think of it this way. If I say the word "Tree," some of you may picture a maple tree, while others may picture a snow-covered pine or a thin spruce, yet we know, essentially, what is being communicated by that word: A natural thing with roots in the ground, a wooden trunk, branches, and some type of foliage.

If I play a piece of music for you (even one with words), the association, personal meaning, and imagery may be completely different from person to person. Music that could soothe or give hope to one group might strike fear in another (Cohen, 2015).

While it may be reasonable to assume that a group of people within one culture may have a similar understanding of a piece, such as a group of teenage girls commiserating about breakups while listening to Olivia Rodrigo singing "Driver's License"

(2021)—a song that describes a breakup— an eighty-five year old Indian man living in Bangladesh would not necessarily relate to that same song with the same understanding, especially if he doesn't speak English. He might hear it and focus on the rhythm, or hear the vocal melody and imagine his granddaughter celebrating her birthday. This is why we can have a situation wherein Miriam Makeba's war song to end Apartheid was interpreted by my Queens College students as being a party song.

Leonard Bernstein, in his search for universals in music, made this same point: we can't completely understand another culture's music unless we have lived it ourselves or take time to deeply get to know it (1973).

Music empathy researcher Laurence explains that music "may well have the capacity to strengthen feelings of similarity, through shared experience and participation" (2015, p. 22). To achieve communal understanding or empathy for another through music, there needs to be a specifically constructed framework—an intentional and thorough attempt at building understanding. In other words, there needs to be a shared goal or some piece of common ground to begin with. This is why the common ground of stress and loneliness during the Covid-19 pandemic, for example, allowed people to connect strongly through music. Music, during that time, expressed a language of a difficult shared experience: *We are all going through this thing, and I'm sharing a musical moment with you in place of physical closeness.*

Researchers Hendricks, Finn, and Freeze, who studied conflict-transformation through music, showed us that to have authentic connections through music, there must be compassion (2023). Laurence also confirms that music does have the capability to strengthen feelings of similarity through shared experience, but this is different than a universal language. This feeling of "oneness" actually comes from one's own set of feelings and experiences and is not necessarily shared with others. We might feel immersed in an "emotional bath," but a shared musical event doesn't automatically make for a shared emotional experience or common understanding (Laurence, 2015, p. 20).

Let me tell you a story from my own musical past. In the spring of 1994, during my freshman year at the Indiana University School of Music, it was announced that the great conductor Zubin Mehta would be coming to conduct Mahler's "Symphony #1"(1887) with one of our five orchestras. This was a piece of music I knew and loved, having played it several years before as a violinist in the New York Youth Symphony.

I was thrilled to learn that Mehta would indeed be doing this with *my* orchestra. Even though I was seated at the back of the second violin section, I felt I was living my dream: to be a violinist and play at the highest level that I could achieve. But in the middle of our second rehearsal, my world and my dream came crashing apart. Pain suddenly shot through both of my forearms and all ten fingers with a throbbing stiffness that I could not play through. I set my violin down on my chair and went to the bathroom to run cold water over my fingers. I massaged my arms and tried to shake off the pain. Though I made it through the rest of that rehearsal, the pain persisted. I could not practice my usual three or four hours a day, let alone even fifteen minutes, without pain. I could not dial a phone number, squeeze my tube of toothpaste, take notes, or twist open a door handle without pain. I simply could not play the violin.

After two medical consultations, a teary phone call home, and a nearly musicless meeting with my violin teacher, I found myself sobbing on my advisor's couch as she described my only option for staying in music school: I would need to drop orchestra and violin lessons, and switch over to voice lessons and choir.

It felt like the death of my career, my dream, and my identity as a performing musician. The following week, I showed up to choir rehearsal in a room I had never been in before. The group was preparing to sing Benjamin Britten's "War Requiem" (1961), a ninety-minute choral piece I had never heard before. I was placed in the soprano section for rehearsals. Meanwhile, in my voice lessons, I learned to breathe from my diaphragm, open my throat, and release my jaw, allowing my voice to find new heights and depths.

Three weeks into the rehearsals, I found myself loving this powerful and unusual requiem, as well as the feeling of singing in a large group. In week four, the week before the concert, our choir was joined by a large orchestra on stage to put the whole piece together. Though I ached inside to be playing with the other violinists, I was curiously enjoying making music alongside them as a singer. The emotional upheaval of not being able to play the violin is not something I want to gloss over, and I will return to it later. But right now I want to show you something else about this singing story.

Much of Britten's "War Requiem" is not peaceful or jovial at all. It is ominous, angry, and tremendously dark. I began to feel my own anger and darkness spill forth. On the day of the concert, something inside me broke free, as I opened my throat and sang through the musical war taking place in my heart. I could feel the vibrations of the timpani, brass, and the entire orchestra moving through my body, as my single voice became one with the singers around me.

I was transported, carried on a powerful musical wave of what felt like a collective energy, to a place beyond words. After the piece ended, I could barely step down from the risers. I was practically shaking with what I can only describe as one of the most profound musical experiences I have ever had. I made my way backstage to collect my things and saw one of my violinist friends zipping up his violin case. Wanting to share in the exhilaration, I approached him.

"Oh my goodness!" I said, searching for words. "That was just so...I can't believe—" He cut me off, finishing my sentence with his own experience, "Such a drag, right? I can't wait to get home and pop a beer."

There was no universal language in that shared experience. Yet I do believe it *is* possible for each person in a large group to feel their own sense of musical "oneness," however different and unique the experience is to each person.

We know that the power of music to bring people together and form deep connections that transcend words is there. Yes— transcend words. Music is not a language because it can move us *beyond* language. It is because of this powerful transcendental capacity that music can be a great influencer on group dynamics, social change, politics, and peace efforts. For anyone who has ever felt unmusical because you don't understand certain aspects of music, or you feel you can't "speak the language" of music, know this: You have your own musically communicative language living inside you. You speak your *own* musical language. You don't need to (nor can you) speak *every* musical language.

Just because my students from Queens College could not distinguish a Caribbean party song from a South African freedom song does not mean they are less musical. It only means they have not had a chance to become familiar with that particular musical material or its context and history.

Many people I have spoken to claim to be unmusical because they lack an understanding of the Western classical music language. Can you see how limiting that is now? The music that you are most at home with and understand most deeply is no less important. In my twenty-plus years of teaching, learning, and researching musical experiences, I truly believe this about universals:

The only aspect of music seen in every culture ever studied is the musically interactive way that caregivers communicate with infants and babies.

We will explore that universal phenomenon in Chapter 5.

Music in Politics

In March of 2024, I opened *The New York Times* to see the headline "Could Beyoncé and Taylor Swift, with Their Tens of Millions of Fans, Sway the Presidential Election?" While the authors determined that famous pop stars are less likely to want to sway their fans, and are mainly swayed *by* the opinions of their fans, these writers agreed that politicians are incredibly hungry for any kind of mention by major artists. Taylor Swift's music has created a "rabid, devoted, emotionally-driven" fan base. When Taylor Swift posted on Instagram, encouraging her listeners to register to vote, 35,000 followers did so in an instant.

Musicians create works that help themselves, and consequently others, to process and form new understandings. Yet leaders, politicians, and those wishing to influence a group understand the power of music to unify toward a common goal. This power has no doubt been used for both good and evil.

Every politician has used music to promote themselves in TV ads and live speeches. Every significant event, protest, victory speech, political movement, or campaign has used music to emotionally influence listeners or to create a lasting effect for an important message. Johan Galtung is the founder and co-director of "TRANSCEND," a peace and development network. He recalls a moment in his childhood in Nazi-occupied Norway when he heard

German soldiers march past his window singing an "incredibly heart-warming tune." He suggests that the music was specifically designed to be uplifting, allowing people, including himself, to believe that the Nazis couldn't possibly be so bad (2015, p. 54). Galtung says that as music sends us into an alternate reality, it also has the capability of allowing us to experience a commonality with others who witness or share the same musical experience. Remember the "collective effervescence" I mentioned earlier? This effect, whereby a group of people is immersed in a type of emotionally influenced "sound bath," does not mean that there is shared understanding or empathy. It operates as more of a contagion, deconstructing, rather than nurturing, individual responses and identities (Laurence, 2015).

Peace Efforts and Activism

The "contagion" effect of music has also played a vital role in changing nations for the good. Take, for example, the Estonian Singing Revolution. Estonians pride themselves on being a singing culture. Since 1869, the people of Estonia have traveled from all over the country to attend a singing festival called Laulupidu, which takes place every five years and is made up of over 30,000 singing participants.

Between 1987-1991, Estonians used the song festival to gather strength and courage, as they sang their banned national songs. In a completely nonviolent manner, their singing played a key part in their successful secession from the USSR, as they formed human chains with their Baltic neighbors and found the courage to speak up about their rights (Tusty and Tusty, 2006).

At the start of this chapter, I wrote about the powerful Freedom Songs of South Africa that acted as a musical force against Apartheid. According to Lee Hirsh, who spent eight years researching and documenting these songs, when people took to the streets singing those Freedom Songs, kicking up their feet and holding spears, the white pro-Apartheid South Africans were truly terrified. The singing caught the attention of reporters on the scene, igniting action around the globe to end Apartheid (Velez, 2021).

In his 2002 documentary film titled *Amandla! A Revolution in Four-Part Harmony*, Hirsh illustrated the role that music played in empowering black South Africans to rise up against the injustices of Apartheid in South Africa. He makes a compelling point that this song, along with several other Freedom songs, actually led to the crumbling of Apartheid.

The songs of the Civil Rights Movement in America were equally empowering. These songs were created from the depths of fury and pain and drove people into the streets with a conviction to fight for justice. The Black Church was the gathering place for the Civil Rights Movement because music was an important part of the struggle, rooted in traditional African-American hymn-style singing. "We Shall Overcome" (1963), one of the most widely known freedom songs, was a product of African Americans and European Americans working together. It was first sung by slaves, then adapted and changed for the Civil Rights Movement. Guy Carawan, a white activist from California, risked his life to spread the song, teaching it all over the South.

There was an intentionality in spreading these freedom songs across the country, church by church, meeting by meeting, and person to person. Mary Travers, of the folk music group Peter, Paul, and Mary, was another white activist who helped spread these songs, saying, "Music has always been the accompaniment of social change. (Whitehead, 2015, p. 84)"

To dig deeper into musical examples from the Civil Rights movement, along with other gripping stories of musical activism and peace efforts, I recommend reading Andrea Warner's book *Rise Up and Sing: Power, Protest, and Activism in Music* (2024).

Music's power to connect us to others and unite entire nations indicates that music is an intrinsically powerful aspect of our human existence. Are you a musical person? Have you ever participated in a protest and found yourself rhythmically chanting or singing whatever song the group has adopted as its persuasive motto? You can't help but become musical when you are called to join in a cause that you believe in through the power of song and chant.

Have you ever changed your mind about an important matter or reconsidered your worldview because of a song? Music's power to change minds and influence policy is an indicator of its universality. The fact that music can do this to us means that we have something inside us that responds to music in a profound way. Harnessing this power has led to many musical "peace-building" projects designed to dispel tensions between groups of people in conflict. The group Musicians Without Borders,[4] for example, trains musicians to work in conflict zones, using musical interaction to bridge understandings through shared meaning-making.

Large-scale efforts to build peace through music may seem too grand or far-removed from your personal life, but let's stop and think about this for a moment. Have you ever used music to try to bring peace to a tense situation or to try to encourage shared understanding in a difficult moment?

My friend Jenny told me that when she and her wife Julie argue, they play the Muppet song "The Rainbow Connection" (1979), which they danced to at their wedding. They have a shared understanding that no matter how angry one of them feels, if either of them plays this song, they drop what they are doing and dance.

Maybe you have a song that you play or sing to snap your tantruming child out of a crying spell. Maybe you created a mixtape or playlist of songs to give to a friend or romantic partner after a fight. The effort is made in hopes of forgiveness. It is deeply human and quite musical to use music in this way. After all, nations and societies are constructed of individual people. If we acknowledge that each of us can use music in this way, we can understand how activism and political change through music can take shape.

---

[4] https://www.musicianswithoutborders.org/

4 — Musicality in Healing

Vignette: Music at the Massage Parlor

The table was warm, the air faint with lavender. Rainforest sounds drifted from the speakers. The sounds of water, wind and distant birds soothed me. My breath slowed. Muscles loosened. I was sinking in. Then the track changed. "Pachelbel's Canon" (1680) came through the crystal-and-aromatherapy surrounded speakers. No. I felt my back muscles tense up and my fingers curl against the sheet as the feeling of *violin* coursed through my ex-violinist body. Every wedding, every background playlist, it's that same syrupy loop. And for me, it was even worse.

Memories of high school orchestra flooded me. Out-of-tune violas scrambling and flutes floating off on their own. Stuck following Richard, the perennial "Concertmaster," while I couldn't seem to rise above second chair. The sting of competition. Feelings of frustration. Pure ugliness. The music kept winding on, pretty to anyone else, unbearable to me. Finally, I lifted my head from the lavender towel and whispered, "Please... change the music."

Singing Bowls and Meditative Music

In the summer of 2023, my friend Lisa and I wandered into a small Tibetan store near Harvard Square. Scarves and silver jewelry caught my eye when I entered. Lisa headed straight for a shelf lined with singing bowls. The shopkeeper, warm and unhurried, invited us to try them. Each bowl rang with its own pitch—bright and delicate in the smaller ones, deep and sonorous in the large basins resting on silk rings.

"Do you want me to do a healing session on you?" he asked. Lisa, without hesitation, said yes.

He set a low stool in the center of the room. As she closed her eyes, he circled along the rim of a bowl behind her head. A resonant hum swelled, vibrating in the air between them. Slowly, he lowered the sound, pausing at points along her body. When the tone reached her lower back, it deepened, pulsing through her spine. He lingered there, as if the bowl had found something hidden. When he stopped, Lisa opened her eyes, startled. "How did he know?" she whispered.

That brief session may or may not have eased her back pain— but the memory lingers, a reminder of how music and healing have always been entwined. If you are unsure about how the music-medicine connection relates to *you* being musical or reclaiming your musical identity, stick with me! The research and the stories I am about to share with you are quite illuminating!

Music and Medicine

Picture this: A patient lies on the operating table with an expert team of surgeons focused on removing a tumor. Suddenly, something goes wrong—machines are beeping; vitals are looking weak. The head surgeon commands, "Suction! Gauze! Mozart's Third Piano Concerto!"

Of course, this scene is imaginary, but the idea behind it isn't far-fetched. Across cultures and centuries, music has been used to steady bodies, calm minds, and support healing. Direct connections between human health and music can be found in many ancient and indigenous traditions, as well as throughout Western civilization.

As we think about what it means to be a musical person, it's worth remembering that our most powerful encounters with music may not come from performance at all, but from the way music supports our bodies and restores our balance. In that sense, the music–medicine connection may be where many of us feel most deeply musical!

In Ancient Greece, certain musical scales were thought to stir particular moods and conditions. Physicians would choose melodies for patients the way we might choose medicine, aiming to shift the body toward balance (Lippi, de Sarsina, & D'Elios, 2010). Centuries later, in the early Middle Ages, the philosopher Boethius imagined the "Music of the Spheres," where the same harmonies that governed the cosmos also resonated in the human body. To him, perfect chords were both beautiful and a force that could steady both the universe and our own health (Farrar, 2017).

I was fascinated to learn from Dr. Wyatt LaCoss, an expert in Chinese medicine, of similar theories about the musical tones of the planets, which have existed in Traditional Chinese Medicine (TCM) for thousands of years. While chatting over a cup of tea, he told me that "In TCM, there were said to be five tones in the universe, which were later proven by science (astronomy and physics) that come from the distance of our planets from each other and their gravitational pull. Each planet whirls at a different speed, which has a tone associated, and these five tones are associated with the five healing elements in Chinese medicine: wood, fire, earth, metal, and water." Dr. LaCoss explained that, in turn, each of these five elements had specific musical tones that could be used to heal specific conditions. These healing tones are still used by classic Chinese medicine practitioners in England and France.

Music's use in balancing or healing the body continued in the Western world as well, through the Renaissance and into the 1800s, when doctors used specific sound vibrations and frequencies to redirect fluids in the body (Lippi, de Sarsina, and D'Elios, 2010). During WWII, a scientific approach to music therapy was born when soldiers suffering from PTSD were not responding to other modes of therapy, but would often have much stronger responses to music. Soldiers who were not even able to speak could sing, hum, or would have sudden awakenings of the mind as they connected with specific pieces of music being played for them (Wong, 2013).

If you, like many, still find it hard to believe that music can be clinically healing, listen to this—A study that came out of the Instituto de Biofísica Carlos Chagas Filho, of the Federal University of Rio de Janeiro, Brazil in 2011, seems to indicate that Beethoven's music can fight cancer: "Dr. Márcia Alves Marques Capella and colleagues performed a series of tests in 2010, exposing dish-cultures of both healthy and cancerous cells to audio playbacks of various music genres. In repeated tests, Dr. Capella found that recordings of Beethoven's *Symphony No. 5 in C Minor* destroyed around 20% of cancerous cells within a few days—yet the healthy cells were unharmed." (Gardiner, 2011)

Do doctors believe that music could one day be prescribed to treat specific conditions? Dr. Michael Barnett, an oboist in the Longwood Symphony, thinks it is possible, especially when it comes to rehabilitation. Listening to or creating music is something that doctors are likely to recommend because music has a powerful effect on and involvement with the way our brain circuits connect and are wired.

Dr. Wong (2013, p. 113) writes about flautist Dr. Daniela Kraus, who specializes in leukemia research. Wong quotes Kraus as saying, "I am too much of a medically trained person to say that we can cure cancer with music, just like we can't cure cancer with just herbs. But I think that as an adjunct therapy to cancer treatment—or as adjunct therapy to almost any kind of treatment, really—music is the way to go." In fact, the rise in research studies about the healing powers of music, along with advocacy from groups such as the Society for Arts in Healthcare, indicates that prescriptions for musical healing are not far out of reach!

Doctor-Musicians

Jeffrey Allen, MD, is a retired pediatric neurologist and neuro-oncologist. His musical story starts with parents fostering his and his sister's early interest in music:

> My older sister was offered piano lessons in early childhood, and by adolescence, she had mastered a large repertoire, practicing four to five hours a week. Our house was always filled with piano music of many classical composers. She graduated from Syracuse Music Conservatory and spent her musical career teaching children piano and playing organ in churches and synagogues. As a child, I played the trumpet and loved it. I often played duets with my sister. In high school, my band teacher introduced me to the baritone horn, which I grew to prefer to trumpet because the larger bore of the

mouthpiece was easier to blow with my braces, and I enjoyed playing the counter melody in the band and orchestra. I have continued to play the baritone in college and community bands and orchestra for the rest of my life. One of the major purchases of my life was a silver-plated euphonium in 1971, which I continue to play.

I am impressed with how many physicians are also music aficionados and accomplished musicians. Although music appreciation is often a passive experience, I have experienced greater satisfaction and personal impact from playing or singing in groups. I believe the latter provides an opportunity to acquire a deeper appreciation of the music and impart a personal interpretation of its outcome. Music continues to serve as a great source of relaxation, distraction, education, and accomplishment for me. Our house is always filled with classical music from WQXR, and I continue to play my euphonium at age eighty-two in a local concert band in Pleasantville, NY.

You know, music is a respite for many people. In medicine, you need to try hard to understand everything. Everything needs to make sense. But with music, you don't need to understand it—you can study the theory if you want to, but you don't need to understand. You can just enjoy it. It doesn't require much brain power, so it can be very restorative. In medical school, there were many, many of us who were involved with music. One of us was in the Boston Symphony, one of us was a conductor, and several others were singers. The musician-physician connection is very common. There are just so many positives to it. You can play alone or with others, making harmony with friends.

I worked with kids who had cancer, and they often had to undergo frightening procedures. We would bring in a music therapist who would play the guitar and try to calm them down before a procedure. There is a very basic positive feeling there. A non-verbal relaxation. Our musical memories are indelibly recorded in our brains like a circuit that's always there.

Doctor-musicians like Jeff Allen are not a rarity. According to Dr. Wong (2013), 70%-80% of doctors have some musical training. She describes the phenomenon like this: "When you reach out your hand and try to touch the place between medicine and music, some place between the physical and the spiritual, you're coming close to one of the fundamental mysteries of life. It delves close to the core of what makes us human." (p. 8).

Wong writes about the Longwood Symphony Orchestra, which was created as a music ensemble for the many doctor musicians who work near Longwood Avenue in Boston—an area that encompasses several large hospitals. There are many such orchestras around the world, that "tap into an identical yearning among musician-physicians to continue their music" (p. 39). Many musicians in the Longwood Orchestra talk about how music makes them better physicians, as it calms and focuses their minds, and allows them an expressive outlet, but also about how being a physician makes them think about and produce music differently, approaching the music with a similar meticulousness and care that they apply to medicine.

"Cello Medicine—Music in Nature"

The profound connection between music and medicine does not pertain only to the healing of people. Rebecca Hartka is a professional cellist. She told me her story about how her classical training and her connections to indigenous cultures came together to form what she calls "Cello Medicine." Rebecca plays her cello for rivers, streams, and trees to heal nature through sound vibration. I encourage you to read her story with an open mind. What might at first sound like a stretch of the imagination actually seems plausible and intriguingly important:

> It's all about vibration. We are sound, vibrating at the molecular level. For me, music had a very special place in my life because it helped me recover when I almost died at 17 months old. I had a staph infection of the blood and had needles in my arms for intravenous antibiotics. To keep me still, my mom sang to me while she pushed me up and down the halls of the hospital. Her voice showed up as medicine for the trauma. She had a beautiful voice. She loved music and movement and infused it into our childhood. She made everything playful and fun like a musical. Naturally, I felt unsafe in my body after such an illness, and playing cello, beginning at nine years old, really helped me connect to a sense of safety and belonging.

As a child, my neighbors were indigenous Ecuadorians and were constantly bringing Andean musicians over. There was dancing around the fire. I felt the purity of the land through their music. I grew up hearing that music, and it felt like home to me. My grandparents lived in Mexico, and when I visited, I was just surrounded by rich folkloric dances and songs. I remember the gorgeous traditional outfits and how they would dance with water on their heads. As an adult [after going through formal cello training and conservatory], I finally came full circle. When I went to Mexico, I went to a small town in the Yucatan with my colleague, Jose Lezcano, who is a Cuban guitarist. Mayan people were reclaiming the musical instruments from their ancestors by looking at pictures and studying surviving examples, recreating the old instruments. We played a performance with Mayan musicians who had reclaimed some of their traditional music. We mostly improvised with them. The scales were so different. It wasn't a perfect performance, but the audience loved it because they could feel the connection across cultures and the sense of Mexican belonging.

Western culture has been separated from nature for a long time. During the pandemic, when I didn't have concerts, I got in touch with how much classical music and our Western view of it had formed my very identity. I took the invitation to just learn how to be a human. To just be. I love playing cello, so I thought, "I'm going to just play outside." I started by playing for a tree. It felt like an audience. Like the tree was a collaborator. I felt like I was reaching to understand across different relations. What could the tree teach me? I would improvise and feel something in the tree actually influence how I was playing. The straightness of the trunk or the way the leaves moved. But it was sometimes more ephemeral than that.

Then, during the Black Lives Matter movement, I found myself questioning what reparations mean to me. I discovered that I had a direct ancestor in the Revolutionary War who was from the Hudson area of New York. Apparently, he was one of the soldiers who actually helped drive out the Haudenosaunee, what we call the Iroquois in NY State. I went through a process of wanting to repair. My sister works with an organization that does a lot of Indigenous work, and she put me in touch with the Schagticoke First Nations Chief. I wanted to work in a way that would be directly involved in that region. They were doing a land reclamation project, planting native, pre-colonization plants. I engaged various people who were fans of mine—concertgoers—to support me in playing in front of streams, waterfalls, and riverways, with the intention of purifying the water and raising money for environmental cleanup.

Have you heard about the Japanese researcher, Masaru Emoto? He did all these experiments with water and showed scientifically how kind words and music can positively affect the molecular formation of water droplets. I raised money and donated it to the Schagticoke First Nations, and I worked with my own ancestors, who were Celtic, and who have a deep connection with the ocean and the land. My ancestors had also had their own traditions colonized, forbidden, suffocated, stamped out through violence. So there was a deep sense of reclamation—wanting to belong to the trees and plants and world around me. So out of that, I developed "Cello Medicine."

Soon after that, I was invited to play at a glass festival in Turkey. I played for a Yew tree and water, and started to create layers with a loop pedal. I felt I could finally take this back to audiences. I performed about three hours of music over three days, mostly improvised while my husband demonstrated glass sculpture. It was a beautiful experience. Whether playing Bach or improvising, I try to bring that sense of play and joy into the music. While the Western worldview of music is so tiny, it does contain magic and beauty. But it's good to remember that we have probably 200,000 years of land-based music. In a lot of pre-modern cultures, musicians are also healers, priestesses. The best I can do with Cello Medicine is to be an example of this.

Music for Soldiers, Prisoners, and the Homeless

The healing effects of music make it well-suited for therapeutic purposes. While this book does not delve into music therapy, per se, music is only healing or helpful to those in distress or dealing with trauma when an emotional connectedness to the music or musicians is present. There has to be a genuine reason to care. Mickey Katz, a cellist in the Boston Symphony Orchestra, spoke with me about a time early in his career, when a lack of connection and care resulted in a painful, rather than healing, musical experience:

> When I was 18, I was deemed to be a "talented" musician. Growing up in Israel, if you are a tax-paying citizen, you go to the army at that age. A small group of us "Talented Musicians" auditioned to be part of a small group of artists who were allowed to continue practicing our art during our time in the army. We had to do basic training and guarding, too, but we were allowed to keep playing. We were asked to play for military ceremonies and events, like for a dinner for the Prime Minister of Turkey. They asked us to play when dessert was served. But we wanted to do something more educational and meaningful. My small group of four musicians proposed playing chamber music for soldiers. But we were talented little jerks, and we just basically entertained ourselves and joked around. We experimented with playing different types of pieces, inviting people to sing along, or inventing ways to teach the soldiers a little bit about the music we were playing.
>
> One time, we played at an outpost near the border in the north. The audience, a group of soldiers, seemed completely dead. No interest. It was very frustrating. We had a meal with them after the concert, and we could feel their open hostility towards us, privileged musicians doing an army job with zero risks. One of them yelled at us, "Our friend was just killed in the line of duty! He was shot in the head!" What did they care about how the melodic line is repeated in the second movement? Their friend was shot in the head! We were just 18. We had no training on how to connect with them.

André de Quadros, a professor of music education at Boston University, has spent the majority of his career working with marginalized communities, including projects with prisons, psychosocial rehabilitation, refugees, and victims of sexual violence, torture, and trauma. His work crosses race and mass incarceration, peacebuilding, forced migration, LGBTQ+ people, and Islamic culture[5].

He and his colleague Emilie Amrein developed a framework called "Empowering Song," based on years of experience in musical healing and interaction with traumatized and struggling

---

[5] https://www.andredequadros.com/about-4

populations. Put simply, de Quadros and Amrein realized that people have a deep psychological need to tell their stories and have their stories be heard. They start each session by trying to create a hospitable and safe space for stories to be shared. Sometimes this happens with closed eyes and hand holding in a circle, sometimes through playful games and acting. Storytelling, they write, allows us to "author ourselves and the world around us," and "position the past to spring into the future" (2023, p. 91).

Starting with dialogue and storytelling, then finding musical ways (rapping, chanting, song-writing, rhythmic improvisation) to include, connect with, and express these stories, can have life-changing effects on the entire group involved. When a group of people understands the vulnerabilities, tender feelings, traumas, joys, and the identities held among themselves, their shared musical experience takes on a depth that can be completely absent when there is simply a one-way performance.

When people think of music as a way to "even the playing field" or bring people together despite their differences, it only works when an effort is made to seek out commonalities. If power dynamics enter in, the possibilities for connection, openness, and trust become dead ends. Consider a situation where a music teacher tries to come into a prison to teach guitar, for example, without asking what kind of music the incarcerated participants are interested in learning. Allowing them to exercise personal choices and preferences can be particularly powerful in a place where most choices are made for them.

Or think about a group of performing musicians who enter a prison to entertain or soothe a group of people, probably selecting musical pieces that don't relate to prisoners' personal experiences. This is often experienced as an infiltration of white culture as a preferred or higher art form into a space that is disproportionately made up of people of color. Felicity Laurence writes about music in conflict resolution and states that throughout history, music has unfortunately been centered on power relationships—the symphony orchestra, the "accepted epitome of Western musical culture, is entirely based on a rigid hierarchical structure" (2015, p. 23).

Laurence also states that a true empathic relationship is non-manipulative. It is cooperative and involves personally knowing another, enhancing feelings for another, and fostering tolerance and appreciation for differences. Our intentions—the *way* we make music together, the extent to which we allow for agency, are all significant in our ability to draw forth or create empathic experiences through music.

Musicians who invite collaborative music-making experiences with prisoners, on the other hand, not only work to decolonize musical experiences, but they also model the idea that prisoners' musical choices are valid and interesting. Trusting that the incarcerated participants can make musical choices also means allowing for a widely diverse sampling of what counts as "good" music.

Violinist Adrian Anantawan is the artistic director of Shelter Music Boston, an organization of musicians who play over eighty concerts a month in homeless shelters and substance abuse rehabilitation centers in the Boston area. The key to their success is in the ongoing relationship and respectful dialogue with those whom they serve. Residents say that they look forward to these visits each week, and that they feel a sense of dignity and hope during a time in their lives when feelings of depression, shame, and uncertainty seem to reign[6]:

> *"The music captured my emotions and transformed rage to peace. Thank you."* —Dimock Center guest

> *"You might have saved a life with this concert!"* —CASPAR Shelter guest

> *"When you play, I know it ain't over; the music gives me hope. Your playing makes me feel alive."* —Pine Street Inn - Shattuck Shelter guest

The musicians from Shelter Music Boston make regular visits to each place that they serve, which establishes consistency and allows for a relationship to develop. In addition, unlike a typical concert scene, where the audience is far removed from the musicians, the Shelter Music Boston musicians interact with residents, answer their questions, and even take song requests. This approach helps to break down any barriers and creates a

---

[6] Shelter Music Boston, "Impact," accessed March 7, 2025, https://www.sheltermusicboston.org/impact.html

sense of comfort or safety. After each performance, the musicians often ask those who are present to reflect on what they heard using "feeling" words.[7] Taking part in these concerts sends clear messages to those suffering from home insecurity and substance abuse: You matter. Your feelings and experiences matter.

Are We All Musical Healers?

Let's get back to reclaiming our musical identities! Here is the connection that I wanted to show you through sharing these stories. The inclination to soothe suffering through music is in our human nature. We pick up a crying baby in the middle of the night and sing them back to sleep. We might help an anxious child feel braver by improvising a little song for or with them as they go to school or prepare for their first haircut. When a friend is going through a hard time, we might send her a meaningful song. It is common to hear end-of-life stories where we help our loved ones transition into the afterlife by playing music or singing to them.

Being musical in these ways has nothing to do with perfection or performance. We don't need to practice or be taught how to be musical healers. The ability to sing in tune becomes less important here. It is shadowed by what we instinctively know is most important: love, caring, connection, and healing.

If a group of incarcerated people can be guided to express their stories through invented songs or raps, so can you. If you are yearning to use music to connect with others or to help people around you understand each other's perspectives better, you don't need to be a professional musician. You just need to listen and make space for each story to be expressed safely. What kind of music do people want to share, connect with, or express their feelings with?

If you have ever felt musically shut down, silenced, or belittled by a music teacher or musician, you can now understand the role that power dynamics play. What does it look like when everyone's musical voice matters (not just those deemed "talented")? What

---

[7] Shelter Music Boston, "Shelter Music Boston Concert Experience," accessed March 7, 2025, https://www.sheltermusicboston.org/impact.html

does it look like when we assume that everyone is musically competent in some way?

Part Two:
Rewriting the Score on Our Musical Development

5 — Our Musical Beginnings

Vignette: Bach in the NICU

Baby Violet (not her real name) was born at twenty-nine weeks' gestation, weighing just 2 lbs., 12 oz.—only a few ounces past what might have been a miscarriage. Before entering the NICU, her mother, and my good friend, Amena (also not her real name), had to scrub her hands, nails, and up to her elbows in antibacterial soap for two solid minutes. She wore a hospital gown and a face mask to be sure no extra germs entered the space.

On Violet's second day of life, Amena invited me for a visit. I scrubbed up and nervously entered the soft-lit room, where four or five other incubators sat, emitting occasional beeps and displaying vitals on individual monitors. I stepped close to Violet's incubator. With a breathing tube around her nose, heart monitoring tubes attached to her chest, mittens around her wrists, and bandages from various blood draws, I could barely recognize this little bundle as human. Violet's vitals were shaky. Her heart sometimes skipped a beat or fluttered; her breath was uneven.

When she made it past her first few weeks, she was transferred to a different room. She was stronger, but her vitals still needed monitoring around the clock. Amena, who is a violinist, was permitted to bring her violin into the room. She played what she considered to be soothing music—some Mozart, and one of Bach's sonatas for solo violin. The music she chose was structured, melodic, and tonally predictable in the way that classic European music of the early 1700s was designed to be. Violet's breathing and heart rate regulated as Amena played, her entire body responding to the music. Amena then looked around at the monitors on the other incubators in the room and noticed that all of the other babies' heart rates and breathing rates had regulated as well!

A week or so later, Amena invited me back into the NICU. "I want to show you something," she said. We scrubbed in, and she placed the violin on her shoulder. "Keep your eyes on her breath rate," Amena told me.

She began playing a section of a Bach sonata that she often played in that room. As the musical chord tension naturally built over the course of several measures, Violet's breath regulated. Then, something incredible happened. Just *before* the end of the musical phrase, Violet inhaled sharply, then exhaled as Amena's bow landed on the dominant "home" chord of the phrase. Violet had learned to anticipate exactly when the dominant chord would be played. It had become a part of her body's inner knowledge—a relaxing return to her home base.

Violet is now nineteen years old. Though she is more interested in fashion design, she also plays the violin and considers herself to be a musical person. I recently asked her to tell me about any significant musical memories from her life. Without knowing anything about what I intended to write about her, she said that her most salient childhood memories of music were, "Listening to my mum playing violin."

This is striking because most people who answer the "tell me about significant musical memories or moments from your childhood" question tell me about their own musical experiences. People talk about embarrassing moments on stage, a harsh word from a teacher, an invitation to play with specific people or at an important event, or making it into a special performance group. When people have talked about listening to special music as a core memory, it is usually about what inspired their own love of music. Yet Violet simply stated that listening to her mother's violin playing in and of itself is her most meaningful musical memory. Having heard her mother playing in the womb, and then having her mother's playing regulate the very breath that kept her alive, I cannot help but think that Violet experienced Amena's playing as an embodied sense of self in a way that nothing else could match. This is her sense of home.

Womb Music

Dr. Sheila Woodward is a professor of music education at Eastern Washington University whose research on prenatal, fetal, and newborn music experiences is widely known among academics in early childhood music education.

When I met her as a guest lecturer at Teachers College, she had some very compelling stories to share. She spoke of a woman who would mysteriously feel like weeping each time she heard Latin choral music. This woman spoke with many relatives and friends as she later investigated this emotional reaction, and discovered that her mother had gone through a personal tragedy while pregnant with her. Her mother, who loved listening to Latin choral music, used to play those pieces and weep.

Another interesting story was about a professional cellist who discovered a piece of orchestral music that, although it was new to him, he somehow seemed to know already. Dr. Woodward explained that this cellist seemed to recognize the music internally, on another level. His mother, it turned out, had been practicing this piece as an orchestral musician while pregnant with him.

Are you curious now about the music that may have surrounded you in utero? While it may not be possible to ask someone who remembers, or to clarify what might feel like an out-of-focus picture, it is interesting to ask ourselves whether there are specific pieces of music that seem to feel more like "home" to us.

Babies Make Us Musical

Imagine for a moment that you are holding a baby in your arms. You lovingly look down into their eyes, which openly meet yours in an expectant gaze. You do *not* say, "Hey, what's up? How are you today?" Instead, your eyebrows arch as you smile and nod. Your voice takes on a higher pitch and comes out in a slow melodic arc: "Helllloooooooooo..."

Can you imagine this exact sound? I would guess that you can. Dr. Lori Custodero, professor of music education at Columbia

University's Teachers College, writes that in every culture ever studied across the globe, adults make wider, more open facial gestures, nod their head, and emote musical speech phrases or sounds as they communicate with babies (2002). When adults speak to babies, we instinctively raise the pitch of our voices and "speak" in shorter phrases with distinct musical contours: A rising shape is used to arouse attention; a falling shape to calm. These very musical phrases inherently invite a communicative response from the baby, who begins not only to expect and predict these melodic signals but also to deliver their musical communications, inviting a musical response from the adult.

Custodero calls this type of melodic parent-infant interaction a "dialogical duet." The specific rhythm and pacing of these musical conversations is particularly attuned between the baby and their primary caregiver, setting it apart from the types of exchanges that the baby has with other adults.

Studies by Trevarthen and Malloch (2002) reveal that in all healthy parent-baby relationships, this "communicative musicality" allows the pair to spend time together meaningfully. Specifically, musical gestures are jointly created and strung together, building companionship which can be sustained and revisited over time. We can think of it as a two-way mirroring that happens where infants will imitate the pitch and timbre of the parent's voice, and the parent will mirror the response back to the baby. This reciprocal exchange helps form a trusting relationship—what psychologists call "attachment," which leads to healthy child development.

In addition to these early musical conversations, Custodero (2024, p. 8) points out that "Many cultures have traditions involving parents swaying or rocking infants in their arms, laying infants across their laps and gently bouncing them on their knees, or carrying infants on their backs and walking, in each instance, accompanied by singing." As adults combine music and movement to help regulate babies in our care, we instinctively draw from our personal musical histories, memories, and music-making abilities. We understand how to do this because the combination of music and movement also helps *us* to regulate, as we use it to calm ourselves, increase motivation to get through an exercise routine at the gym, or get into a flow of household chores.

The universality of musical communication and regulation that we engage in with babies shows that musicality may be biologically necessary for a baby's survival, growth, and development. As the baby grows into a child, communicative relationships are what help the child to begin functioning in society. Two points from this research are so important that I want to restate them for you explicitly:

1. We are all very musical beings by nature in the first months of our lives because our survival depended on bonding with our caretakers, which happened for us through musical conversations.

2. Adults instinctively make themselves into musical communicators when they interact with babies. We already have this ability inside us!

Family Music, Home Music

In Part One, you may remember Lauren's description of the "unabashed joy" of making music together with her family. I asked you to consider the fact that most families make some music together, even if it isn't to the extent that Lauren's family did. I asked you to recognize that it isn't the amount of music that families engage in together at home, but the fact that it happens in most homes.

Perhaps you wondered whether this is actually true! Custodero and Johnson-Green (2003) interviewed over 2000 parents of infants, illuminating how and when parents chose to use music with their babies. They found that even though most parents didn't consider themselves to be musical, almost every family sang or danced with their babies regularly to soothe, bond, play, and communicate. In fact, as children age, the adults in their lives seem to instinctively understand that music is useful in helping children through their day. From the emotional regulating lullabies that we use with babies, to clean-up songs with young children, music often functions as a transitional object (like the comfort of a special blankie or stuffed animal) in families and in preschools.

"Because of its social nature, music also may lie at the heart of family coherence, which is integral to a healthy upbringing and critical for mitigating the stress inherent in transitions" (Zur and Johnson-Green, 2008).

Custodero noticed that mothers instinctively use higher-pitched singing with their babies to establish emotional connection, but use a lower-pitched voice with toddlers, allowing for more clearly enunciated words, and shifting towards teaching concepts or ideas (2006).

Interestingly, it doesn't seem to matter to babies, toddlers, or young children whether the adults in their lives sing "in tune" or not.

When parents sing to soothe, excite, play, or give directions, they are creating musical relationships that help regulate daily life and bond with their little ones. Caregivers and teachers instinctively know that singing, rather than speaking, will have a much stronger effect. This adult instinct to sing songs to babies, toddlers, and young children has anthropological roots, as we saw in Part One of this book. Furthermore, when parents or caregivers sing regularly to babies and young children, they are modeling the notion that it is normal and "okay" to be a musically expressive person.

When people talk about "exposing" their child to music by taking them to music classes or signing them up for lessons, they often don't realize that young children already possess a world of musical knowledge and experience from their home lives. They may not even remember the frequent musical interactions that they had with their caregivers when they were little. I cringe when I hear music teachers talking about the importance of teaching kids how to keep a "steady beat!" Do they not realize or remember all of the rocking, bouncing, soothing, and energizing music that babies and young children have already received before entering the music room?

It is beautiful to witness, instead, when early childhood music teachers acknowledge the wealth of babies' experiences in their classes by asking caregivers to share what music they engage in at home. These music teachers will build musical knowledge from those previous experiences, or skillfully weave in songs or music from home to make connections with what is happening in the room at the moment. Preschool and elementary school music teachers also have many opportunities to invite children to share or teach the class about their family's musical culture. When teachers and experts in music build from there (rather than from a "blank slate" lens), we are creating a two-way street that allows young children to also feel like capable and respected music-makers.

Are you wondering now what *your* early childhood musical experiences were? All of the music that you truly engaged in but simply can't remember because those experiences fell under the category of *play* or *caregiving,* rather than "music-making?" Custodero suggests that a powerful tool for recalling these early childhood musical memories is autobiographical writing: "Autobiographical memories of our earliest years provide windows through which we can examine how our past still lives in our present, to have a sense of ourselves as complete historical beings with promise for continued growth" (2024, p. 55).

Custodero explains that talking with parents or caregivers can help bring musical memories to the forefront and give us new understandings about our musical childhoods. There is usually something there, even if our memories have pushed them too far back to recall. She found that in actually writing down your "Music Autobiography," sometimes the memories that arise can bring up feelings of surprise, confusion, or missed opportunities. But why not give it a try?

If you have older family members who are alive and available to delve into your past with you, ask them what they remember about your early musical experiences. Start writing down your musical story! And if feelings of regret arise, just stick with me—I will show you later how we can begin to reclaim our musical selves.

"I Think She's Asking You to Dance"—
Tuning into Toddlers

It was my third or fourth session teaching in the beautiful home of a young Palestinian mother who offered her living room in East Jerusalem for our baby and toddler music classes. One of the mothers had asked if it was okay to invite her father along, and I eagerly agreed. He took a seat on the couch, while the rest of us sat in our usual arrangement—a large blue mat on the floor with cushions.

Various instruments, puppets, and dancing scarves were available, as always, for the babies to play with through our first few songs. The toddler (I will call her Yasmin) glanced back at her grandfather several times as she shook her small maraca. She even held it out to show him, or perhaps invite him to join. After our first activity, I sang our cleanup song, and we cleared the mat for dancing.

Yasmin stood up on wobbly legs, toddled over to her grandfather, and tapped her hand on his knee. Her grandfather gave her a big smile before her mother lifted Yasmin back onto the mat to get ready for our usual circle dance, a Greek folk song called "Tik Tik Tak" (1999) in which I typically invite the babies and toddlers to participate as they wish. Some babies usually enjoy sitting in the middle as we circle them; some prefer being held by their adult, and some, like Yasmin, like to move on their own with the circle. As the familiar sounds of the accordion filled the room that day, Yasmin left the circle again to tap her grandfather's knee, this time adding a verbal "Uhhh uhh!"

"I think she's inviting you to dance," I prompted. Yasmin and her grandfather each lit up with glee as he joined her and her mother in the circle.

Yes, even the youngest humans understand that bonding and connecting through shared musical experiences with those we love is essential.

"You Have to Sing!"

Five-year-old Erica was singing to herself as she cut, colored, and glued geometric shapes into her notebook. She had been singing almost nonstop for nearly an hour of this kindergarten "work" period. Nearby, Troy sang "Zig Zag Zig" to the tune of "This Old Man" as he colored a large letter Z. Meanwhile, Spyro and Lila worked side-by-side, standing up at their work table as they drew with colored pencils. Their hips were moving to the rhythm of their song, "I Like to Move It, Move It!" (Morillo, 2005). They were singing at the top of their voices.

Suddenly, Lila stopped singing, which caused Spyro to stop

coloring. Spyro, looking confused, turned to Lila with agitation and commanded, "You have to sing!"

This was a scene that I witnessed in a kindergarten classroom in Darwin, Australia, in 2006 as part of my doctoral research. My aim at the time was to spend a month in each of three different kindergartens in three very different cities, observing and documenting children's spontaneous singing: the unprompted song inventions that stream forth from children's mouths as they play, work, and interact socially throughout their day. I wanted to learn about how local culture could influence the content of children's spontaneous songs. What I learned instead was something entirely different.

I had already spent a month in a New York City classroom and another month observing kindergarteners in Singapore. I had compiled several notebooks full of descriptions of these types of spontaneous songs, and I had noticed the many ways in which young children were using songs to help with emotional regulation, schedule transitions, social interaction, and cognitive processing. When Spyro told Lila, "You have to sing," he summed up my entire research study. I realized that the act of singing together was helping him work. He *needed* to keep singing with her to finish. Children singing to get through their day is nearly universal, as I will soon show.

Researchers who study young children in their classrooms and homes have described the many contexts and conditions in which young children sing, dance, and chant spontaneously. From emulating a rock star to being soothed by a mother's lullaby, playful musical expression is the very means through which children come to understand and create their world. Since Moorhead and Pond's first studies of young children's invented music in 1941, many researchers have contributed to our understanding of the many reasons why songs seem to naturally spill forth from young children as they go about their day. Researchers Marsh and Young (2016) provide an in-depth review of this material, covering studies that illuminate age-specific characteristics, interpretive lenses, psychological conclusions, and socio-cultural influences. From coloring and working to imaginary play, to bath time, and bedtime, children use music to process the events and emotions of their lived experiences.

Spyro's statement, "You have to sing!" was like a shockwave

through my system—its truth so stark:

Children need to sing to help them get through their day at school.

Through my own research on children's song inventions (Zur, 2007), I found that the children who had the hardest time following directions or finishing their work quickly were, in fact, the students who sang the most! These were also the very same students whom the teacher labeled as problematic, disruptive, or hard to handle. It became apparent to me that a child's need for extended creative play is closely tied to the amount of time spent singing. Children who were quick to respond (the first to line up, the first to know the answer to a question, or the first to complete work) barely sang at all during my observations. Though other factors may have been in place, I couldn't help but be mesmerized by the notion that young children were using music as a tool for self-regulation.

Kindergarten often marks the first year of formal learning in school settings, which often means less time for play and more hours spent carrying out teacher-led work and activities. Since many preschools and kindergartens like to state that "play is the work of children," I want to clarify that when I say "play," I am talking about the free-form, open-ended, and often imaginary play where the teacher is not directing or expecting a work-related outcome. When kindergarteners struggle with the higher expectations and scheduling boundaries of a school setting, their music-making connects them to their playful nature. It helps children to elongate their playful world where time feels endless and more relaxed.

In fact, humans everywhere across the globe, no matter their age, turn to music to help them get through the tedium of their day as well. Consider the office janitor with his headphones on, vacuuming to the beat of his favorite tunes. Consider the early morning jogger, listening through a Bluetooth speaker headband, or the subway rider, tuning out the world as he makes his way home after a long day.

What happens to the outpouring of young children's invented songs when a teacher or caregiver repeatedly demands quiet? Are quiet classrooms truly the mark of focused attention? If singing (or dancing) really does help a child to finish their work, or enter into a state of flow with their work, how can we support this without it being disruptive?

Is the quieting of children in school settings part of what shuts down their natural music-making abilities?

I am not suggesting that teachers allow for constant singing and chanting, but I do believe there is a way to respectfully ask for quiet attention when the teacher needs that. For example, instead of saying something harsh like, "Stop singing. It's not music class!" we could say, "You're singing so beautifully! I love hearing you sing, but right now, I need quiet attention from everyone." This simple statement acknowledges to the child that it is okay to be musical. The *you-are-musical* recognition and appreciation for the child's singing helps children to understand that their singing or rhythm-making isn't something to be embarrassed by. We will dive deeper into the topic of nourishing, rather than squelching, young children's musicality later in this book.

It's Not "Cute"—Recognizing and Honoring Children's Invented Songs

Let me ask you a question: If I were to ask you to think of "children's music," what comes to mind? And if I were to ask you to imagine "children's art," what jumps into your mind? I would venture to guess that when most people think of "children's music," they imagine music made by adults *for* children, such as songs from Raffi, *Sesame Street*, or *Barney*. Meanwhile, the words "children's art" often conjure up images of sloppy watercolor paintings or crayon doodles made *by* children. Why is it that children's art tends to be something made by children, yet children's music is something made *for* children? To move away from quickly labelling a child as "talented," or not, and just appreciate their musicality or artistry as a normal part of life, we might need to reframe our perception and appreciation of young children's vocal play.

When asking young children to draw or paint something, an art teacher might simply provide a prompt and allow the artists to create a scene. As adults, we appreciate children's artwork as beautiful, even magical, visions of the way that they see, interpret, and express the world around them. We honor these pictures by hanging them in our homes and saving them in portfolios.

Where is the musical equivalent? How do we honor and savor the uniquely magical music made by children in their everyday lives? Instead of laughing at the songs that children produce (calling them "cute" or "silly"), could we listen intently and appreciate these vocal doodles? Instead of judging whether or not a child is a "good singer," could we encourage them to explore their singing range, improvise on a melody, or play around with dynamics? Could we model a sense of curiosity and help them develop vocal explorations by asking questions such as, "What would it sound like if a dolphin could sing?" or "How does your voice feel when you stand up tall like a tree?"

The word "cute" is often used in association with childhood in general, when adults see children through their adult lens. What I mean by this is that few adults would lay their winter coat on the ground face up, stand behind it, stick their arms in the sleeves, and flip the whole jacket over their heads just to make sure it goes on correctly. We may see it as cute because the child is very seriously trying to do this thing that we adults have mastered long ago. But if we take a moment to look at this task from a child's perspective, they aren't putting on their jacket in that way to be cute. Their intention isn't cute—it is a focused effort to gain mastery. If we want to encourage children to develop their musicianship, calling their music (or art, or dance, or anything) "cute" is detrimental and demeaning.

"What a Wonderful World"—A Non-Verbal Singer and Dancer Who Can't Walk

When I began my teaching career, I had a lovely music classroom in a public school just outside New York City. I remember being excited to hang up my colorful poster of a Zimbabwean proverb that read, "If you can walk, you can dance; if you can talk, you can sing." I thought it was inspiring. I thought it was true.

Amit, age six, came to my music classes with a huge smile on his face. He would park his walker at his music spot and take a seat.

On one particular day, we were learning a folk dance that involved alternating sections of dancing in a circle and then moving inward and outward, closing and opening the circle as we raised our arms up. I had thought of and designed an accommodation that I thought might work for him. As I started to teach the dance, I explained my idea to him.

Amit shrugged his shoulders. "I can do it," he said. "I can do the dance." My proverb poster clearly didn't account for Amit's ability to dance, even though he couldn't walk. His legs may not have worked, but he had no problem dancing along with the rest of the class.

And now I must tell you the story of Daniel. Once a week for the past five years, Daniel attended my music classes along with his one-on-one aide and six classmates. This self-contained "special needs" class was composed of students who were not integrated into typical classrooms at all. Each student was non-verbal and needed frequent one-on-one assistance to move, eat, and function throughout the day. Molly was in a wheelchair and could only move her head and hands a little bit. Matthew moved freely and used a tablet to communicate. Daniel, who was ten years old at the time, had low-functioning autism (LFA). Sometimes he blurted a word out here or there, but was mostly silent and had not said more than one or two words in a row in his entire life.

As their music teacher, I had prepared a set of about twenty laminated and magnetized picture cards on the board, which these students could select at the start of class to communicate which song they would like to engage in. Some of these were game songs, some included instruments such as shakers or hand drums, and some had picture books associated with them. "What a Wonderful World" (1967) by Louis Armstrong was one such song, which has a beautifully illustrated picture book (Weiss, 1995) to accompany the lyrics. It was a song that Daniel had selected every time for the past several years.

A few weeks prior, I had introduced some toy microphones called "Echo Mics" that slightly amplify the voice. Though most people would not likely call it "singing," Molly and Matthew, two slightly more verbal students in that class, enjoyed experiencing the amplified effects of these plastic mics as we sang through various songs.

I will never know what was different about that particular day in March. Whether Daniel made some type of connection with these simple toy microphones, or whether something inside Daniel was different on that day. Upon entering the music room, he placed the "What a Wonderful World" picture card on the board, picked up one of the echo mics, and sang the song by himself from beginning to end, exactly on pitch in the sweetest voice one could imagine. The paraprofessionals in the room had tears streaming down their faces. It was the first time anyone had really heard his voice. That day, I tore the poster with the Zimbabwean proverb off my wall.

I taught Daniel and his classmates for one more year after that, before I left to begin my doctoral work. I never heard him sing again, but I learned something that will stick with me for the rest of my life: We simply don't know how or where music resides inside others. What someone overtly exhibits may not match their *actual* inner musical world. And what a wonderful world that can be! Nearly twenty years later, I still hold back tears each time I hear that song.

6 — The Spaces and Places Where We Feel Musical

Vignette: "You Should Stand Outside the Bathroom..."

When I first became interested in studying young children's spontaneous singing, I was teaching in an elementary school just outside New York City, working toward a master's degree at Teachers College. I had just read a fascinating book called *Songs in Their Heads* (Campbell, 2010), which describes the richness of children's spontaneous singing in their daily lives, and I was eager to see what kinds of singing my students would do. At that time, the school had eight separate kindergarten classrooms, and I asked each of the kindergarten teachers if I could sit in on their play time and listen for any songs that might occur.

In one of my first observations, the class was playful, but I wasn't hearing very much in the way of singing. The kindergarten teacher in that class was curious to know more about my research, and I explained that young children often invent songs and sing spontaneously throughout their day. A wide smile spread across her face as she leaned in to whisper, "You should stand outside the bathroom. That's where I hear the most singing! I think they like their privacy..."

The Musical Clubhouse

We often think of young children as being expressively free and uninhibited. Up until about the age of four, they seem completely unconcerned with telling Aunt Jody that she looks enormously fat, or taking off their pants in a room full of people, for example. Yet it turns out that when young children are offered private spaces or are left to play without an adult gaze upon them, their creativity soars.

Danette Littleton, a music education specialist, is widely known for her research on young children's musical play. As part of her doctoral research, she conducted music play experiments in the preschool where she taught, which sparked an array of interesting follow-up studies. Littleton (1991) set up several music free-play sessions with four- and five-year-olds to find out how different settings influenced their musical creativity. She placed small percussive music instruments such as hand drums, tambourines, shakers, triangles, and xylophones around the preschool room and observed how they interacted with the materials, as well as what kinds of songs they created.

As part of her experiment, Littleton also experimented with the role of the teacher (herself). In some sessions, she acted as an encouraging, supportive teacher, making suggestions and directly interacting with the musical play. In other sessions, she stood nearby, quietly observing. Lastly, she allowed the students to play with the materials while she pretended to be doing "busy work" at her desk, essentially staying out of the picture. Can you guess which sessions produced the most abundantly creative musical expressions? Upon reviewing her data, Littleton could clearly see that her absence yielded the highest forms of creativity.

Taking the concept of privacy a bit further, music education researcher Allison Harmer noticed that most preschool settings are large, open-concept spaces. This makes sense, since teachers and early childhood caregivers should be able to see and easily access the children under their care. But young children also like to be cozy and seem to have a natural inclination to make clubhouses, tents, forts, and other secretive, womb-like or den-like spaces. Harmer wanted to see what would happen if she created an intentional clubhouse for students ages three and four. She placed a large tablecloth over a small table and attached a hidden camera to capture any musical happenings within. She made sure that an equal number of small instruments were available within and outside of the clubhouse. She noticed that the intensity and duration of musical expression under the table went far beyond what she had ever heard in the open-plan room (2011).

Let's face it—adults respond constantly to children's music-making. All it takes is the tiniest little song to trickle from a child's lips for an adult to comment, "What a nice little song," or "What are you singing?" or "My oh my! Such a voice!"

And never mind a spoon banging on a pot, or a ratchety rhythm made with a stick on a corrugated metal fence. Musical play is noisy. It is not intended to highlight a skill or to please others as in a performance. It is the musical equivalent of a sloppy finger painting, where the joy lies in the physical sensation of producing wet, colorful marks on paper rather than in producing a fine piece of art (though sometimes it can evolve into the most sophisticated and refined work). Most adults would probably not even perceive these sounds and rhythms as music in the first place, and I'm guessing young children, sensing that is the case, feel more comfortable singing and "musicking" in private. In truth, young children might not call it "music" either. They might just be having a pleasurable sound-making experience! But if we let them do that, who knows what musical learning and growth can transpire?

Shower and Car Songs

As we know, adults prefer singing in private as well. The closest thing we often get to a clubhouse is usually our car or shower.

In these private spaces, it's okay to go off-key, botch the words, flub a harmony, or have our voice crack. We have to be allowed to be bad at something before we can get good at it. When I'm driving, I can try to locate and sing along with the lower harmony of an Indigo Girls song I love 423 times if I want to, and maybe I will finally get it the 424th time!

In this sense, our cars and showers are like the practice rooms where we hone our skills. Yet the idea of a practice room implies that we are practicing for a particular purpose or performance. I will never need to belt out one of those low harmonies, but it feels so good to just open my mouth and let the sound come out!

Here is another intriguing point. If all we need is privacy to allow us to open our mouths and sing, why don't more people sing in their office with the door closed or when they are home alone? Or out in an open field when no one is around? Showers and cars are more than just private spaces. They are small and enclosed spaces where we cannot do anything else but finish the task at hand—getting to our destination or washing ourselves. Both in the car and in the shower, we are free from other distractions and to-do lists, and we are not being stimulated in other ways that are interesting to our brains. We are forced to simply be where we are. Singing helps us regulate, thereby turning a mundane experience into something more pleasurable.

I believe there are other elements at play in these particular enclosed spaces: sound and movement. The sound of the highway and the sound of the shower immerse us in a womb-like space that is aurally and physically soothing to our bodies. I have not seen scientific studies about this, but my instinct is that the vibration of the car engine as it glides over the highway and the sensation of water moving over us each have the capacity to wrap our senses in a blanket of safety and familiarity that somehow brings us back to our earliest childlike state—a time when singing and being sung to was a natural part of our being.

Conversations with Kids

In the spring of 2024, I decided to start asking students at my school (roughly ages five through ten) about the spaces and places where they felt the most and least musical. The fact that I was doing this in a conversational way, in a place where students know me well, along with the fact that I only spoke with about twenty or so children, means that I can't really classify these conversations as "research." Yet some intriguing points emerged.

At age five, Enid (not her real name) was a gentle and sensitive young girl who came to school each day wearing a large colorful bow in her long brown hair. Enid could be overheard singing as she worked and played in her kindergarten classroom. Her mother liked to send me videos of the songs that Enid would invent at home. One day at recess, I asked Enid if we could spend a few moments chatting about music. "Sure!" she said as she jumped off a swing and walked with me to a nearby bench. This was our brief conversation:

Me:
What is a "Musician?"

Enid:
Someone who plays an instrument or sings.

Me:
Is everyone a musician?

Enid:
Everyone is if they want to be.

Me:
Where are you most comfortable being musical?

Enid:
In my bedroom with the door shut because I don't like people hearing or seeing me.

Me:
Where is the place you feel least comfortable being musical?

Enid:
In front of my mom and dad because I have stage fright. It comes from a lot of people watching me.

I had many other such conversations with students during their recess time as well as in their music classes. Here is a sampling of what I heard.

Places where children felt the most musical:

- When I'm with my guitar--it gives me all this musical stuff.

- A bright sunny afternoon and no one is out there but me. I can just lay in the grass and watch the clouds.

- When I'm outside. There's so much inspiration, especially when it's quiet and I can think of other things.

- Outside. The fresh air and trees make me think clearer and I feel most musical.

- In the shower.

- In the car. It makes me feel like life is good and there's a straight path ahead. It triggers something in my brain. I like to listen to music to get me ready and pumped up before sports.

- My basement, because that's where my drum set is.

- The car, when my family puts music on.

- An empty parking garage--great acoustics!

Places where children felt the least musical:

- In loud public spaces.

- When there are lots of people around and noise.

- When I *have to* do music and it doesn't come so naturally like when it's forced upon me if someone asks me to sing. I get nervous at first.

- At swim camp by the pool. Too many shouting kids.

- On the sports field.

- In public spaces.

- If I feel sad or tired.

- During meeting time at school.

When children are free to be on their own and aren't worried about their surroundings or distracted by too many people, they can feel more musical. When they are put on the spot, observed, or when life feels too busy around them, they feel less musical.

This matters because if we think of the ways that we are asking kids to show up musically in their school years, it is often in the form of school concerts, auditions, and being put on the spot to express something through song, instrument, or dance. We rarely offer private spaces where singing or other music might happen more naturally, and we don't really have ways of assessing students' musical abilities according to the music they might produce in those private spaces (and I am not suggesting that we should!).

We judge children's musical abilities in public and performative spaces, where they are often least comfortable, and then they are led to believe that they are not musically "talented" when they can't perform under pressure.

I don't know how to fix this, but I do know that it needs to be acknowledged and that we need to consider that there are many other ways that a child can be or feel musical besides what happens in music class or on a stage. If you have more ideas about how to make larger changes to school systems, I invite you to be in touch. I would love to hear your ideas!

Musical Space Invasion?

We feel safe singing alone in our cars and showers because we know we aren't bothering anyone. Wouldn't it be wonderful if we could just feel free to sing anywhere and not worry about what we sound like? Not necessarily! We have all experienced sound as an invasion of space. You're sitting on a bus or subway, trying to rest your eyes or read a book on your way home from work, when your sacred quiet space is suddenly disrupted by someone's boombox, whistle symphony, or solo singing.

It happened to me just recently when I was browsing for

holiday cards in a shop in Cambridge. The young male worker was just starting his afternoon shift and turned off the background music that had been playing. He was mumbling to himself about what to play and then said out loud, "Why not just sing?" He opened his mouth and started filling the space with his full and expressive singing.

What had felt like a peaceful shopping experience became a showground for his voice. While there was nothing particularly off about his singing, I found myself instantly irritated: *I'm not in the mood to hear someone singing loudly right now. I just want to browse for cards, and now I can't focus on what I want to buy. Why does he think it's okay to infiltrate this space? Is there something mentally wrong with him? Is anyone else bothered?* No one else appeared to be particularly bothered. I left the shop without purchasing anything, feeling shocked and angry at my intolerance. Here I was, the writer of a book about expanding definitions of musicality and the importance of self-expression, and I just couldn't take it! I felt ashamed on my ride home, wondering if I should rethink my judgmental attitude.

Later, I spoke about this experience with André de Quadros, professor of music education at Boston University, wanting to make sense of this experience and of my shame. De Quadros is internationally celebrated for his outspoken research and pedagogy in the areas of civil rights, anti-colonialism, and inclusivity of those who live on the margins of society. He chuckled when I relayed this card shop incident:

> Well, you're a human being just like I am, and you have things you like and don't. As adults, it's too late for us to rewire our sonic values. There are things we like and things we don't like. Sometimes people talk about things as if they're facts. They might say, 'This dish is delicious,' but that is actually not a fact. You might like the texture or taste. Someone else might not like it at all. The fact is, there's no such thing as delicious. Only how it tastes to you. Those tastes are only partly to do with enculturation and some to do with what you're born with. This is the same as how we feel about sounds. Maybe our likes and dislikes are related to what we experienced in utero or during our early childhood experiences. So if someone says, 'that's beautiful,' well, it's entirely individual.

Perhaps our musical preferences are a sign that we are all musical in some way, because we know almost instantly what our response is to music that we hear:

- Yes, this music will help me relax while I study for the Bar exam.

- Yes, this music is perfect for my dinner party.

- Yes, this music will motivate my two-mile run today.

- I didn't feel like dancing before, but this song makes me jump up and join in!

- No, turn that off! I can't focus.

- No, this song reminds me of my loneliness.

- No, I think this song will scare my baby.

Johan Galtung (2015) points out that it is a human right to say, "This did not touch me." We can be at a concert or look at art and not feel a thing. Nothing moves us. We can wonder if there is something wrong with us or with the art or with the relationship between us and the art, but it may just not be the right art for that exact moment. Music and art in the public arena each have an immediate effect on the surrounding area. Performing musicians on street corners or train stations can instantly change the mood of passersby, bringing on a feeling of liveliness, joy, melancholy, or any number of other emotive responses. With visual art, you can look away if something displeases you; with music, you are sensorily affected whether you like it or not, until you are out of earshot.

GeO "GoFive," Luis "TakeOne," and Pheebz are the Boston-based graffiti artists whom I referred to in Chapter 1. After Luis left our conversation to put his daughter to bed, GeO and Pheebz began talking about singing. We spoke about this feeling of taking up space:

Pheebz:

There's something just really intrusive about sound versus drawing. I'm a vocalist, but I don't tell people that because I don't like how it takes over all the atmosphere around people, versus having my voice heard through visual art, because it's a quiet practice. Even though we're really loud when we're all yelling at each other on the lift and spraying our cans and the motor's running and the speaker's going, I feel like it's an easier way to just blend into it and be outside of myself. Whereas singing and performing, it's like, "Look at me!" I don't like being put on the spot.

Me:

That's true about sound taking up space. But the murals take up a huge amount of space…

GeO:

With murals it's a lot less vulnerable because they're not viewing *you*, they're viewing your work. It's a different dance that you're doing with people. Even if you're painting and someone's there viewing you, it's not the same as singing where everyone stops and watches you. There's no conversation. It's just different.

Me:

It's also the timing aspect because once you've put something out there vocally, you can't take it back, whereas with painting, you could always go back and go over it or touch up this or that.

With thoughts about "space invasion" in my mind, I realize that I may need to think differently about the young subway singer I mentioned in my introduction. Perhaps her older sister wasn't simply hushing her and telling her to sit down because she was being judgmental or mean. Could it be that she was looking out for her well-being and the comfort of those around them on the subway? Not wanting others to feel irritated by the young girl's song? She may have been trying to teach her little sister a lesson about proper social habits: singing a song out loud in public is not often socially acceptable!

An Anti-Racist Public Piano?

Walking through Boston's newly renovated Logan International Airport, a mini grand piano sits at a hallway intersection of the departure and arrival halls. I have walked past this piano several times over the past year, picking up or sending off various friends and family members. I pass the piano upon entering and leaving the space. It is either silently empty or occupied by someone playing an expertly polished, usually classical music piece. I am sure that you have also encountered pianos placed in public spaces: malls, hotel lobbies, parks, bus stations, business centers, and more. Some are painted in bright colors with the words "Play Me"—an open invitation to passersby to noodle and make some sound.

Yet, according to Friesen and Menard, who studied this phenomenon (2024), the public expectation for who is allowed to play and what is socially acceptable to play centers on the expertise of Western classical music, such as Chopin or Beethoven. A silent expectation for whiteness resides among those 88 keys. They write, "Although it is unintended, the sounds of this piano playing perpetuate the embodiment of what is and is not music and who gets to be heard and who does not" (p. 69).

Pianos are loud and imposing instruments both physically and aurally. Approaching a piano to make sound on it, one knows that whatever they play will be heard by many, from quite a distance away. Our society values sounding "good," and we are accustomed to hearing the product, rather than the process, of musical learning. Sounding "good" is the product of dedication and time. Menard and Friesen's work reminds us that all of the noodling and experimentation, failures, and time spent repeating phrases and ideas to our liking happen, typically, in the closed space of a practice room. Time and space for practice, as well as the availability of a piano (or other instrument) on which to practice, are, of course, factors of privilege and class.

Menard pointed me toward a book called *Just Vibrations: The Purpose of Sounding Good* (Cheng, 2016). The author warns us that the concept of "sounding good" can be exclusionary and shaming to others if we don't critically examine it as coming from a position of power and social standing.

Classical Western-European music-making (both colonialistic and white), continues to be held in the highest regard as the most respected genre of musical learning. This is why our school systems continue to offer chorus, band, and orchestra as the primary ensembles and why music teachers continue to teach terminology, theory, and concepts based on that genre of music alone. André de Quadros, who chuckled at my card shop incident in the previous section, spoke with me about this seemingly unshakeable core aspect of music education in America:

> The band-orchestra-choir thing is so embedded in American culture, I'm not sure you can change it any more than you could change the NBA! Some of these programs, like in Texas, can be fantastically well funded, and they're phenomenal. I'm not saying it's great that students are *only* doing that, but all students there can have the experience of playing in an ensemble. But there's a tyranny in that also. And universities are the most rigid organizations! Impossible to make changes. Bruno Nettle said that trying to change a college curriculum is like trying to change a graveyard.

Classical music is all about perfection, impressive skill, "talent," competition, and mistake-free performance. Friesen, who teaches music composition at the University of Toronto, decided to take on the challenge of critically examining power positions in music-making with his students. Together, they came to an agreement, which they posted publicly in the classroom:

> I acknowledge that THE major developments of music in North America have come from often appropriated, racialized communities, and that institutional music education is complicit in systemic racism by still continuing to hold white Western European Music at the center and above all other practices. I hope we can push back on/disrupt this together.

Can this acknowledgement allow for more experimental, less perfection-based forms of music making? If we, as a society, can recognize and hold other forms of music-making in equally high regard, would people feel more free to noodle around on a public piano? Make mistakes? Improvise? Worry less about sounding good and instead start to feel good about enjoying themselves?

Dare I suggest that the next time you encounter a public piano, you take a small moment to "Tune in" with yourself instead of worrying about impressing passersby on their way to airport check-in counters? Maybe if you do, others will be encouraged to enjoy their soundings as well.

I cannot answer the question for you about the boundary between "space invasion" and free expression when it comes to such things as public pianos, but I do encourage you to notice your own feelings and your own playful exploration. Somewhere between being sensitive to those around us and pushing the racial and cultural boundaries of what is considered acceptable sound, we might find some musical joy.

Music Playgrounds?

In Part One, we explored the playful, musical worlds of young children. We saw how music seems to spill forth from children as they go about their day in their classrooms. If we are talking about music-making in public spaces, we need to consider what happens on playgrounds. Do children sing, tap rhythms, and chant as they swing, slide, and tumble? What about music playgrounds, which we see popping up in various outdoor spaces and integrated within playground structures? What kinds of musicality do those spaces invite?

In 2014, I was invited to help build a "music wall" at my daughter's preschool. Her teacher and I invited families to bring in materials such as PVC pipes, corrugated tubes, plastic tubs, and anything else that might make an interesting sound. After several weeks of gathering materials, one of the class fathers brought in his drill, and we attached the objects to one of the stone walls of the playground area outside.

Our basic preschool "music playground."

We thought carefully about what should go where and how children might interact with the "Music Wall." When we opened it up to the students the next day, we placed a bucket with sticks, spoons, and other mallet-like objects that they could use to "play" on the wall.

I visited the school during their outdoor play time several times over the next few weeks. In the first few days, it was very exciting. The children explored every possible way of tapping, scraping, and shaking the materials, trading sticks, and showing each other their discoveries. Yet by the end of that first week, the "Music Wall" was pretty unmusical. It was no longer a novelty and only received occasional attention. By the end of the second week of school, it seemed to be merely a decoration, as students resumed running around the structure and engaging in pretend play with some dolls and kitchen items in the corner of the yard. Why had the children lost interest? And could the tapping and scraping even be classified as "music?"

I spent the next year visiting many different types of outdoor playgrounds, as well as some "music playgrounds," to try to answer my questions. I spent hours sitting on benches next to fancy playground structures with pirate themes or animal shapes. I stood near the fences of basic structures with just a bridge, steps, and a slide. I visited playgrounds at the beach, outside the mall, ones with large sandboxes, innovative swings, and one with open foam mats and blocks for tumble play. I followed leads from friends and colleagues who told me I *had* to see this or that incredible park or outdoor music playground.

What I found is that musical expressions on playgrounds (invented songs, chants, rhythmic movements, or sounds) are directly linked to creativity and imaginative play. When a playground has a fixed structure or fixed expectation for what the play should look like, the play tends to be more physical: *Climb the ladder here, cross the bridge, hang on the bar, and slide down over there. Run around and repeat.* To be clear, this type of physical play has its own value, but if we are looking at musicality and creativity, a play space needs to have items that can be manipulated and shaped, moved, and constructed. We are much more likely to hear songs, chants, and other musical expressions in those types of play spaces (Zur, 2016).

One of the oldest such playground spaces in America opened in 1979 in the Marina area of Berkley, California. This "Adventure" playground has a rough, hand-made, rather than manufactured, feel to it, with rope swings, crooked wooden ladders, wooden planks, and junkyard items scattered around. Paint and tools are available for common use in the tool shed. Children can create forts, move large planks or tires around, and work to fulfill their imaginative ideas. In the same way that adults use music to motivate their work experience, children can often be heard singing and chanting as they construct their play space.

Some of the most creative and musically rich playgrounds I have ever seen are in the "Junkyard" playgrounds in Israel. These intentional outdoor play spaces are unique to Israel's *kibbutz* preschools. As defined and explained by Malka Haas (2016), the goals are for children to explore, play, create, and destroy using real-life local materials with minimal supervision. Objects such as broken stoves, farm crates, hoses, fax machines, teapots, and CD players are intentionally placed in the (usually sandy) yard according to a democratic class discussion of where and how the space should be used.

In contrast to indoor play spaces, where children play with toy phones, toy cribs, or toy tools, everything about the Junkyard is real. Consequently, real-life objects that are usually out of bounds allow children to enter into an adult sphere where they are trusted to create child-centered play themes. Children's concepts of reality are intensely intertwined with their fantasies and feelings. Several times a year, the space is cleared and cleaned, and new decisions are made.

Children used sheets of fabric and pillows to make this "Junkyard Playground" space cozy.

*Parts of old tractors, computers, and other junk were
arranged by children for their dramatic play.*

In comparison to more typical outdoor play spaces, where songs or chants might be heard in short, quick bursts, I observed long, flowing, and socially interactive songs streaming from children as they played in the Junkyard playgrounds. Even though this wasn't a "music playground," I heard more music coming from the Junkyard than any other play space I had encountered!

Susan G. Solomon's extensive studies of American playgrounds (2005) may help shed light on why Junkyard play inspired greater creativity. Describing American playgrounds, she explains, "Today's playgrounds guide kids in how to perform and leave little room for fantasy or spontaneity." She describes modern plastic playground structures as "...overly safe and terminally boring..." (p. 207). Junkyard playgrounds, where children can get dirty and experiment with everyday, and sometimes unsafe materials, allow children to create their own play world. It is, in the words of Haas, "...their own microworld in which they may freely express their feelings" (p. 349). These types of playgrounds (Adventure and Junkyard) represent the ideal playground for child development.

Even though we might realize the value of such play settings, Solomon points out that modern playground construction is primarily concerned with safety, made extreme by decades of lawsuits and bureaucracy. Working within these limits, attempts to make play spaces more imaginative and creative have led to constructions of playgrounds with embedded musical parts, or "music playgrounds," which I described at the start of this section. With pots and pans, PVC pipes, and other low-budget or recycled objects affixed to fences and walls, the look of a "junkyard" play space is evoked. But unless children are free to construct and manipulate their own musical instrument playgrounds, generating ideas and co-constructing the space with others (as they can in Junkyard or Adventure playgrounds), the quality of children's music making in these spaces can't develop as richly as we hope.

Playground Songs and Clapping Games

Kathryn Marsh, Professor Emeritus at Sydney University, has spent years researching the hand-clapping and jump rope songs that take place on playgrounds across the globe. Having worked with ethnomusicologists, documenting and analyzing playground songs across a wide variety of countries and cultures, Marsh explains that these songs represent a unique tradition that is "...owned, spontaneously performed, and orally transmitted by children and usually involve text, movement, and rhythmic elements" (2009, p. 4). These songs can be quite musically complex, with polyrhythms and dynamic melodies that adults usually assume to be too challenging for children to be able to understand.

But here is what I find most fascinating about Marsh's studies. She noticed that as children were singing many of these hand-clapping playground songs, their voices hit notes that fell outside of the classical, Western musical scale. Non-standard pitches. She explains that while some music teachers might equate this with singing out of tune, we should be thinking of children's playground songs as being in tune with their own playground culture, reflecting local culture.

In other words, Marsh asks us to widen what she calls our

"adultocentric" view of being "in tune," and to accept child culture with its own set of musical qualities. I love this because if we think about it, why does it really matter if children are singing out of "key," which is really quite a Eurocentric set of pitches in the first place? Even if they were failing to stay within a Western scale, as they jump, clap, chant, and sing, why is this important to adults?

Isn't the point of music to feel joy? To feel a sense of belonging within a community?

7 — School Music Programs and Private Lessons

Vignette: The Seventh Floor Piano Player

From the eighth floor of my apartment on 187th Street in Manhattan, I could hear the sounds and rhythms of everyday lives happening all around me. On warmer days, with the window open, I might hear the same two strollers being pushed up the hill every morning, along with the voices of two Jamaican nannies discussing when to meet at the playground. The voices of a small group of seniors speaking in Russian would drift up to my window around midday, and then the sounds of spatulas and spoons hitting the sides of pots or pans would emerge in the early evening.

There were several months when each evening I would hear someone (presumably a child) playing the piano below me on the seventh floor. Each time, it would begin with *playing*—an unorganized, improvisatory exploration of sound. It felt joyous and unburdened. I imagined tiny hands gliding across the keys, exploring all the possibilities of timbre, dynamics, and mood. There were light, delicate flavors intertwined with dark clusters of notes: fast, exciting sounds; slow, long notes; and plenty of musical surprises.

This exploration would last anywhere from two to fifteen minutes, before the "real" practicing set in. I imagined a parent coming over to the piano at that moment, and saying something like, "Okay, now it's time to practice..." Suddenly, the artful exploration would stop, and I would hear the familiar notes of "Hot Crossed Buns," the three notes mechanically punched out, like someone tallying points. There was no passion, flow, or, dare I say, "musicality" to be heard. I remember thinking at the time, "That is not music. If only people could recognize how musically gorgeous the prelude to the practice was! If only we could call *that* music!"

Should My Child Take Music Lessons?

Year after year, I hear from parents who genuinely want to give their child the opportunity to learn a musical instrument. Some parents want to give them the "gift of music." Others worry about missing the window of opportunity. Some parents are convinced that music lessons will teach their child patience and the meaning of hard work. They understand that in an ideal situation, their child would have an inner motivation to learn the piano or violin (or some other highly-respected orchestral instrument) and ask to start lessons.

But what happens if their child doesn't want to? These parents often say that they themselves feel so unmusical that they don't know how to foster their children's interest in music.

In these conversations, there is so much I wish I could express. I want them to consider their own childhoods and help them to redefine what they mean by "musical." Did they dance in the kitchen with their grandmother or hold a hairbrush in front of the mirror to belt out show tunes?

I also want to reassure them that their child is already a "musician," and suggest that they work together to find an instrument that feels like the best pathway forward. Sometimes I mention that it can be inspiring to attend concerts—I try to provide examples of the many types of musical performances they could seek out. Gospel choirs? Middle Eastern duets with a *doumbek* and an *oud?* A jazz band, an orchestra, or a Japanese *Koto* performance? Yet most parents imagine a "classic" instrument such as piano or violin. I remind parents that learning a musical instrument and finding the motivation to practice can be really challenging, *even when the child is passionately excited about learning.* What will it look like if they don't want to learn?

If I aim to suggest a broader definition of what it means to be "musical," it may seem wrong to state what music is *not*. Yet I feel so strongly about this, I must say this here, even though I am sure many could argue against this: Music is not the black and white notes written on the lines and spaces of a staff. Especially for young children, those black and white lines on the page can almost be seen as prison bars if that is their first formal introduction to music lessons.

If a child's first music lessons are about the notes of the staff and note-reading, they are learning from an expert musician that there is a right and wrong way to play notes, and playful musicality, which is natural for children (as well as the basis for improvisatory forms of music), is lost. To me, it makes little sense for a child to develop a belief that their explorations and experiments are not as real or valid as learning to find Middle C with their right thumb.

I am not suggesting by any means that music teachers turn away from note-reading and theory lessons. There are fabulous methods for teaching note-reading to children, from Orff, Kodaly, Gordon, Fierabend[8], and beyond, as well as a plethora of resources that make note-reading playful, fun, and child-centered.

What I am suggesting is that curiosity and musical play should precede or be used to introduce note-reading. I am suggesting that children may already have confidence in their own beautiful and natural musicality, which can be nurtured and acknowledged as "real" music, and act as a pathway into more technical and theoretical learning.

We must allow children the freedom to "scribble" and make messy musical masterpieces in the same way we allow them to draw and paint. The motivation to hone more technical skills and to seek out better fingerings, hand positions, and note-reading skills will likely develop as a natural result of these joyful explorations, especially when a music teacher is there to offer technical suggestions as the need arises.

And if it doesn't develop? If someone never learns "proper" fingering techniques or note-reading? Perhaps they may not have the fluency on the clarinet needed to get into their high school marching band, but does it mean they aren't musical? Of

---

[8] For those familiar with music education, these are each well-known methods for teaching music to children in school or group settings.

course not! Let us not forget that for thousands upon thousands of years, musicians have created music without the Western-European framework of the music staff. They did this through communal creation, imitation, exploration, spiritual inspiration, and self-mastery. They did this through an almost entirely aural tradition whereby the roots of local culture were passed down from generation to generation. Jazz musicians such as Dizzy Gillespie, Louis Armstrong, Thelonius Monk, and others learned music mainly by listening, trying to replicate, and joining in with others as their skill sets widened.

From the singing cultures of South Africa to Eastern Europe to the music made in Irish pubs, everyday people gathered together (and continue to gather together) and just participated. I remember reading about independent folk singer Ani DiFranco, who taught herself to play the guitar by listening and watching other masters. When Prince asked her to jam with him one day and suggested a sequence of guitar chords, she was too scared to admit that she didn't know the names of the chords. But she used her ears to figure it out, and they had a blast! (DiFranco, 2019).

Western music notation was invented in large part so that musicians could preserve, share, and play a set of sounds together. If children are interested in writing down the music that they have created, whether on pots and pans or on a piano, why not ask them to invent their own notation system as well? A "listening map" of their piece might be much more meaningful and can make a lot more sense to a child than the five lines and four spaces of our adult-centered music scores.

This "Listening Map" below was created by a fourth-grade student named Mimi. Can you follow it and imagine what her composition sounded like?

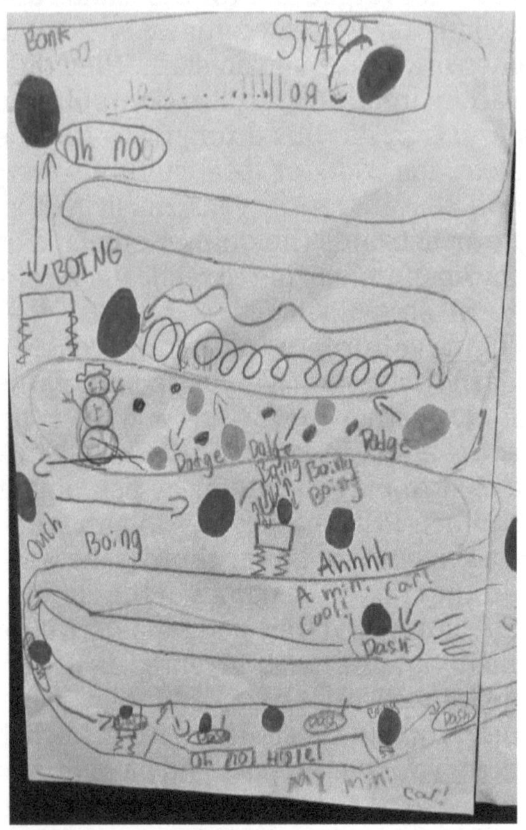

This "Listening Map," created by a 4th grader, acts as a musical score.

What Counts as a "Real" Instrument?

I teach at a prestigious independent school in Cambridge, Massachusetts. Every fall, hundreds of families attend our Open House event, where they can peruse the campus, meet teachers, and learn about the way their children will be educated if they send them to our school.

Year after year, I have come to anticipate the same questions when parents enter my music room. The primary question is this: "Do the kids play instruments?" I gesture to the maracas, xylophones, metallophones, rhythm sticks, rain sticks, steel drums, *djembe* drums, triangles, and more that we are privileged to be able to use in my classroom. We create soundscapes, *Orff* ensembles[9], folk song arrangements, and creative improvisations. But this is not what most parents mean by "instruments." They often nod and smile, and ask the question differently: "Do they play any, you know, *real* instruments?"

I explain how band and orchestra instruments are introduced and modeled for students, but private instrument lessons are pursued outside of the curriculum.

Each year, this question raises more questions in my heart. Why are rain sticks and Irish Bodhran drums not "real?" Why is a silver orchestral flute held in higher regard than a Cherokee flute, Japanese flute, Iranian flute, or an Andean Ocarina flute? Why is a violin or cello more celebrated than a ukulele? Why are they among the most highly regarded in the realm of "The Arts?"

In a conversation with Rebecca Hartka of Cello Medicine, she explained that the elitist attitude towards classical music is an American phenomenon: "Americans wanted to separate themselves from snobby Europeans, so they rejected classical music. This forced classical institutions to have to appeal to the wealthy elitists to stay afloat."

Perhaps another reason why classical instruments are regarded as higher up on the "impressive" scale is that success on these instruments is more measurable ("I'm on Suzuki book #4!"). Pianos and violins seem to be the shining lights of the elite Westernized music world—the winners of competitions and the gold stars of resume builders. Surely, if someone is "successful" at playing the violin, it means they are a high-achieving, hard-working individual with artistry in their blood!

John Fitzgerald, a widely known drum circle facilitator who is well-versed in educating the masses about different aspects of musicality, spoke with me about the allure of studying Western classical instruments.

Our brains provide the conscious filters through which we see the world, as well as the aperture to receive information.

---

[9] The "Orff Schulwerk" system for music education was developed in the 1920s and 1930s by German composers Carl Orff and Gunild Keetman at the Günther-Schule. This system, used by thousands of music teachers around the globe, allows even the youngest children to engage in playful instrumental ensembles with stories, chants, and movement.

Speaking very broadly, the left brain is rational, reductive, and linear, and seeks control. The right brain is where empathy is fired. It's holistic and experiential—it does not have language. The allure of acquiring technique and of reading music is that they want something they can grasp, that they know and believe is an accomplishment, something that can be measured. We think what is important is reading notes and musical technique. But that's all left brain, which is basically about control. I think it is also because the "West" has exported its culture, and others have bought into the idea that it is superior, partly because of the traditional and economic power differential.

Why is control, and the perfectionistic competitiveness that comes with classical music, equated with better artistry or more musical worth?

This art form, reserved for those who have the opportunity and resources to spend hours a day practicing and biting their nails through auditions, somehow continues to be what parents want for their children. If this is the case, that we value talent and competition over community music-making experiences and folk music, what is my role as a music teacher? Do I satisfy parents or stick to what I know all children (and humans) need in order to thrive and be able to express themselves musically and creatively? Of course, I continue to choose the latter!

"Doesn't It Feel Like Something You Love?"

Many years ago, at one of my first teaching jobs in a suburb outside of New York City, I was waiting in the doorway of my classroom for my next class to arrive. I could see them coming as I looked down the long hallway—a group of twenty kindergarteners, with big smiles on their faces, excited for music class.

As they approached, their excitement built, and two of them started skipping. Their teacher stopped the class and admonished, "Stop skipping. We walk down the hallway."

Why, I wondered, was skipping not allowed?

On another day, I passed a first-grade class in the hallway.

They were in a neat line on their way to the library. One of the children was running their finger gently along the rough painted bricks and commented to her friend, "Doesn't it feel like something you love?"

As her friend and then another friend each lifted their fingers to experience the pleasure of the rough wall, their teacher said, "Hands by your sides. We do not touch the walls."

I began to wonder if certain rules were in place simply to ensure control and whether these types of rules were getting in the way of children's natural artistic and experiential exploration.

Dana Bentley, an early childhood specialist, explores this topic in depth in her book *Everyday Artists: Inquiry and Creativity in the Early Childhood Classroom* (2013). She makes the point that children's artistic thinking goes beyond painting or crafting, but is embedded in the very fiber of what it means to be a child engaging in the world. Bently identifies "art" as "children's process of 'making beautiful'" (p. 7). In other words, as children go about their day, they act as artists by reshaping the things and experiences they encounter into beautiful possibilities. For example, "an unwanted plate of broccoli becomes a magical forest, the child, a brachiosaurus who must demolish the trees. The dreaded walk back from the park becomes a princess parade in which we point out the different 'castles' that are our homes" (Bentley, 2013, p. 54). In this way, the commonplace elements of daily life come alive through artistic, playful processing.

When the young girl at my school wanted to experience the pleasure of a rough wall, she was exploring her world through joy and artistry. Similarly, young children's music-making in the form of humming, chanting, dancing, skipping, or rhythmic tapping is an artistic way of shaping and experiencing their world.

As adults, we need to ask ourselves whether the rules we put in place for children are important for their learning and safety, or whether they are squashing natural curiosity and creativity.

Does a child's singing or chanting *need* to be hushed? If it does, could we at least say, "I love your singing, but right now we need a quiet space," rather than simply saying, "Shhh!"?

If children are not allowed to experience "something they love" by humming, skipping, or touching the crease in a brick wall, how can they figure out other preferences or make good artistic decisions?

"The Cello Won't Fit on the Bus!"

The making of artistic decisions (having an inner knowing about what you love and don't love) is extremely important in figuring out which instrument to play if someone has an opportunity and the will to play one. Children often have a strong sense of preference when it comes to instrument selection.

Deb Wilfond, an MSW Fellow at Merrimack College, talks about the importance of agency when selecting an instrument:

> As a child growing up in the UK, my mother was a "Type A" personality who thought it was good for children to learn an instrument. She took me to the instrument store and told me to think about what I wanted to play. I had been to some concerts and had seen some kids playing instruments too. I really wanted to play the cello, but Mum said, "Too big. We can't get that on the bus. You're going to play the violin." It would have been better if my parents had listened to me and if my wishes and desires had been heard. Sure, the cello might not have worked out for practical reasons, but my agency was taken away from me, and I think when these decisions are made for children and not with them, it is problematic. I played violin all the way through high school and college orchestras because I loved the music, and it gave me social opportunities. However, playing the violin was always a love-hate relationship as a result of how it all started. In terms of playing an instrument, it should really blossom from the inside out. Unless the motivation comes from the child, it's not going to go so well.

Many times, when a student gives up on an instrument that they were told to play, rather than choose to play, they are left feeling unmusical for the rest of their lives.

"Boring, Boring, Boring!"

Being told what to do or how to play on an instrument can also lead to a sense of boredom and, consequently, failure, if there is no room for personal growth. Carol McGonnell, a professional clarinet player based in Ireland, spoke with me about the way that most music lessons feel and a particular teacher whose comment changed her trajectory for the better:

> "Boring, boring, boring." When he said that, it was the most important thing in a way because it resonated with something deep in me. I didn't want to be boring. I knew I wasn't inherently boring, but I had allowed myself to be guided by these teachers who were these really strong music personalities who were basically telling me what to do, and I was willing to give up my natural instincts and just go along with what they had. Maybe it was a slight laziness on my part, but on the other hand, it was feeding into my insecurities because they were so strong. I also had this ability to just emulate and be what they wanted me to be, so I was able to do that and produce good results, but at some point, that wasn't going to work anymore. And at that point, I really had to find where I was.

On a podcast called "Harmonically Speaking,"[10] Carol described how focusing on what something *should* sound like, versus your own core expression, is the "death of musicality."

I asked her, "Isn't this how music lessons with kids basically work? A teacher saying, 'No, play like this,' or 'No, it should sound like that.' Aren't kids trying their very best to sound like what the teacher is telling them to sound like?"

This was her response:

> Those children are trying to keep their teacher happy. They get on stage trying to fill a set of criteria for what it means to be a good violinist or whatever. It is the death of creativity. I mean, who wants to hear that? My daughter is six. She's been taking violin lessons for two years. Her teacher is pretty

---

[10] Hosted by clarinettist Macdara Ó Seireadáin, Season 1, Episode 5, July 14, 2024

wonderful with that. There's so much that needs to be learned in terms of technique. My daughter is very naturally expressive, and the teacher is very aware of that and doesn't want to interfere with or destroy that. So when the teacher is articulating how she should hold her bow or place or fingers or whatever, she does it with the caveat "So that you can express yourself more clearly," or "So you can make these kinds of sounds that you're trying to make." Technique often becomes about itself. We're only building technique so that we have things in our toolbox to get to expression. It can be so simple. That small addition as to why we're learning these things and practicing these things, can make all the difference in the world. I was also able to find a piano teacher for the girls who always improvises with them in the last 10 minutes of every lesson. That makes all the difference!

Stop That Noodling!

Christopher Serkin is the great-grandson of one of the world's most renowned violinists, the late Adolf Busch. Chris's grandfather, Rudolph Serkin, was a well-known pianist. Together, Adolph and Rudolph founded the Marlboro Music Festival, which continues to attract some of the finest classical musicians from around the world each summer in Marlboro, Vermont. It has hosted such classical music stars as Midori, Emmanuel Ax, Joshua Bell, Mitsuko Uchida, and countless others who grace the world's stages as top award-winning musicians.

Chris, who is a professor of law at Vanderbilt University, has attended the festival nearly every summer since he was a child. I wanted to hear his story because I was curious about what it was like to grow up with such musical fame around him and what his own musical story was.

My father once played "Twinkle Twinkle Little Star" on his violin for Toscanini, right? And my grandfather was so nervous, he had to leave the room. But Toscanini gave him some advice: "You know you can play two notes in one bow, right?" At age five, I started violin lessons with a neighbor down the street. I had to use a book with pictures of birds landing on wires to symbolize the four strings. Even then, I thought it was infantilizing. I hated that book, and I hated the violin. I consider that a failed attempt at music lessons. Then I tried piano for a few years. Everyone kept asking me about the piano and whether I would one day take lessons with my grandfather. But I found the whole thing so stressful that I didn't want to play. I hated practicing. My family just had this attitude of excellence for music playing. It was easier not to play at all than to play poorly. They felt that music was extremely important and that if you were going to play, you had to take it very seriously. If someone came over and casually played around on the piano, my grandmother would scold, "Stop that noodling!"

One day before my lesson, I felt like I really didn't want to go anymore. I finally got the courage to tell my parents, and they just said, "Okay. You don't have to if you don't want to." This was such a shock to me! I had no idea that I could have the power to make that decision or that they would so easily just allow me to stop. I kind of felt bad about it. Maybe if I had known that they would allow me to stop, I might not have asked to stop. Part of me almost wishes that they had made me continue.

At Marlboro, at the end of the summer, they have a tradition of having everyone come together to sing Beethoven's Choral Fantasy. Even as a young child, this was the highlight of my summer. Then, at age twelve, my aunt and uncle took me to see a Talking Heads concert. It was the first non-classical concert I had gone to, and it blew my mind! People got to dress up in fun clothes, and it was incredible! After that, I spent many summers at Marlboro, just not wanting to go to any of the concerts. I would go off to play ping-pong or pool during the concerts. I had no interest. But as I got a little older, I began to be friends with a lot of the musicians. It started becoming interesting to hear the concerts when I had friends who were playing. Then, during one informal concert in the dining hall, some of my friends were playing a Fauré piano quartet, I think it was, and something just clicked inside of me. I took much more of an interest then.

In high school, I decided on my own to pick up the violin again because I was interested in learning more about music. I asked one of my Marlboro friends for advice, and she suggested studying with her. I decided, after some time, to take violin lessons with my grandmother. This went really

> well, and I just loved being at my grandparents house and spending time with them, having dinner afterwards. The lessons felt very special because I was playing off the same sheet music that my great-grandfather Adolph had used. My grandmother kept bringing me the same little piece over and over again—a short Schubert song. I couldn't understand why she wanted me to play this, but one day she said, "Okay. I think you're ready to play this for your grandfather." I was so nervous that my bow was shaking. After I played, he said, "Again!" After the second time, he leaped up out of his chair and said, "Christopher! This is wonderful! Already you're making music and you play so… relatively in tune!"

Though Chris went into law rather than music as a career, he considers himself to be a musical person. He just didn't enjoy the pressure and seriousness that surrounded his family's musical legacy.

Motivation—It's Not About Star Charts!

Yonah, a professional violinist in his late forties, has always struggled to find the motivation to practice. With a father who was a professor of music composition, he had a lot of early exposure to orchestras, and he remembers that he was most drawn to playing the French horn. His parents preferred the violin and signed him up for lessons at age six. He recalls being told to go down to the basement to practice:

> They would set a timer and I was supposed to stay down there and practice until the time was up. Sometimes I would get so angry, I would punch the wall. My parents would say, *You'll thank us later.* This would make me angrier than anything. Do you think that now, as an adult, I want to thank them?

Even though Yonah continues to earn his living as a violinist, he finally bought himself a French horn and gets more pleasure in trying to play it than he feels for the violin.

In my twenty-plus years of being a music teacher, the number one question that parents want to know is, *How can I get my child to practice?* They try star charts, pennies lined up on the music stand, or some other reward system, but it doesn't seem to make much of a difference. Why is practicing an instrument sometimes such a teeth-grinding experience? What helps students not only maintain motivation but also keep wanting to actually play their instrument? There seem to be two clear motivational themes that emerge from the stories I have shared as well as from research on this topic: agency and peer/family connection.

Let's talk about agency first. Agency is allowing children (and ourselves) the power of choice. What type of music draws you in and makes your heart sing? What instrument are you excited about trying? This is another side of finding what I call the "musical fit"—what works best and feels most musically right for *you.*

Deb dreamed of playing the cello but was told she would play the violin instead. She struggled for many years before "tossing it in the bin." Chris wanted nothing to do with the seriousness of piano playing that his family hoped would grow on him, but being at a Talking Heads concert blew his mind because it felt so free and fun. It felt like *him.*

Let me tell you a story. I once had a young student whom I will call Graham. He was one of those boys who struggled to stay still in class and whose natural way of moving in the world seemed to take up space. His teachers were somewhat concerned about his body awareness. To me, his movements felt large and indelicate. When asked to play a melodic pattern on the xylophone, for example, the bars would fly off and hit the floor. While dancing, he needed reminders to be aware of friends around him so that he wouldn't crash. Graham's parents approached me during his final months of second grade to ask what I thought about Graham taking some music lessons.

"He loves music, and we thought maybe we should try having him play an instrument. Do you think we should try the violin?"

I was grateful that they were asking this question. Picturing Graham on the violin, I just couldn't see it as a good fit.

But I remembered that when we had free choice time in the music room, Graham gravitated towards the drums each time. His mother cringed slightly when I suggested the drums, but relaxed when I told her that a digital drum set with a set of headphones would allow her to maintain a quiet home.

Two years later, and no longer his music teacher, I had largely forgotten about that conversation. I showed up to the winter concert for grades 3-5 to support my colleague across the hall (I only teach up through grade two at my school). The fourth graders were performing last. What was that drum set doing out front? Unbeknownst to me, Graham had been taking drum lessons and would now perform on the drums along with his class to the piece "Glowing" by Great Big World (2022), from their album *Particles.*

The lights in the noisy gym dimmed as the students turned on their little battery-operated tealight candles, which they held in their hands.

At first, it was just piano and voice. Then Graham began to play. Allowed to finally take up space and move in a way that was so beautifully *him*, he crashed and smashed his way into everyone's hearts that day. The audience, including me, was moved to tears.

Later, I found his parents. Graham had started playing drums a few weeks after I had made the suggestion. He dove into it with his whole being. His parents described how he played (with headphones on his digital drums) each night in the basement, practiced on his lap or notebook at school, and was flourishing.

When families understand the importance of their child's musical engagement as a soul-energizing force of personal connection, rather than a status symbol or college-application checkbox, they realize that a violin or piano is not "better" than a drum set.

Using agency or choice as a motivator can empower children to take ownership of their music making so that it feels like part of their identity rather than something that will earn them a star sticker.

Here is what it can look like when parents talk to their children in a way that gives them agency:

- We have set up trial piano lessons for you with three different teachers. We would like you to figure out who feels like the best teacher for you and who you're most excited to study with.

- Let's go see a concert together so you can hear some instruments up close and discover which one you think you would want to try.

- Your teacher said that you should be practicing every day. Let's experiment together to figure out what time of day works best for you. Before school? Right after school? Before dinner?

The other very important motivating factor is having a social or familial web of connection and support. Practicing alone in a basement is a very lonely business, even for the most engaged young musicians. Unless there are friends who come over to jam and create music together, such as with a garage band, why not have the practice space be in the living room? Or even in the kitchen if space allows. This way, there is an opportunity for the child to feel that they are contributing something meaningful to the fabric of their family life: "Oh, Skylar! I just love cooking dinner to the sound of your guitar!"

Playing music for others or together with others is crucial to sustaining a desire to play and practice.

A number of professional musicians I interviewed mentioned that if it had not been for their friends, they would have quit playing. Any opportunity for students to play in an ensemble, join a group class, have an informal jam session, or even a pretend group "talent show" for an audience of stuffed animals can go a long way towards a feeling of internal goodness and belonging. *Music belongs in me, and I belong with others through music.*

8 — Moving Towards a "Musical" Identity

Vignette: A Black Dress and My Violin

I was six years old, standing in front of the large mirror in my parents' bedroom, with my mini ¼ sized violin tucked under my chin. I was practicing the "Happy Farmer" tune from my Suzuki Book 1 of beginner violin pieces[11].

In the traditional Suzuki method, a piece is learned aurally, by repeatedly listening and trying to repeat the piece, phrase by phrase, until it is completely in your ears and body. At that moment in front of the mirror, after having played it with the recording many times, I felt powerfully ready to try it on my own. I could hear the piano accompaniment in my head as my bow dipped onto the D string. I swayed with the music, playing the second phrase more delicately, and finished with a strong finale.

Electrified by my success, I played it again and again, dancing passionately in front of the mirror. At that moment, I was the best, most beautiful violinist in the world that everyone wanted to hear. I imagined I was wearing an elegant black dress on stage, and the audience was mesmerized. I played until my mother came into the room and told me to stop.

"It's bedtime," she said. I imagined the concert was over—time to remove my black dress backstage.

---

[11] The Suzuki method of learning violin was developed by Shinichi Suzuki in Japan in the mid-20th Century. The system has eight books of short songs, each progressing in difficulty.

About a decade later, the New York Youth Symphony was rehearsing for its first concert of the season at Carnegie Hall. My audition got me in the last seat in the second violin section, and we were told we must wear all black. For me, this was a dream come true. I don't know what it is about the idea of wearing a black dress, slinging my violin case over my shoulder, and heading downtown to play a concert, but this romantic image was in my mind from a young age. At age six, and still at sixteen, this was what it meant to be a "musician!"

"We Are All Drummers"

Our ideas about what it means to be a musician are fascinating! The images and ideas associated with musicianship are often rigidly stuck in our minds and have been there as long as we can remember. Yet these ideas and definitions are also malleable. John Fitzgerald, internationally known drum circle facilitator, told me about how drum circles give people a chance to feel like musicians even if they have never played before:

> Drumming is deeply somatic and has that quality of novelty which our brains thirst for. Brain science tells us about all these neurological chemicals that fire off when we are engaged in playing music. I realized [while leading workshops] that these everyday people are touching the thing that I longed to touch constantly as a musician, but was often kept from it because of my ego and need for perfection. All these people who'd never played before come together in this context. By the end of that hour, they'd been playing full on and wildly. They get into it! An hour goes by, and they say, "Wow—that was an hour!?"
>
> One of the first experiences I had with this was in Japan, facilitating a drum circle from a stage, which is not an ideal setting, but that's what we had. The participants were a bunch of Yamaha store personnel from Tokyo, all in ties, all sitting very quietly in attendance. They seemed very stiff. The person in charge introduced me, and before he left the stage, I asked him to ask the people, "How many people here are drummers?" There was silence, and then one or two guys sheepishly raised their hands. We passed out the instruments, and we got

started. They got way into it. Each of us facilitators took turns leading, and then we did a big closing. At the end, I said to their translator, "Can you ask them again how many people here are drummers?"

At this point in our conversation, John's voice caught in his throat with emotion:

And it makes me cry. *Everybody* raised their hands. And the social connection was profound. They were talking with each other, exchanging instruments, and we had a hard time getting them to give the drums back! In the corporate world, especially in Japan, there is a strict protocol about behavior and everything. They are being watched. They are being judged. They are being assessed. These are adults who have built their public persona over decades, and here they are sitting in a drum circle. So they stepped into an entirely different territory of being. I expect that they went back to work the next day, and they may have told a few people about it, but I'm guessing they went right back into their slots. To really get people out of that—it is a healing act that needs to be repeated and brought to conscious awareness by asking, "Hey—what happened here? What happened to you? What did you experience?" When I ask these questions, rarely does that conversation focus on music. They say, "Connection happened here." They always talk about unity, peace, and connection.

Music is a legacy of the human race. So there's something really powerful and important about music and traditional music making, for most of our time has been learned in a relationship with somebody who already plays. It's not about learning notes. Music is not notes. Music is a map. And it brings all these benefits that you can then enumerate: social, emotional, and physiological. Making music together triggers a neurological response that releases serotonin and other chemicals, which helps us bond, which is how humans survived. Without that sense of place and social bonding, how much value is your intellectual musical knowledge?

As a drum circle facilitator, John realized that something transformative was happening among his participants that he himself couldn't feel as a solo musician: a deep sense of connection with others and to himself. The very shape of a drum circle symbolizes equality and unity. I asked John whether there was any overlap with or borrowing from African drumming traditions. Here is what he said:

> For thousands of years, African cultures and cultures all over the globe have had traditions of music making—some of them purely drumming. They carry rhythms and music traditions that are specific to particular uses, passing on cultural traditions. I've never heard of a traditional culture where music is just jamming and making stuff up. It may happen, but the preponderance of that music is recreating and moving forward a tradition. And there may be new creations or patterns that get created within that tradition, but it's not just jamming. By and large, they're playing set rhythms that are meant to be played together in a particular way for a particular purpose.
>
> The contemporary drum circle came out of the counterculture of the 1960s. In the 60s, the counterculture developed in response to the 50s. The hippies were going, "Wait a minute, what is the truth?" They started honoring or exploring their unique personal values in opposition to the dominant culture. Materialism was suspect. Corporations were suspect. Politics was suspect. Big companies were pushing oil. The government was in Vietnam napalming innocent people. And the counterculture got together as a large tribe and bonded together in large groups. As a way of connecting, they found themselves in gatherings where people were playing drums. Most of them were not trained drummers. Here were 200 people all camping, coming together around the fire, and they'd just start drumming. And nobody was trying to copy traditional rhythms. They were playing from their unique experience in the moment.
>
> To me, that drum circle represents a unique innovation in the history of mankind. Playing together without a reference to any traditional music of any kind. They're not jamming to Country Western tunes or a Jazz tune, or Ragtime. It's not a Gypsy folk melody that somebody is improvising over. It's just people coming together. Emergence is the word that comes to mind. And with instruments that are so intuitive that anyone can do it. Music for the people. All free improvisation.

When I asked John whether there could be a "non-musical" person in such a drum circle, he shook his head:

> I thought it was all about drumming. Nope. Then I thought it's all about rhythm. I finally came to the conclusion that drum circles are not about drumming or music. They're about relationships. About connecting people to their own unique value. They are witnessed by others in their own unique value, and they witness others. To bring people into the experience of their own expressive capacities with simple tools. With fewer people, you have to create an environment where everyone feels safe. Where people feel less self-conscious. But in a group of fifty, we're all going down the river. It's a rhythm river and we're all wet.

What Comes Naturally?

New Hampshire native Joseph B. Carringer plays the didgeridoo, an ancient Australian instrument made from a hollowed-out eucalyptus tree. The "didge," as many call it, has been played for over 60,000 years by indigenous Australians and is known to have healing properties in its deep, resonant tones. The player must learn how to use a technique called "circular breathing" to maintain a constant flow of air so that it can be played for many minutes at a time.

Since learning to play the didgeridoo, Joseph divides his musical time between playing in bands and playing for healing. I met with Joseph after attending one of his healing sessions to ask him more about his story:

> I never thought of myself as a musician until I started playing the didge. I just kept failing miserably at being good enough to feel comfortable. I failed miserably at guitar. I struggled to understand fingering and the coordination for that. I started playing the saxophone at age twelve, and again, I could hear things I wanted to do, but I couldn't make my fingers do the things I wanted quickly enough. I stopped playing music for a while, and then in 1997, I got my first didge and could just play. I instinctively knew you were supposed to circular breathe. And I realized early on that nobody else played it,

so I wasn't being judged. I love the freedom of not having the rules that everyone else has to deal with. That's actually what made me musical. I never thought I was a musician or a musical person. I appreciated music and knew what good music was, but it wasn't until then that I felt like, "Wow, I can do this!" People thought it was amazing, but I've always played for myself. I like the sound of the instrument. That was what drew me to it. I've always wanted people to like what I was doing because that feels good, but at the end of the day, I can play for myself, and it feels good. It's for me. When I play with electronic dance music, which is what I love to do, that's when I'm in my Zen. In my groove playing the didge.

What if we kept trying instrument after instrument until we found one that worked for us? Throughout our school years, we are invited to explore different activities from chess club to debate club, and we are encouraged to try different sports teams from fencing to football. If someone doesn't make the ski team, she might try the soccer team, swim team, basketball team, and more before self-assessing her sporting abilities.

Yet with playing an instrument, we are often assigned at school (*Your hands are big—you should play the viola. We need a trombone player in the band, so you should play that...*) and if we can't do it the way we imagine we should, we rather quickly self-assess as being "unmusical." Give yourself a break! Or, rather, why not give yourself a ukulele, or a djembe drum, or an Irish flute? Who knows?

"Come This Way to Music"

Lauren Cregor, the professional singer and songwriter whom I quoted towards the beginning of this book, also described finding her own path. In her case, she felt she was musical but kept hitting roadblocks until she figured out what worked best for her. I am including her full story here, even though I have already shared the first part, because it now takes on new meaning:

There was a lot of music and joy within my family growing up—it was unabashed joy! At family gatherings, people would just jump onto the piano and play. I could be a part of it because it was all around me. Playing piano for my *Nonna* at age four gave me immediate positive reactions. There was both a physical and emotional joy to playing for her, seeing how deeply she felt the music she was hearing. Then, once I started school, people seemed to recognize me as being musical. Playing music was living—a beautifully alive way of living. My grandfather's mother was a professional musician who started a music competition in Indiana. She was a family legacy. From there on, it trickled down, and the whole family could tap into that. They weren't professional musicians, so it was very casual and free.

At age nine or ten, I hit a wall. I declared, "I'm never playing piano again!" My music teacher had a strong intuition and suggested that we start working on musicals. She began teaching me how to sing while I played. This helped me to figure out how music played into my identity—into my life. Music really brought me through those shaky years—the age of being embarrassed even by your own breath! I remember I went to an audition in seventh grade feeling like a real star—a Badass! It was an audition in front of the whole school. When the song got to the high part, my voice cracked, and all my classmates laughed. I paused and breathed and then just laughed right along with them. Then I tried again and kept going. I got the part! You really need to understand that mistakes are normal. Nobody is perfect. We need to allow ourselves to let those creaky moments show because that is what makes it so identifiable. So spectacular and real! As a singer, music became a powerful way for me to feel both vulnerable and confident.

Thinking back to my musical training, I didn't want to go to college for music because I knew the expectations would be too high and the pressure too great to make it my career. I wanted music to be "mine." But after college, I went to grad school in London for an intensive one-year program in drama, theater, and music. There was a very "large and in charge" old-school woman there who gave us exercises for a monologue. First, you would sing an excerpt of a song over and over as she told you how to move. Then all of a sudden, she'd tell you to jump into the monologue. We had to sing, speak, sing, speak, while many acting directions were given to us. When I would speak, the woman would say, "STOP! I don't believe you when you're speaking! I believe you when you sing, but not when you speak." It was a lightbulb moment for me—Come this way (through singing) to music, not through drama or theater. And that led me eventually to becoming a singer/songwriter. I had auditioned for Broadway shows. It was dehumanizing. A drummer in a group I played with told me that I had very original spins on cover songs— would I consider writing my own songs? That's how it began for me. I could now have a way of "owning" my own music— making it "mine." If you think about it, music is already there. It is already yours. You have to figure out the most natural path for you. Music unlocks something inside you. It all comes down to joy. There has to be an "inviting in." A web of energy that already exists. "This is yours! Do it! Play with it!"

Lauren was resilient. How many of us might have run off stage when our voice cracked at that high school audition, believing that we had failed? Lauren's confidence came from years of playing music casually with her family in no-pressure situations and from having teachers who opened new doorways for her when she felt she had hit a wall. Lauren's lightbulb moment, "Come *this* way (through singing) to music, not through drama", led her to uncover what worked for her as a musician.

Normalizing Musical Mistakes

Like Lauren, Brian Karzen, fitness coach and singer, also grew up in a home where music was a regular part of life, and where making mistakes was considered a normal part of performing. His story helps us to understand why these two elements helped build resiliency and helped him return to singing after a long break:

Growing up in Chicago, the Ravinia Festival was a regular family destination throughout the summer. Ravinia is a nightly concert series with a wide array of musical genres. My family took me to hear Ella Jenkins, Tom Chapin, and other children's concerts. At age six, I remember I loved singing along with lots of music. It was fun to sing! We also went to see *The Nutcracker* and watched *Fantasia* annually. These were family traditions for us, which I've now passed on to my kids. At age five, I started playing the piano, but stopped at age eight because I had a lot of other schoolwork and didn't want to practice an hour a day. I just wanted to run around outside with my friends! But I do feel that having played the piano contributed to my feeling of being a decent musician—I had a smattering of musical experiences that shaped who I am as a musician and that made me feel I was capable.

The cantor at my temple was male and had a big influence on me. He had a big booming baritone voice, which made it feel like it was cool for guys to sing, and it's not just for girls! He commanded the room. After my bar mitzvah, at age thirteen, the cantor took me aside and said, "I think you have a future as a singer." This man's daughter was later my high school choir teacher. She was a huge influence on me as well, always encouraging me to sing. At the end of my freshman year, she pulled me aside and said, "You are the future of the tenor section of our high school choir." She painted a vision of success for me that helped broaden my horizons. I started voice lessons during my sophomore year. My voice teacher had a degree in psychology and had a knack for understanding kids and meeting them where they were. She could sense what I needed as my voice changed. I felt like she had a full grasp of me as a person, not just a singer. I left there each week feeling like a million bucks! She encouraged me to just keep going and not dwell on slip-ups or what went wrong.

After college, I had the opportunity to sing with the Navy Pier Players, an *a cappella* group at a large year-round tourist attraction in downtown Chicago. One Halloween, we were on TV! I remember I had such stage fright. I was supposed to sing the lead on "Monster Mash" (1962), and I had a massive moment of panic in the middle of the song—I completely blanked on the words. It was so embarrassing! I screwed up despite having sung the song so many times before. We should normalize making mistakes. It's part of growth, and music is central to shared experiences. There are these mental narratives or stories we are given from the time we are born. I think a lot about how we talk to ourselves. We are given so many micro-messages about music that are reinforced through society and media, which become real for us. Inhibition and shame for being vulnerable—music is so vulnerable! But playing or singing together connects people and creates empathy, which helps people navigate uncertainty in their lives.

I spent a few years after my undergrad as a struggling stage performer. I sang and danced in assorted musicals and light operas (along with plenty of time waiting tables to make ends meet). Those years were deeply fulfilling, though I eventually made a change because I wasn't making a living. I left music behind as a professional endeavor, but there hasn't been any time since that it wasn't part of the fabric of my day. I listen to music, sing in the shower and car, and now get to introduce my kids to a world of awesome experiences through sound.

Music is a central part of life. It's all around. But our society has its normative ways of being, and when it comes to music, we easily label and judge.

A year after my interview with Brian, he wrote to tell me that he started singing again with a nearby community choir.

"It's so much fun. It's tremendous. It's an excellent challenge to rise to, and I'm enjoying the healthy struggle. Aside from the obvious physiological benefits of singing for a few hours every week, I also have something to look forward to on my calendar. The sense of belonging I found was immediate. It took less than a minute for me to think, 'Oh, these are my people. I belong here.'"

With a childhood filled with a "smattering" of musical experiences and family traditions, as well as teachers who painted a picture of musical success for him, Brian's identity as a musical person formed easily and stayed at his core despite setbacks and a hugely embarrassing blank moment on TV. The feeling of being at home with music happened naturally because positive musical experiences surrounded him at home, and were nurtured in him at his temple and school.

What can we learn from this? How can we reclaim our musical selves so that we can feel those incredible feelings of connection and community that music can provide? What is the type of music that you connect most with? That can make you feel like *these are my people—I belong here*? Can you find concerts to attend? Can you play that music for yourself often enough for it to feel like a part of you? Can you sing along? Grab a drum and play along? And if you have children, can you find concerts to go to together? Start your own family musical traditions?

You can model your resiliency in making mistakes as well as your own enjoyment of what you're listening to or dancing to.

Perhaps you can even lead your children on their own musical scavenger hunts, experimenting with different sounds, going to different types of concerts, or trying out some instruments in a music shop, to find out what kind of music feels like home to them!

"It Felt Better than Anything Else"

Earlier, I shared part of Carol McGonnell's story—how her teacher's comment "boring, boring, boring" led her to dig deeper in her musical expression. Here she is again, describing what kept her going as a clarinet player that led her to make it her professional career:

Music has been a way for me to connect with energy and the power that we have naturally in our bodies and with each other. That's been an incredible journey. Deep inside me, there was my natural way of being and my own kind of instincts and reactions that were very much dampened as a child. During my whole childhood, for reasons I won't get into, I had the feeling that I needed to hold my emotions in check. I felt as if controlling my emotions was important to my family's well-being.

When I had the clarinet, I could just be me. That was my thing. Just for me. Not for my mother. When everyone would leave the house, as I got a bit older, at age eleven or twelve, I would sing at the top of my lungs. I would never do that when others were around. I always felt I was a really bad singer and didn't trust my voice, but somehow I would be alone singing at the top of my lungs. I would just love that. As I got better at the clarinet, I could sing through the clarinet. It felt so free and so good. It felt really good to play. It felt better than anything else. And that's what I kept following—that feeling.

I saw the *Barbie* movie. I came away thinking it was probably the best movie I'd seen in my life. It was done so beautifully. There's a moment when Barbie has a decision to stay in Barbie Land or become human. She said she wants to become human because she realized she wants to feel. To me, that was mind-blowing. That's why we're here. To feel. As a child, feeling wasn't allowed. It wasn't a possibility.

Through the clarinet, I could feel. I could feel good, and that was the hook.

Peter Erskine: It's Not About Impressing the Universe

Peter Erskine, a professional jazz drummer and percussionist, offers us yet another window into becoming a professional musician. He had incredibly supportive parents who went to great lengths to get him auditions and lessons with the right teachers. For Peter, letting go of his ego and learning to normalize mistakes made all the difference for him:

The urge for self-expression is hard to extinguish. Most of us have something to say, but might be admonished. Musicians are not only judged but are their own worst critics. I was a very fortunate product of supportive parents, and drumming was something I always wanted to do. I discovered music early on because my father was also a jazz bassist. I was the embodiment of his dream. I asked my mother to bring me back a trombone when she went out shopping one day. But we had a Chinese tom-tom [drum]. I played along to my father's recordings and learned early on how to turn on a record player. In my imagination, I thought there were tiny musicians in the speaker cabinet who played for my listening pleasure! Concerns about my mental acuity led to tests, and I tested very high, but they did note that I showed an inordinate amount of concern for how I compared to others. Was I smarter? Was I liked? With that indication, my father gave me a lot of attention, and he would tell me, "Not everyone's going to love you." Because I wanted to be a musician, he knew what I was in for.

I loved playing. My parents sought out great opportunities for me. My mom sent a telegram to a summer jazz camp about me, this marvelous kid drummer. It was an arduous two-day drive to get to the audition. When we arrived, they saw I was only seven years old and said I was too young. But they held a special audition for me because they saw a press opportunity. Stan Kenton was there as well as a journalist and photographer, and it became part of the local press. Lots of well-known musicians go to that summer camp, and it became my summer fix. I loved being around these older musicians, and I was pretty good at surviving the slings and arrows from people who didn't like my playing. But I auditioned for a local TV talent show, which was humiliating. They wanted to know, "Does he dance or sing?" I had told my friends I'd be on TV, but I wasn't.

I got to the point that when my parents took me to the summer camp auditions, I would place in the top band. When I was twelve, I began to transition from an accomplished child to something else. At that point, I went to a different branch of the camp in California. It was more jazz-focused. The first time I auditioned for that, the auditioner put his head in his hands. When the results were posted, I had gotten in the wrong group. They placed me at the bottom, but it was a blessing in disguise. The faculty there gently took me apart and put me back together towards becoming a more mature musician. I now have an appreciation for the role of ego. In later years, I came face-to-face with a very macho self.

At the Thornton School of Music, my approach in my teaching studio was "I've never met anyone who walked out of an audition saying 'that's the most fun I've ever had and the best I've ever played.'" But students may not realize we're rooting for them and want them to be the answer to the search. You are here to make mistakes because that's how we discover. In the jazz world, I call it the "fuck it" response. You make a mistake, who cares? That was partly thanks to my mom. It's not going to matter. While my housemates at Indiana University [in the classical division] were pulling all-nighters and taking performance-enhancing drugs, my mom said, "Just do the best you can."

At age nineteen, I had my first lesson at another summer camp in Morehead, Kentucky, with George Gaber from Indiana University. He was aware of my anxiety, wanting to do well and be praised. George put a piece of music in front of me and a snare drum. He said, "If you play any of it *correctly*, I'll hit you with this mallet." I played all the rhythms wrong and backwards. He puffed his cigar. He told me to go over to the window and look outside. "What do you see when you look out the window? Trees? Blue skies? The Earth is still spinning. You played worse than anyone could have, and nothing happened. Now let's begin."

John Wire is a wonderful percussionist who was a timpanist in the Toronto Symphony. He'd worked with Seiji Ozawa and was also part of the ensemble Nexus, which had an astonishing range of musical ability. They could play West African drumming and virtuosic mallet pieces like Ragtime styles or marches. I was fortunate to work with them a few times. John had to leave because of cancer, and he settled in Nova Scotia. I was on tour with Diana Krall, and we had a free day to visit John. His living room was filled with an incredible structure made of all his chimes and glass bowls—sound-producing things. He asked, "You want to mess around on the improv machine?" We went to the basement, and there was a large, rudimentary, primitive marimba thing. The wood was redwood, I think. The bars reached across so you could stand on either side. The tuning was sort of pentatonic-ish. John loved his microtones. He handed me a pair of mallets and told me to start. "What's John doing?" I wondered. He was playing slow and simple, and he wasn't taking any of my beat. I calmed down and started exploring this simpler thing, and he began to smile. There was this idea that it's more about listening—not so much about impressing the universe. Our desire or need to impress usually comes from some level of insecurity. The irony of ego is that when we surrender ego, we can often bolster it.

There Must Be a Typo

This is an incredible story that made my jaw drop and had me wondering all about access to talent. Albert Frantz, now an internationally recognized virtuoso pianist, remembers a musical toy that he received as a gift on his fourth birthday. Several weeks later, during the holiday season, on this toy piano, he sounded out a Christmas carol by ear that he had heard around him. Albert still remembers the beaten-up, yellow upright piano that sat in the corner of his kindergarten classroom the next year. One day, his teacher asked his mother, "Where did Albert learn to play the piano?"

Dumbfounded, his mother replied, "You must mean some other kid. We don't even have a piano."

The teacher explained, "Every day the principal comes into the classroom, plays a melody on the piano, and Albert plays it back."

His mother didn't believe her, but she thought that the kids, including Albert's two brothers, adopted from Vietnam, should at least try piano lessons. One brother liked it; the other hated it. Albert was indifferent.

The family moved around a lot, and there were a couple of on-and-off attempts at piano lessons before an exasperated teacher told his mother, "You take your money every week and throw it in the garbage. Albert will never be able to play the piano." She thought this was true because Albert had gotten as far as level one, but couldn't read music.

Many years later, as a high school junior, a teammate on Albert's track and cross country teams inspired him to try his hand at music one last time. This is Albert's account of what happened from there:

He was a jazz guitarist. We would go on long training runs together, and he'd talk about the jazz greats the whole time: Miles Davis, John Coltrane, Pat Metheny. Sometimes we would run past his house, and we would stop, and he would play his guitar to demonstrate something. I figured I had tried—and failed—to learn piano as a child, but maybe I could at least learn a couple of pop songs? So I signed up for lessons with someone named Mrs. Pellett, who lived down the street. I used to be her paperboy. She introduced me to classical music right away and assigned me a piece by George Gershwin. She did show me the sheet music, but she allowed me to be guided by my ears.

Wanting to know more about George Gershwin, I went to the library to do some research. That's where I discovered his *Rhapsody in Blue* (1924). It immediately gave me goosebumps—I recognized one of its melodies from the United Airlines commercials! It was so incredibly moving. At my next lesson, I announced, "I'm learning the *Rhapsody in Blue*!"

Mrs. Pellett tried to calm me down, explaining that the piece isn't for beginners; it's for professional concert pianists. Undeterred, I naively replied, "I already bought the sheet music," to which she retorted, "But you can't even read music." Then she did something very wise. She let me learn it. She knew I'd make all sorts of mistakes. I had little sense of rhythm, I didn't yet know chords and keys, I hadn't yet developed a technique, and I knew nothing about how to play beautifully. Still, Mrs. Pellett could see that I was discovering not just my passion but something about myself—my emerging identity as a musician. I learned all thirty-one pages of Gershwin's original masterpiece by memory within months and performed it for my first concert. Musically, I'm sure it left a lot to be desired, but the audience gave me a standing ovation. It was such a joy to get to share music I loved with an audience. I was hooked for life.

The next year, Albert went off to college at Penn State to study engineering. He was particularly interested in sound engineering. He took piano lessons on the side with Professor Steven H. Smith, who became his mentor. In his sophomore year, Albert won the university's concerto competition with Ravel's *Piano Concerto for the Left Hand* (1921), written for a pianist who lost his right arm in World War I.

At the dress rehearsal, the conductor stopped him:

Conductor:
Albert, there's a typo in the program. It says here you just started playing four years ago.

Albert:
That's not a typo.

Conductor:
But this is one of the hardest pieces in the piano repertoire. That's impossible.

The performance was a big success. Afterwards, Albert switched his major to music, with no family support.

"I figured I had lost my whole childhood, not practicing. It was now or never."

Albert continued to play and perform some of the most challenging and impressive piano repertoire imaginable, and was later awarded a Fulbright scholarship to study piano in Vienna, one of the most musically rich cities in the world for classical music.

While living in Vienna, Albert made a startling discovery: He had been lied to about his very identity. It turned out he was the product of "third-party reproduction." In other words, his biological father was an anonymous sperm donor. Between DNA tests, tracing information in government records, and many years of research, he found the proverbial needle in a haystack: his biological father. His newfound family was incredibly warm towards Albert and was eager to meet him. Albert learned some jaw-dropping facts about his family:

1. His grandmother played the piano throughout her life. Incredibly, her favorite piece was Gershwin's *Rhapsody in Blue*.

2. His biological brother was an engineer and scientist in the field of the physics of sound.

3. A branch of his family of origin was from Vienna.

4. He could trace his ancestry to Vladimir Horowitz, one of the greatest pianists of all time.

If Albert hadn't taken up running in high school, would he have encountered the jazz guitarist who inspired him to try his hand at playing piano again? The magic of his story leads me to believe that he would have found the piano and his passion for piano music one way or another. Yet I can't help but wonder how many piano teachers out there discard or discredit highly motivated players because of their inability to read music! I want to believe that most music teachers these days can see musicality beyond the bars of the five lines of a printed staff.

Circumstance plays such a big role in leading us towards or away from a musical identity.

What were the musical beliefs of the family you grew up with or the teachers you encountered? Did you have access to something like a piano in your home or classroom? Did you have just one person who could sense your musical tastes and lead you in the right musical direction? Albert's story shows us that talent isn't the only variable in leading someone towards a musical identity, and that someone might embody incredible musical abilities and never come to know that about themselves.

"I Can Do That!"—Picking It Up Again as an Adult

Where Albert's story highlights the importance of access, Kim Sauder Stoeckel's story demonstrates why community connection and opportunity matter in sticking with playing an instrument:

I grew up in the Mennonite Church community, singing four-part harmony *a cappella* hymns, which I still love and appreciate. The Mennonite school I attended had a lot of singing at its core, and I liked being surrounded by that world. They had a Christmas concert every year. My family had a friend who used to play the violin, and when she died, her husband gave it to my dad and said, "I'd like Kim to play this." My dad put a lot of pressure on me to play it and fulfill his friend's wishes. I didn't have time to practice, and there was a lot of crying and tension. There was no culture around me of ensemble or orchestra playing, so playing the violin was very lonely. My family couldn't have understood how to make that door open for me. There was no framework for even looking for ensemble opportunities. Being in a group would have made a big difference for me, but my parents couldn't conceive of the type of world needed for violin success.

When I got to college, I found that I had a sense of pride in the church music I grew up with because not many others had that kind of experience. I knew music was something I had inside of me, but there weren't opportunities to really continue with that type of music, and it didn't feel like something I could pursue. I also lacked the confidence to pursue playing violin in a college ensemble because I had never been a part of any formal music ensemble. But then one day, a friend of mine decided to start taking violin lessons as an adult, and I suddenly thought, "Hey! I can do that! I could learn to play the violin again!" I took lessons for a few years after college graduation. I had a friend who played in a local ensemble, and she encouraged me to join her community orchestra. It was a welcoming environment, and the pace of learning new music fit my skill level. It was such an amazing and fun experience to play in an orchestra! When I moved away from that area, I was not able to find another community orchestra that fit my skill level.

> But then, as a mother, I found myself singing those church hymns to my children to soothe and nurture them. Now they take lessons on piano, and they sing and we sing together as a family.

Kim's story offers us an opportunity to consider the difference between the music that surrounds us in our home culture and the musical worlds that we are invited into by others. Her world of beautiful church hymns that filled and nourished her as a child is the same musical world that she later introduced to her children upon becoming a mother. That is the music through which Kim felt musical and alive.

While those hymns created a sense of home for Kim, playing the violin or piano was not a natural part of the world that surrounded her. It felt lonely and tense. Her parents, not having a framework themselves for creating a natural, joyful experience on those instruments, were not able to envision how an ensemble could help. How a friend or peer could provide the motivational scaffolding needed to keep going. Yet as an adult, when Kim's friend invited her to join the community orchestra, that provided the community and connection needed to create an "amazing and fun experience."

The other important element that brought Kim from pain to pleasure as a violin player was that the community orchestra was a good match for her skill level.

How many of us have quit playing in an ensemble, thinking, "I don't have what it takes," rather than asking ourselves, "Where can I find an ensemble that plays my kind of music at my level?"

And while there may be more opportunities to find a "matching" ensemble in larger urban areas, whether it be a West African drum circle or a tin-whistle marching group, the point is that we can recognize musical "lack" as having more to do with rightness of fit and opportunity rather than our musicianship.

Part Three:
Rewriting the Score on Our Musical Definitions

9 — Judgment

Vignette: The Twelfth Audition of the Day

Several years ago, I was invited to listen in on violin auditions for the Boston Youth Symphony Orchestra groups. During the "audition week," an average of 350 violin students play in front of a panel of judges who use an evaluative rubric to decide who's in and who's out.

I sat several rows back behind the judges, curious to hear part of the process. I listened to fifteen middle and high school violinists, many of whom were understandably quite nervous. Nearly all of them had chosen to play the same suggested excerpt from Vivaldi's "Winter," a technically challenging movement from *The Four Seasons.*

Some made minor mistakes; one or two were clearly not prepared. Most of these young violinists, however, were impressively in tune and precise with their rhythm. After hearing about eight of these auditions, I was beginning to zone out. How would the judges decide among so many seemingly qualified hopefuls? And then came violin player #12, a young girl with straight black hair and large brown eyes.

She played the same excerpt as most of the previous violinists, but something felt different. Her playing was expressive—full of passion and nuance. I sat up in my seat and my heart beat faster in my chest. Her technique was somewhat sloppy. She made several big mistakes and botched up an entire passage, yet I loved every moment of her playing. *This is a violinist I would want to hear in a concert!*

When she was finished, she slinked off with her head hung

low. She knew she had made mistakes. We both knew she probably would not get in.

I wanted to run after her to tell her it was the most beautiful playing I had heard all day!

I wanted to cry! Would she ever try again? Would she stop believing in herself? How could the "best" violinist not get in?

I think back to the time when I identified as a "violinist." When I carried that romantic vision of myself dressed in black with my violin case slung over my shoulder, heading home from the symphony. I never questioned whether I was "good enough" until I started to audition for specific orchestras.

Though I was accepted into the New York Youth Symphony, I was placed last chair in the second violin section. I began to feel embarrassed about my sound and my mistakes, yet I felt passionate about playing and performing, and continued to pursue my romantic vision.

When I auditioned for the Manhattan School of Music high school division, the director stopped me after a few measures and asked me with seeming disbelief, "Wait—so you want to be a musician?"

Though I was accepted, I will never forget the way he laughed at me.

When I relay this story to other classically trained musicians, they often laugh and shake their heads. Almost all of the classical musicians I spoke with seemed to have had crushing moments like this or teachers who terrified them. Yet this type of abusive teaching was new to me at the time.

Fast-forward about 25 years, and I found myself teaching music in a private school in Cambridge, Massachusetts. I encountered a first-grade student whom I will call Anand, who thought of himself as a "very good piano player." He would often walk into the room with an air of superiority because he identified so strongly as an excellent musician. He would saunter over to the keyboard and ask if he could show his classmates the very beautiful piece he had just learned. On occasion, I would allow this.

Though he played the correct notes, Anand lacked what many would call natural rhythm. I felt the cruel critic in me rush to the surface. Perhaps because we often teach in the way that we were taught, my cruel violin teacher from college seemed to have perched himself on my shoulder. I found myself wanting to tell Anand, *you have a long way to go—a lot to learn. You aren't as good as you think you are. Don't be so arrogant—there are many first-graders who play much better than you!*

Where was this coming from?! If even I could so easily fall into the role of a cruel musical critic, when I so strongly believe that everyone is musical in some way, how possible could it be to actually broaden the wider world's definition of musicality? Was I simply trying to humble his arrogance, or did this prove that classical music training is naturally prone to competitive one-upmanship? Was I projecting my own painful story onto him? And if so many musicians and music teachers carry these painful stories around, how easy can it be to break the cycle? To teach with pleasure, love, and exploration?

I decided at that moment to focus on Anand's fingers gliding over the keys. I focused on the incredible drive that a child can have to look at these 88 black and white keys, play with the puzzle of note and finger patterns, and learn how to create or recreate a piece of music.

The fact is that we are all prone to judgment. Musical learning can be quite competitive. Yo-Yo Ma described it to me like this: "The world is full of people constantly judging or being judged, and as a child you play the 'brain real estate' game—how much of it are you doing for your own pleasure; how much of it you're doing to please your parents or teacher."

He described how, within American education systems, we are often rewarded for comparing ourselves to others and feeling superior. "We are constantly competing—*We're number one! We are the best!*"

Yo-Yo explained that in Finland, a country whose citizens are said to be among the happiest in the world, three things are held dear to life: 1) they don't compare themselves to others, 2) they value spending time in nature, and 3) they never break the circle of community trust. By frequently competing and trying to feel superior, we Americans are constantly breaking "community trust," which doesn't lead to much happiness.

Aren't people judgmental about other subjects as well? Math? Sports? Conversational skills? Yes, but musical judgment is directed differently and is felt differently.

Other subjects, such as math, science, and language, are taught to everyone. It is assumed that everyone can be taught these skills, and if they work hard enough and practice a lot, or have the proper tutors, they can improve and acquire the skills they need. Just because some people are genius mathematicians doesn't exclude others from trying. Even when someone fails at math or science, we make them repeat the course, and they *must* keep learning.

As a student, math was usually a struggle for me. Despite sitting in the front row of class, raising my hand each time I didn't understand something, and seeking extra help after class, I failed many math tests and rarely received an overall grade higher than a C. Yet math was required in school. I was not allowed to simply quit.

I could say, "I'm not good at math," and I had teachers who continued to encourage me and take time to teach me because our society deemed math to be important for survival in our modern-day world.

Isn't music vital as well? Its ability to connect us with others, express our inner worlds, and feel a sense of joy and belonging in a community are the qualities that made music biologically vital for our survival in ancient and traditional cultures. But these days, a failed audition or embarrassing public performance can make someone turn away from ever trying again. In fact, I will add that orchestras, bands, and choirs at the upper levels are precisely designed to weed people out! School ensembles do create and sustain our need for community, but *only for those who can make it in.*

Like music, sports can be unforgivingly competitive as well. However, young children tossing a ball around outside are allowed to just goof off and play without adults circling to judge whether they are talented (well, at least most of the time)! With sports, we can also acknowledge that some people play professionally and others just do it for pleasure. You don't necessarily need to be talented at kickball or basketball to join in a low-key community game at the rec center or local park.

Some traditional cultures have this same attitude about

music—you can just show up at an Irish pub with your fiddle and join in! In most modern-day societies, these casual community music happenings are very hard to come by, though it seems that we may be turning a corner. More and more people are realizing the importance of these casual music-making groups. We just have to seek them out, find our bravery, and take the leap to join in.

Being judged for our musical abilities also feels different than other subjects because our musical connections, expressions, and yearnings come from deep within our human souls. Music's profound ability to cut straight to the heart of our identity makes it feel extra vulnerable to put a musical sound or expression out into the world. This is especially the case with singing, as previously mentioned—a sound that is produced by our own unique bodies! Our voices represent who we are. So when we are judged for singing poorly, it can evoke the deepest sorrow and shame.

I never followed up to ask who that "Twelfth Violinist" was or whether she kept pursuing the violin. I will never know if she kept trying and eventually "made it" or whether she put her violin in her closet until its strings came loose from disuse. If she's reading this, I want her to know that I loved her playing. That she didn't fail that day. She just stood out too much to fit into an orchestra whose excellence placed perfection in higher regard than expression. In a way, we could all be that failed violinist, slinking off backstage with our mistakes weighing us down. But maybe, just maybe, we moved someone in the audience and made them feel something beautiful. Even if we will never hear that feedback.

America's Got Talent?

The word "talent" looms large. It is often the first word that comes to mind when people think of professional musicians. Elitist attitudes and judgments about what makes a "Good Musician" can make or break one's motivation or shape one's entire musical identity. We forget that we can value music within ourselves. We forget to trust our ears and hearts and instead place our trust in the hands of judges who may only hear us once in our lives.

Consider the impact of *America's Got Talent*, created by Simon Cowell, which premiered in 2006 and attracts an audience of around 10 million viewers per season. Dancers, singers, and other performers compete on live television in front of judges for a chance to win a $1 million cash prize. No one could have predicted how popular this show would become.

I remember watching it for the first time with my friend Sue, our jaws dropping with each incredibly rude and painful blow of judgment doled out to the teary-eyed hopefuls on stage. Yet as we witnessed these painful musical moments, we couldn't help but be captivated.

What was it, we wondered, about watching these musical "failures" that kept us glued to the screen? Did it appeal to some twisted part of ourselves that wanted to feel musically superior? Was it just the fact that drama itself is captivating, or was the experience of judging someone as being *unmusical* somehow gratifying? Could it be possible that *America's Got Talent* is so popular because so many of us resonate with the painful experience of auditioning? Carrying a hope that we could be good enough and then being humiliated or rejected?

Jazz singer Melissa Karger recounts her experience singing on *American Idol*, a similar show that preceded *America's Got Talent*:

> *American Idol* was a way for emerging artists to get started. It was kind of like the TikTok of its time. Their contracting was very limiting for artists. If you won, *American Idol* would take 50% of your check, and you'd be beholden to them for those two years. And there was a lack of support for these artists after they received fame. They were left on their own. *American Idol* was basically a money-making machine and not setting you up for success because contestants who make it far enough are required to sign paperwork early in the process, agreeing that they won't sign with other record labels for the first couple of years after the show, when they agree to compete. This effectively locks them into a multi-year contract with *Idol*—often ranging from four to seven years—where the production company and label maintain significant control over their careers. Most artists feel compelled to accept the deal because they need to capitalize on the exposure while they're still "hot" from the show.

Unfortunately, this often sets winners up for failure. The label dictates what they release, controls their schedule, and stifles their creative freedom, etc. Ultimately, *Idol* seemed more focused on scouting contestants who were controllable and predictable, rather than supporting long-term artistic growth.

I was sixteen years old— a needle in a haystack out of 40,000 people. When I arrived, I had this moment of doubt: Am I here because I'm talented or because I'd be good entertainment? And there's a lot of production behind the scenes that never makes it on TV. In my case, after I sang, they had the judges talking with me backstage about my stage presence. They said I had good musicality but that I was very young. They suggested I come back next year. But the only thing they showed on the actual TV was Randy saying, "Sorry Dawg, it's a no." Randy never even spoke to me! It was all staged.

I remember feeling sad and tricked that what was portrayed on the show wasn't what happened. They were making fools of people! I mean, these are people's lives! For example, they would actually separate the talent behind the scenes. If you had skills, they would tell you to come back and bring outfit options and prepare new material. The sorting happened as early as Gillette Stadium when they were cutting down in large numbers. It was wild. Almost like being marked with a scarlet letter if you were for entertainment. But they would tell the other group to come back and wear the same thing and sing the same song, just to make them look bad. I had wanted to audition because I thought I could do it! I had worked with a vocal coach for three months just to prepare for that audition. After *American Idol*, I felt like I wanted to reinvent how I pursued music. I felt like an artist, but it made me sad for people who loved music and were cast badly on the show. I do love being able to say I had that experience.

Really, to make it as a professional singer, you need perseverance and good marketing. So much of the hard work kills the passion. You also need really good connections to make a living out of it. I had an internship with EMI Music years ago and saw how they dealt with artist royalties. I realized that artists earn .004 cents *or less* for every time their song is played on the radio. I noticed that artists composing their own music were making more money and had fewer people to pay out. And then you have the problem as a listener of being told what music to even like! Unless you're carefully choosing your own music, what you hear on music streaming platforms is based on what a company is selling. It's popular because you're told it's popular. There's a lack of support for other artists to thrive. So the problem with a lot of these artists failing is that they lacked the mental and emotional support to be their authentic selves. And people do want authenticity. They seek it out. The artist's dream is to have it fund their lives, but when you get stardom overnight, what does that feel like? You're exposed to even more judgment and control. You really need that inner confidence and positive self-talk to carry you through.

I personally love the creative elements of music making, and so I prefer not to be famous because I can have more control as an artist and with the audience. I listen to music every day and always try to learn more songs. And I make music with my kids. What is a musical person? It's somebody who wakes up wanting to listen to music. Anyone touched by music is musical. It's not limiting.

Melissa's story illuminates some of the darker aspects of music competition, where someone's musical "goodness" is almost entirely wrapped up in what kind of entertainment ratings they might receive, how controllable they are, and how much money they might rake in for the show. Melissa was lucky enough not to let her negative experience turn her away from making music. She had a strong inner feeling that she was good enough to keep going and was able to reinvent herself to hold on to the more creative and enjoyable aspects of her music-making.

One thing that Melissa's story makes clear to me is that while it may be true that a singer who "wins" on *American Idol* probably has a voice that others enjoy listening to, we cannot say that those who failed did not.

Pop Music's Double-Edged Sword: AutoTune

The invention of AutoTune initially gave singers an edge and allowed their mistakes to be digitally fixed in real time. I interviewed two people with differing opinions about how AutoTune affects competition or alters judgment. I wanted to know if AutoTune evens the playing field, allowing more singers to have the confidence to get in front of a microphone, or whether it sets impossible standards that young performers now feel they have to live up to. In other words, does it make singers feel better or worse about their natural abilities? Here is Paul Karger, an investor in AutoTune, and also the husband of jazz singer Melissa Karger:

> AutoTune started around 1997 and boomed over the last ten years, especially during the pandemic. Artists were using similar technology in the '70s called the EvenTide H9-10 Harmonizer. The tech evolved to where you could use it in real time (Autotune). It uses an algorithm to shift sound waves to obtain perfect pitch. It's controversial, like the use of AI by artists, or using Photoshop/filters on a picture. It became a music tool— an essentially musical quality in itself, as artists intentionally altered their sounds. People say it influences the creative process, but it also removes authenticity. You can take a song, which is basically a data set, and manipulate it. For instance, AI can take Snoop Dog and make him sound like Sinatra. But I think you still need talent, as it's hard to replace raw talent and creativity. Artists won't go away; they'll always be there. AI will serve to enhance, similar to the rise of DJs in the live music scene. Yes, they are using sound equipment, but I think it's hard to argue that David Guetta or Calvin Harris are not creative artists. You still need stage presence and artistry, which is something you're born with. Think of AI like skiing—skiing has evolved as the equipment has evolved. Current equipment technologies allow people a smoother and better ski experience. You can do things on new skis that you couldn't do with older types of skis. It's the same with music tech and AI. It allows you to do more than you could before.

Courtney Kaiser-Sandler is the Associate Director of Contemporary Music and Collaborative Projects and founder of the Singer-Songwriter program at the Interlochen Center for the Arts. As someone who teaches young musicians how to create songs and put a successful band together, she has a rather different opinion about Autotune:

I'm not into it! It's good for moments when you're exhausted and there's that one little section you just keep trying to get and can't, or when what you're trying to do isn't working and it's compromising the integrity of the piece because you can't get it in tune. It's good for tiny things that bother the singer. But for someone to use it all the time does not make music more accessible. On the internet, everyone is putting their art out there on TikTok and YouTube. What happened to just enjoying making music and making songs for yourself? Does it really need to be put out into the world for all to see? If you're hoping to be the next Jennifer Lopez or be discovered, no. An artist needs to learn resilience, how to improve, write for their voice, put in the work, and understand what their artistry means. If everyone is using AutoTune, how do you even know what's good anymore, or what's real? It's also a form of entitlement and privilege—who has access to that expensive technology?

Just because you have access to impressive tech tools doesn't mean you get to suddenly be a good singer! Plus, does that feel good?! To be called a good singer when you didn't put the work into it? Didn't earn it? These days, being a singer/songwriter is drowning in privilege. It's all about monetization and capitalism. Human imperfection is more real and enjoyable. AI actually makes it harder to have a musical career, a) because now there are so many other people out there trying to make it—thinking they can, and b) because people aren't learning technique and skill, and the struggle with dedicating yourself to an art form.

I want to make a distinction: Everyone can make music. Music is accessible to everyone, and kids should all believe that they can write songs, invent songs, and be musical. But not everyone needs to become a professional musician and share their music with the world.

I shared these two opinions about AutoTune to help you realize something: Most performing singers use corrective technology in some capacity when they get behind a microphone. When you compare yourself to a professional singer, you aren't hearing their natural flaws, missed notes, or limits in their vocal range. You are hearing what technology has enhanced. Just like looking at an airbrushed magazine image of a woman with perfect skin, teeth, hips, and hair, witnessing the brilliance of something that has been digitally enhanced can make the rest of us feel less than capable. Another important point to consider is that even the most famous musicians compare themselves to others, judge themselves harshly, and wish they could be better at *something*.

Five-Star Reviews: Judging Others and Ourselves

Peter Mulvey is a touring solo folk guitarist with over 20,000 social media followers and several albums available for purchase. Peter talks about the very real aspect of how all musicians judge themselves and negatively compare themselves to others:

> I was really lucky in that I had very supportive parents, but I started to tell myself, "I'm not a good improviser," and so I wouldn't take guitar solos. It becomes a way of specializing. Like I specialize in accompanying myself as I sing. But why not work on those things? This stuff (judgment) doesn't stop in childhood. My friend Megan Burns is an absolute killer lead soloist, but no one throws the solo to her. She still doesn't feel like she qualifies! We (professional musicians) judge ourselves.

When do we ever feel that we are "good enough" as musicians? Someone who can barely fumble their way through a few notes feels that they aren't a good enough guitar player to continue taking lessons. Someone else takes guitar lessons, but doesn't feel "good enough" to play around a campfire with friends. Someone else can play around a campfire with ease, but has never won any competitions or been invited to play any solo shows. And now we just read about Peter and his friend Megan—two professional guitarists, with tens of thousands of followers and large-scale tours, who don't feel "good enough" to play a solo. We can always look for and find reasons to believe that we aren't qualified to do something. And certainly, the invention of five-star reviews or rating scales doesn't help! Here's Peter Mulvey again:

> One of the biggest sadnesses we have created with our productivity-obsessed society is to convince so many people that if they aren't an MTV-level dancer, singer, or guitar

> player—if they're not a professional, well then they're not
> good at it. Commercial music in the 80s figured out in their
> surveys that if you rate something from 1-10, some people's
> tens were other people's ones, so they decided to make the
> rating system in fives and sixes. This rating system was
> created to sell advertising. So even as a listener, you can
> judge. You can think, "It's not exciting." They might love or
> hate [a song] and make decisions to listen to more of what
> they like, rather than being exposed to all kinds of music. I
> hate to say capitalism ruins everything, but it kind of does.

These days, "liking" a song or adding to your smart playlist means that the streaming platform you use will suggest other similar songs. Peter's sentiment about rating scales makes me realize that the era of browsing in a record store and coming across something different just by chance seems to be over. We have been well-trained at forming quick judgments about the songs we hear. If we do encounter new songs or musical material that feels foreign, offbeat, or even off-putting to us, I wonder what it would take to remain open and curious towards it, rather than judgmental!

I sometimes lead my elementary school students in guided listening activities, where I invite them to listen with "open hearts." I introduce it like this:

> I'm going to play something for you that might be really
> different from anything else you have heard! Use the pencil
> and paper in front of you if you want to write down any words
> or draw any images that come to mind. I know that
> sometimes if something sounds surprising or uncomfortable,
> it can make you want to laugh or giggle. That's okay and
> normal. You don't need to hold it in, but please don't share
> any thoughts or words about it out loud so that every
> person's heart and mind can feel something for themselves.
> We can talk about what we heard when the music stops.

We do not *rate* or judge what we hear. We simply share what we notice. I make it clear that they are allowed to like or dislike the music that they hear, but I ask them to just take it in and *notice.* What, specifically, do they not like? Why might someone else like it? What is one quality or aspect of the music that they find interesting? Is the music energizing to them?

Calming? Does it paint a scene in their minds?

I don't know whether there is a way for us adults to listen with "open hearts" in the same way that children can, but I encourage you to try! Take out your paper and pencil and see what words or images pop up as you listen to something completely random. Maybe, just maybe, you will discover some new sound that delights you. But in doing this experiment, we are both challenging the "musicality" system and honing our musical listening skills!

The Subway Concert Experiment

Even the most attentive listener might be reluctant to stop in their tracks during rush hour to hear a street performer. On the morning of Friday, January 12, 2007, one of the most well-known virtuosic violinists, Joshua Bell, opened his violin case in a DC Metro station and began to play. Over a forty-five-minute stretch, he played a variety of pieces. Of the 1097 people who passed by, according to reporters on the scene, only seven stopped to listen (Weingarten, 2007). Later, and for the next several weeks, as people reacted to the media's coverage of this performance, many harsh statements were cast:

- *Do we live in a world where people can't recognize talent?*

- *Does no one have the time to stop and listen?*

- *How can people care so little about such gorgeous playing?*

- *Have we become a cultureless society?*

There we were, placing judgment on each other for some lack of artistic knowledge or appreciation. Something about this experiment—this test for attention during rush hour—felt wrong to me. When we decide to go see a performer, we check our calendars, hire babysitters, and put on fancy clothes. We make time, purposely, to sit and listen. We may familiarize ourselves with the pieces that will be played before the concert, or we may leaf through the concert program to learn more about what to expect. It is a dedicated time and place where social cues and personal choices play a significant role. During a Friday morning rush hour in the Metro, people have not carved out time in their day to stop and listen. The context is all "wrong." People are trying to get to work on time. Speed takes precedence over pleasure on most busy work days.

What someone wants in any given moment of their life is entirely dependent on time and context. What I want upon entering a subway station on a weekday morning is to get to work quickly so I can prepare my material for the day. What I want at a fast food restaurant is to pick up my bag of fries and my milkshake and be on my way. That doesn't mean that I wouldn't occasionally love to linger over a long and luxurious three-course meal, but I don't enter a fast food restaurant to linger, savor the food, or admire the wallpaper and lighting.

Laura Menard works at SoundLife Scarborough—a research center dedicated to music and community engagement, at the University of Toronto. She researches sound and music-making in public spaces. In our conversation, I asked her about whether the Joshua Bell experiment could tell us about how people engage with or appreciate music. Menard agreed that the experiment was unfair, and added, "You can never know what's happening in someone's head and how certain music impacts people, or whether they are listening. There's an arrogance in assuming we can understand all the implications of the way people behaved [while he was playing]."

Menard and her colleague Friesen explain that the same individual may hear the same sounds differently at different points, depending on what is happening in their lives at the moment. They give, as an example, the sound of a fire truck siren. If one's house is burning down, it will be the sweet sound of relief and hope. If that same person is stuck in traffic, running late for their daughter's final soccer game of the season, that same sound might elicit anger, frustration, guilt, or grief. And, even though people may have appeared to rush by without a moment's pause, what Laura is saying is that whoever might be potentially touched by the music playing might still have been deeply touched, even if it didn't appear that way.

Menard also spoke about democratizing access to sound and musical experiences. "What is our role as educators to allow different ways in—different experiences? For some people, there is a real affinity to high performance; for others, it's not their thing."

In other words, we need to ask ourselves why the designers of the experiment chose a classical violin master as a standard for testing the general public's appreciation for "good" music!

André deQuadros, a professor of music education at Boston University, has spent a good portion of his professional life trying to dismantle just this type of colonialist and hierarchical standard for what "good music" is. Why not a Cuban drum ensemble with a singer, shakers, guiro, and claves? Why not a Chinese Erhu player or a teenage African American *a cappella* group? The "good music" could have been anything, and that "anything" might appeal to certain people and not others.

In their book *Empowering Song* (2022), de Quadros and his co-author Emilie Amerin explain that we have come to fetishize sound norms for what is "good" in music that are heavily embedded in whiteness and exclude many cultures, communities, and potential audiences.

This was evident to me when I went to an international music education conference in Pretoria, South Africa, in 1998, and met a man from Ghana—a country known for its deep traditional musical roots in drumming. When we spoke about music in school settings, he told me that much of Africa was behind because they didn't have many good music conservatories or people trained to teach orchestral instruments.

I was in shock! This conceptual separation between traditional/folk music and "advanced" music left me feeling incredibly sad. Our human captivation with fame, "talent," and high achievement is understandable. Most of us want to feel like we have achieved something or be recognized for our efforts and hard work on something that we care about. Music is no exception to this. We imagine how wonderful we would feel if only we had been accepted into that elite choral ensemble, or if only we hadn't messed up that piano recital in front of the whole school. We might understand that the heart of music is in connection, tradition, or personal transformation—a soul-quenching goodness.

But we also wish we were "good!" Even top musicians who have played on the world's most acclaimed stages can't help but notice that there is always someone better than them. Someone more "talented" or who won more competitions. Perhaps it will help to read the following story, which Yo-Yo Ma told me himself: even he was judged early on as being untalented!

Yo-Yo Ma Was Deemed Untalented!

Yo-Yo was given a violin at the age of two and a half. Coming from a family of musicians, his parents told him that he wasn't talented when he didn't take to it or gravitate towards it. Yo-Yo chuckled as he told me that when he was four, his family was in Paris, where he quite accidentally saw a double bass and thought it was the biggest thing in the world.

"I want to play that!" he said. His parents compromised by starting him on the cello instead. "Somehow, the violin didn't work, but the cello did. Suddenly, I was deemed to be 'talented,' so I got some attention. People would say, 'Oh, Yo-Yo, you're good!'"

A snap judgment on a very young child could have erased the name Yo-Yo Ma from being the world-famous household name that it has become. If his parents had merely insisted that he continue with the violin, or if they had simply looked the other way when Yo-Yo said, "I want to play *that*," the word "talent" might not have even come into play.

I hope that by now you are beginning to see how important the following elements are in shaping musical identity:

- Family support

- Having a teacher or friend who can show you another way when you hit a proverbial wall

- Finding an instrument that feels like the right fit

- Having access to teachers, ensembles, or a community of musicians who match your needs

- Circumstance—being in the right place at the right time when a musical opportunity comes your way

- Being resilient in the face of harsh judgment

In other words, the shaping of your musical identity was not necessarily just a question of talent or skill. If you wound up feeling musically incapable or unmusical, your natural musicality may simply not have had the chance to blossom in the right direction!

Born Musical? When Judgment Begins

If music is so vital and prevalent in our lives, from pre-birth through early childhood, when do these shifts in identity tend to happen? How do we begin to define ourselves as *musical* or *unmusical*? Who teaches us what musicality means?

As we saw in Yo-Yo Ma's story, even the youngest children can be judged as being untalented by others. As children enter school, we know that they begin to take ownership of their musicality, singing songs they know and love, inventing songs which they sing both consciously and subconsciously throughout their day, and making decisions about musical preferences (Zur and Johnson-Green, 2008).

Perhaps this is the time when surrounding adults, namely teachers, hear children's songs and begin to make judgments about their musicality. In our Western Eurocentric world, parents are eager to find, name, and hone what makes their children stand out from others. As Yo-Yo stated, we are prone to wanting to be the best. Can my child run faster than others? Are they learning to read before they enter school? Will Russian math classes at age five allow them to excel so that their college applications will stand out down the line?

Competition and ambition are the baseline for how our capitalist world functions. In addition, parents want to feel that their children are special in some way, perhaps because this reflects on their parenting abilities.

I found myself in this very mindset when I first saw my daughter, at age three, dancing spontaneously in my living room to a recording of a Brahms trio. Surely the grace and expression with which she moved her arms and toes meant that she was a natural dancer, and I promptly found a local ballet class where she would have more space to elegantly float across the floor. If I were parenting in a pre-modern or non-Western community, I would likely have witnessed her dancing and celebrated it as an expected stage of development. Yet there I was, in full judgment mode, prepared to label my daughter as "talented," rather than simply enjoy her natural propensity to move expressively to music as most children do.

The problem with this is that *any* kind of obvious judgment, whether positive or negative, can adversely affect a child's natural explorative enjoyment of the activity they are engaged in. Harvard professor of psychology, Ellen Langer, has studied judgment extensively. In her book *On Becoming an Artist* (2006), she shows how the feedback loop works when it comes to creative expression.

Imagine a young child at an art table, drawing freely with crayons, for example. They are drawing what *feels* right, maybe choosing colors based on a mood or a subconscious thought, or simply to explore what it looks like on the paper.

Now let's say that a well-meaning adult comes over and says, "What a nice picture! This is just great!"

Now the child wonders about what made it great, and the next time they pick up some crayons, they might be more focused on creating another "great" piece rather than on their own explorative yearnings.

Similarly, if a young child is singing or humming away and an adult says something like, "What a lovely little song," the child stops to wonder what was lovely. Their singing may move from a subconscious expression to a fishing-for-compliments exploration.

But we adults feel we must encourage creative expression and appreciate the beautiful artistic outpourings that young children produce. Here are some other possible comments or questions that are less judgmental and more encouraging:

- I noticed you used a lot of colors in that picture!

- Tell me all about this piece of art.

- You feel really good when you are dancing, is that right?

- What does it feel like inside when you play the piano like that?

- I love hearing how you figure out what notes to play!

When I took my daughter to those ballet classes, I admittedly had a hard time with this! I wanted to say, "Oh my gosh, you are just *so* good at this!"

My daughter is currently a teenager who still loves dancing. I can proudly say that she does it because it feels good to her. She calls it her therapy. She is aware that she is not dancing at a professional level, but she knows this isn't the point.

While parents, teachers, and other "experts" deliver summative criticisms or encouraging words that strongly influence our musical identities, we also, quite naturally, judge ourselves. This is simply part of figuring out what we like and don't like; what we excel at or struggle with. What energizes us, or what brings our mood down. This is part of the reason why playtime is so vital to young children.

Do I like cutting cardboard?

How does it feel to paint with my fingers versus a brush?

How tall can I build this tower of blocks?

Is it scary or fun to pretend there is a monster chasing me?

These explorations and wonderings align with how Bentley (2013) describes children as "everyday artists," finding magic in the elements around them. As they explore different materials, actions, and provocations, they begin to identify what makes them unique in the world. Parents in our culture often feel the need to foster this exploration-of-the-self by introducing all kinds of activities outside of the home as well: soccer, fencing, chess, drama, dance, music lessons, tennis, etc., so that their children will find something they are passionate about besides watching Barney or playing games on their iPads.

What about "natural talent," or people who seem to be born with musical abilities? Albert Franz's incredible story, shared earlier in Chapter 8, seems to be a clear example of a child prodigy. I will tackle this in a moment, but first, I want to tell you about Maya.

Maya was one student who seemed to be in another league. A young black girl adopted by Indian parents, she first entered my music room as a four-year-old with a shy smile and many curious questions. During one of our first classes, I was introducing a game song called "Little Horses" by Lynn Kleiner (1998, p. 49). It is a simple tune that moves from a slow pace to a fast pace and back again:

Little horses, little horses, come out of the barn. The door is wide open, and the sunlight is warm. La la la la la…

I handed out drums and toy horses and told the students that their horses could gallop and play on the drums, which would be their "barn." On the "La la la" part, they could move away from the drums, but should come back when they hear the words again. I have done this song for years with this age group, to introduce patterns, fast-slow tempo awareness, and playful drum and movement exploration. But I had never had a student like Maya before.

After a few rounds of the game, she invented a third original verse, complete with rhyming lyrics, which added a new element to our game. The other students were eager to incorporate it, and I joyously did.

Maya continued inventing songs frequently in class. Her voice had vibrato and a wide, elegant range that made her sound like a pop star! In kindergarten, I began recording some of these songs, which were about all kinds of things: springtime, sapphire stones, magic kingdoms, or butterflies. In first grade, she created a song about love that was so gorgeous and profound that I wrote it into sheet music for the entire grade to sing at our spring concert:

When the love comes into my heart,
all I wanna do is shout it out.
But sometimes I don't have the time,
and all the love just goes blowing down.
But when I think about it I just let it aaaall
And when I want it I just go-o-o-o.

Everybody has a part in this world
And that part you just take with you–u–u–u.

Maya stopped creating songs in second grade. When I asked her about it, she said she didn't have time. Less playtime, less recess time, more homework, more stress, and self-consciousness set in. But I knew it was still there inside her.

Then, the following year, when Maya was in third grade, my four-year-old students became passionate about rocket ships. I knew I needed to find a song for them about rockets that they would be excited to sing for their spring concert, but nothing I could find seemed to be quite right. I asked Maya if she could invent a song for us about rockets. With that same shy smile, she entered my room during recess, and we got to work.

In just twenty minutes, we had an entire song with rhyming verses that included a slow "floating" section in a minor key, and even a funny joke about seatbelts. The four-year-olds were enchanted, and it was a hit at our spring concert. When I introduced the composer, Maya shyly stood up and smiled to thunderous cheers and applause.

Would I say that Maya is naturally musical? I can't describe her as otherwise! Her adoptive mother says she has no idea where she got it from. "We're not a musical family," she admits.

Sometimes the word "talent" does feel like the right word to use to describe someone's musicality, yet I continue to find this word irksome. Perhaps "fluency" is a better way to describe it! Sometimes people seem to be born with something extra in that arena that can mystify and stun the rest of us. Perhaps we can call those people "very interested" in music, or "exceptional at musical expression." This feels different than the word "talent" to me because "talent" implies that you either have a gift or you don't. If someone is "very interested," we know that they dedicate a lot of time to that activity. If some is "exceptional at musical expression," it means that they are simply good at communicating and expressing the music within, while others might have a more private relationship with their musical selves. Not every musical person needs to perform and exhibit their musicality.

Can we admire, celebrate, and honor a wider spectrum of musical skills? Or do we see the brilliance of a performing star as shadowing our abilities, negating the musicality that does exist inside us? The choice is ours.

Musicality Versus "Talent"

In the last fifty years or so, attempts at defining "talent" and perspectives on whether musicality is innate or learned have taken many turns. While working towards my doctorate in music education at Teachers College, Columbia University, the resounding opinion of my professors and colleagues, based on years of collective research on young children, seemed to be that we should not be using the word "talent."

The argument goes like this: As a given, all of us are born musical. Infants feel the rhythm of their mothers' heartbeats from the time in the womb, and are born responding to the musical speech patterns of their caretakers (I wrote about this in great detail in Chapter 5). This is how they attune to or bond with their caretakers, which is essential to their survival and development. If a child's musicality is hushed or criticized, that child is most likely to turn away from musical opportunities and will develop into an adult who feels unmusical.

While I tend to agree with the above argument (as you have probably gathered in the title of this book alone), I can't help but think of students I have had like Maya, described above who, even at age 4, could take your breath away with a voice that sounded like a pop-star and her ability to create rhyming songs on the spot. Albert Franz could play entire piano pieces at a young age after hearing them played only once! And what about Mozart? Isn't Mozart the very definition of musical "genius" and "talent?"

Franz, who is also a musicologist, offered an intriguing view of talent that I think is quite relevant. While interviewing him for this book, he told me that the discussion about the nature of musical talent has mostly centered around research by Anders Ericsson, considered to be the "expert on experts."

Ericsson's big conclusion in researching any expertise was

that experts are made and not born. He is known for his statement that it takes 10,000 hours of practice to become an expert on anything (Ericsson, Krompe, and Tesch-Roemer, 1993). However, Franz explained that this research turns out to be dead wrong:

> There's a lot of research that disentangles the nature/nurture debate. There *is* such a thing as musical talent, which is a propensity to develop a particular skill more easily and faster than others and to a higher degree. Of all the different types of skills studied (including chess, math, reading, etc.), extremely high musical achievement can be explained up to 86% by genetics. This is really sobering. Yet talent is nothing more than potential. It has to be practiced and honed. If you get the best training, you can maximize that. Musical talent is not just one thing. It can be a real range of skills, and you can be good at one aspect and not others. It also requires a strong psychological ability, timing, and lots of work.

As I spoke more with Albert, I realized several important points. If it is, in fact, true that 86% of musical talent is based on genetics, there are still many different forms that musical talent can take (dancer, listener, DJ, rockstar, singer, saxophonist, etc.). Having the good fortune to find the right musical path, encounter and afford professional guidance, and having time to hone that skill still play a key part. What if you *do* have a music talent and you just haven't yet found your particular pathway into that arena?

But here is the most important point:

> **If some people are indeed born with a higher propensity to be famous and successful musicians, this does not mean that the rest of us need to feel unmusical!**

Let's go ahead and let those professionals play their scales and arpeggios for hours on end within the walls of their practice rooms. Let's celebrate them on stage, remembering that most performing musicians have their own best musical moments *off* stage, in community with others, or simply listening to music that moves them.

We can be musical in those same ways, too, and enjoy our own musicality through group singing, belting it out in the shower, dancing with young children, or sharing a great song with a friend. "Talent" has absolutely nothing to do with musicality, and we should not be using that word to exclude ourselves from the many ways of being musical that bring us connection and joy.

10 — "I'm Not Musical"

Vignette: You Have a Breathy Voice

I was sixteen years old, nervously waiting in the hallway outside my high school's choir room for my turn to audition for "Show Choir." My best friends, Indu and Mariéve, had already made it in, and they had encouraged me to try out as well.

When I was called into the room, I took a deep breath and tried to keep my voice stable as my nerves jolted through me. I was going to sing "Castle on a Cloud," one of my favorite songs from the musical *Les Misérables* (Boublil and Schönberg, 1980). A few days later, having heard each of us eager singers, my choir director led me into her office with a warm smile and told me to sit down.

"Sara, you have a very pretty voice, but it's too breathy for Show Choir. Keep practicing, and you can try again next year."

Too breathy? What did this mean? I didn't feel brave enough to ask her. The following year, I tried again and was accepted without a glitch. Who knows if I improved or whether she heard me differently on that audition day? Perhaps she had simply had a wonderful morning walking her dog. Perhaps someone had just complimented her on her new colorful glasses, putting her in a more receptive mode.

After graduating from high school, I took voice lessons as an undergraduate and in graduate school. I spent time singing in various choirs and even sang a few solo parts in concerts. I studied vocal pedagogy and conducted both children's choirs and adult singing groups. I sing every day to and with my students as a music teacher, yet thirty-three years later, I continue to wonder if my voice sounds "breathy," or somehow weaker than it's meant to sound.

When we receive feedback from an expert, we believe them *even when we don't know what they mean.* Harvard psychologist Ellen Langer, who writes extensively on the processes of creative thinking in the arts, says that we tend to accept an authority's evaluation as if it were objective (2006). Not questioning that evaluation can be a major roadblock toward creative pursuit because it binds us to a single narrative. We assume there is a "right way" of doing something and that other people can do it better.

It wasn't until after I began my first music teaching job in an elementary school just outside New York City, that I experienced something that made me feel like a good enough singer. I was teaching a song to a class of first-graders when a girl named Anna interrupted me to say, "Sara, your voice sounds so beautiful, it is like God's tears."

I will probably go the rest of my life thinking that my voice is "breathy," but I also know that with practice, my voice has improved. And on days when I don't feel very confident in my singing ability, I remind myself of little Anna, and I must believe that her opinion also counts because children are also experts on what they feel and on the music that they enjoy. And that is good enough for me.

Swing Dancing with Jacob

Every once in a while, I hear about someone who others say is truly not musical or who tells me there's "Not a musical bone in my body." The truth is that only about two to four percent of the world's population suffers from amusia, or tone-deafness (O'Connor, 2022). People with amusia may not be able to distinguish between tones, may not be able to reproduce a melody, or recognize when they are singing off-pitch. Yet this disability is centered on singing and may not affect all forms of musical engagement.

People will often judge themselves or others as being "not musical" if they witness off-key singing, forgetting that there may be other ways of being musical. In addition, approximately 5% of people are affected by Musical Anhedonia, an inability to enjoy or feel any kind of pleasurable response from music. People on the autism spectrum are more likely to have this condition. The phenomenon that makes music undesirable could also be what impairs social bonding, something associated with autism spectrum disorders (Bracci, 2020).

My dear friend Jacob was not on the autism spectrum, but he was insistent that he was the least musical person I would ever meet. While getting to know him, he told me that he couldn't sing, couldn't understand anything about music, didn't like music, and could not keep a beat. Not believing that he could possibly be as "tone deaf" as he claimed, I played two notes on the piano for him, asking him to tell me which was higher. He could not hear the difference. Jacob was a child who was told to "just mouth the words" in choir. When he tried to pick up the clarinet, his band teacher told him, "Just pretend to blow into it, but don't make any sound."

When he joined me along with several friends to attend an outdoor concert at Tanglewood[12], he brought his crossword puzzle and a book, happy to disengage. As a child, Jacob very much wanted to play the piano and worked hard, practicing diligently for his weekly lessons. Jacob told me that at some point, the piano teacher called his mother to tell her she was wasting her money—Jacob would never be able to play well. Why she thought playing "well" was the point, or how she even defined a "good" player, is intriguing in itself, but I digress.

Several years into our friendship, he called to ask for my help: he wanted to impress a girl he had met who loved swing dancing. Would I please take him dancing so that he could learn?

We hit the dance floor as the lessons began, and I was stunned. How could Jacob, a Harvard law student, not have the ability to count to four on a steady beat? We laughed about it over some drinks. Jacob, I decided that evening, would have to find other ways besides swing dancing to impress the girl.

Was Jacob completely unmusical? In my mind, I was labeling him as he had suggested: the least musical person I had ever met.

A few years later, Jacob and I both attended a dinner party with some friends, several of whom happened to be Jewish. The discussion turned to our shared Polish-Ukrainian ancestry and

---

[12] A summer music festival in the Berkshires of Massachusetts

the violent *Pogrom* attacks, which caused Jewish families to flee. Recalling images and scenes of such attacks, someone mentioned the musical *Fiddler on the Roof* (Bock and Harnick, 1964). Jacob, to everyone's surprise, started singing. His grandparents and parents had passed down their love for this musical, and he knew all the words to all the songs, even the sections with Yiddish lyrics! His singing was not particularly tuneful, but it was beautiful to hear—full of expression, love, and joy.

It turned out that Jacob *could* sing. Jacob *was* musical when he accessed and shared this part of himself. Being in tune, in my mind, is not a measure of musicality, but a measure of the ear's trained ability to process a sound and reproduce it. Jacob was in tune with his heritage, and with this musical, which felt like home to him.

For me, this story calls forth the lyrics "What's Love Got to Do With it?" made famous by Tina Turner in 1984. I would like to think that for Jacob, he could not access or feel moved by music that wasn't in his heart. He had likely never experienced musical connectedness through dancing or symphonic concerts. He had not been taught to listen for pitches or recreate melodies. His deep family connection to *Fiddler on the Roof* is what made his heart pay attention enough to learn it and reproduce it so beautifully. His voice lilted and his body swayed as he sang—everyone in that room could feel that this was coming from a special place inside him.

"No One Ever Said I Was Good..."

Without clear and positive feedback from someone, it is easy to conclude that there isn't much good about your musical abilities. Most people tend to believe that they aren't talented. Pat, age thirty-five, works in advertising. She told me about the numerous ways that she felt uncomfortable and unsure about her musicality:

> I don't know when I decided I wasn't musical. It feels as long as I can remember. I was generally a shy and self-conscious child. The idea of performing anything was mortifying. My aunt is a singer, and my uncle is a pianist. My uncle was having one of his recitals, and my aunt insisted that my three

female cousins and I sing with her for one of the pieces. Even though very few people aside from family were in attendance, I was mortified at the thought. I remember being so anxious and not wanting to do it at all, but I was an authority follower and did it anyway. I was probably seven or so.

In middle school, I was in a high honors program, and we were forced to take band and chorus. We had to try out for the chorus, and I was mortified to sing in front of my classmates, even though everyone was in the same boat. I was deemed an alto, and I felt that was just the most boring type of singer. It felt like all the pretty, skinny girls were sopranos with pretty high voices. In band, I was forced into playing the saxophone because that's the instrument I had access to. I borrowed a saxophone from a cousin of a friend. My school was an underfunded city school, and my family wasn't about to buy an instrument when I didn't even want to be in the band. I would have rather done percussion, but there was, for some reason, the perception that the percussion kids were the lazy ones who didn't want to play a "real instrument" and didn't get as good grades. I truly did not like the sound of the saxophone at all. I hated soaking the reed in my mouth. I also have suffered from migraines since a young age, so the noise of the band room, plus the blowing into the sax, physically pained me.

I now know as an adult that I get sensory overload quite easily, so the enjoyment was just not there for me. Thinking about overstimulation now is interesting because I love concerts, and I loved going to loud bars/clubs in my 20s. If I'm having a good time and am there by my own will, it doesn't bother me. If it's at all against my will or if I'm uncomfortable or anxious, the overstimulation is awful. But it is interesting how loud music can be noise or it can be joy. Slight differences in the type of music and other factors can turn it from one to the other on a dime.

I was so excited when tenth grade rolled around and I could elect art instead of band, finally. I truly had a passion for art and went on to take AP art and minor in studio art in college. Art class was a much more introverted and quiet form of expression that I connected to much more. I also received a lot of positive feedback for my art, whereas in music, I never received that. I don't remember being told I was bad, but no one ever said I was good at singing or playing my instrument. My band teachers were some of my least favorite teachers. I wonder how it would have been different if I had better teachers. We also played boring music. Overall, I just did not have a good time trying to be "musical."

In my tween teen years, I would say music was a way to connect. I tended to like the music that my friends liked. That music tended to be slightly different than the majority of my peers but very influenced by a subset of peers. So it was a miniature rebellion for someone who was very unrebellious. For example, I was very into the emo/screamo music when I was in grades six through ten or so. I went to a lot of concerts, and it made me feel cool. I wasn't that cool! My music taste has become much less influenced by trying to fit in with peers and is just based on what resonates with me. I have also used music to focus. I had one song by Big Sean that I would listen to on repeat in college when studying. The song was so ingrained in my head that it was just like white noise and helped me almost lose track of time, so I didn't get anxious about how long it was taking me to grasp something or write a paper.

Do you see yourself at all in Pat's story? Feeling put on the spot or mortified at having to sing in front of others, feeling as if your voice isn't pretty enough to make it into the soprano section, not being able to play the instrument that called to you, not receiving any positive feedback in a sea of struggle and noise, and feeling a lack of connection and joy to the music you were being asked to play? Each of these conditions alone could turn someone away from feeling musical.

Pat's story hits upon a few key themes that I have come across again and again when people tell me stories about how they engage or disengage with music or how they turn toward or away from a musical identity:

1. **Negative comparison or judgment**: Pat compared herself to her cousins when asked to sing and felt judged by her family. Later on, she compared her alto voice to the soprano voices of her popular peers. Being put in the spotlight and being made to feel less worthy or good could have been offset with a lot of positive feedback and with some vital messaging about how each person's voice is unique and beautiful in its way. Being shown examples of different types of singers and how people

use their unique voices in differing ways, along with positive feedback and vocal training, could have helped. No one ever told her she was good at music, so she grew to feel that she was not.

2. **Agency:** Being told which instrument to play can automatically remove the motivation to practice or play it. Being allowed to choose an instrument can be especially powerful for teens who are in a crucial stage of identity formation. This also pertains to the type of music that students are asked to play. When the music is unrelatable, chosen by a director, and feels "boring," where is the joy? Could the band director have chosen three pieces to try out and have the students discuss what was interesting or not interesting about each?

3. **Music as Connection:** Music was important to Pat and played a significant role in connecting her with friends and helping create a timeless soundscape for her studies. Connecting with others and within ourselves through music seems to be the number one factor for wanting to engage with any type of music. I wonder if her band director or choir teachers had created better frameworks for peer connection within those ensembles, if it would have made all the difference in the world. When we look at the stories told by musicians who have stuck with it, their motivation to keep going usually comes from how they connected with their friends and peers while playing.

There are so many factors that go into developing a passionate connection to music that motivates a commitment to practice and continued involvement in music. I'm glad that Pat posed this question!

Can't Carry a Tune in a Bucket

The following few stories come from people in my local community who responded to a post that I shared in a Facebook group for exchanging and donating items. I had never met any of them before, and they were eager to answer my question, "Do you identify as an unmusical person?" I agreed to exclude their last names to respect their privacy. You might begin to notice some common threads that also resonate with Pat's story above:

Vanessa, professional nanny and educational mentor:

> One of my first memories of my dad is me singing in the bathroom and him telling me, "You couldn't carry a tune in a bucket, could you?" I didn't know exactly what that meant, but I got the feeling my singing wasn't great. In sixth grade, when I was in a musical production, I sat by the microphones and several kids told me I was way too bad a singer to sit that close. In middle school chorus, I had to audition solo in front of the class, and I was so bad that the director had me stop mid-song. In college Spanish class, I had to sing in front of the whole class, and the teacher let me stop early. I don't really sing in public, but I do sing frequently with children, as I am a nanny. I sing a lot to them—known songs and made-up songs, silly songs, random rhyming songs, etc. Music just makes no sense whatsoever to me. I do really enjoy listening to music, especially when a song really hits me, and I listen to it constantly.

Kim, self-employed independent beauty consultant:

> I love music, and I sing along all the time, but I just sound terrible. Nobody told me I couldn't sing. I figured it out myself. I can't match the pitch of what a person is singing. I do sing "Happy Birthday" at parties, and I like to join in. I go to church every week, but don't join in there because I don't want to stick out. I played the flute in elementary school and had taken lessons, and also piano for a very short time, and that was it. My teachers never told me I was good or bad, either way. I thought I did okay. I wouldn't say it was hard, but I just lost interest in it. I didn't have friends who played.
>
> My sister and I shared a room, and she had a gazillion records, and there was always music on. I loved Luther

Vandros, and when I went through my divorce in 2018, I remember listening to some of his music and realizing it wouldn't work and I'd have to move on on my own. Music often brings you back to someplace in the past. You could almost close your eyes and be back there.

I do love to dance. When I was a freshman in high school, my boyfriend at the time was a senior, and I went to his prom. One of the friends at our table was trying to get me to dance. I didn't want to, but then I started hearing some songs that I liked and got out to the dance floor! When I got older, I went to clubs and danced until my feet hurt so bad I was crawling out of there. When my kids were little, I used to dance with them in the kitchen. But the singing part just wasn't there for me. It's something you're born with, and I wasn't.

Jassi, drug interaction scientist:

I come from a very musical family. My parents and two older sisters sing beautifully. One of my sisters is now a professional Indian classical musician. As a child, I would wake up to her doing her *riyaaz* (music practice), and I loved that. As a family, we did twenty minutes of prayers in the mornings, and most of that was singing hymns in Punjabi—I am a Sikh. That was how each day began. My sisters are five and seven years older, and they both love music. So I grew up with music all around me, as they both always had it playing. One played hard rock and classical Indian music, and the other was more into pop music. I knew I could not sing well early on, as my sister (the musician) would laugh when I would sing. So I just stopped. I still enjoyed the music, but did not sing. My voice did not have a range. I loved dancing, and she told me when I was about five years old that I was a bad dancer—and I did not dance for the next fifty years or so! Weird how comments made to a child can have such a lasting impact. These days, I do listen to more music because of Spotify and tend to listen to Sikh hymns and also random music that my kids like.

Dana, environmental consultant:

I like music a lot, but I feel like I'm not talented. For example, if I'm at a classical concert and someone mentions a mistake they heard, I can't hear it. I went to a recital of a friend of mine. My mom noticed the mistake, but I didn't. I feel like I'm not very observant when it comes to that stuff. I tried to teach myself to play the ukulele during the pandemic with an online tutorial, but I couldn't do it and got very frustrated. My husband plays the piano, and he remembers all this stuff from when he was a kid. I played violin as a kid, grades three through six, but it wasn't cool in middle school, so I stopped. I never felt like I could do it, but I liked it and appreciated it. I was in the school orchestra, and I tried out for All County and made it in. It just felt like I couldn't keep up. Everyone around me seemed to have more skill.

Chris, psychotherapist:

I have a younger brother, and we both started playing guitar in middle school. I had a couple of friends who I'd play with up until early high school. The guitar teacher would come over once a week, and I liked it, but it always also felt hard, like a struggle. Even tuning it was hard. My parents tried to encourage me, but weren't really involved. I didn't stick with it. But my brother, who started at the same time, still plays today. He was very good at it. It came more easily to him to learn it. I could see that he stuck with it and got so much enjoyment from it, and I didn't as much. I enjoy listening to music, but I don't have music on all the time. As a kid, my parents had a nice record collection, and I remember enjoying that. My dad listened to a lot of classical music on the radio, which I still enjoy listening to. They also loved Pete Seeger and Arlo Guthrie, Peter, Paul & Mary—there was a fabric of listening to records in the living room. I know people who go to a lot of shows, but I don't as much. I have this idea that my rhythm isn't really good. Some of these things are natural and inborn, I think.

Andy, medical training facilitator and professional nurse:

Ever since I was a kid, my father told us he was such a bad singer that his school music teacher used to tell him when the principal came around to observe, he should mouth the words. He thought it was funny, and we did too. We felt we got our terrible music genes from our father. We can't sing "Happy Birthday" without clearing out the room, and we laugh about it and embrace it. He grew up in the 1930s, and the music teacher was probably worried about her reputation.

She was probably worried she might lose her job if people were singing badly.

When I was a kid, my parents signed us up for the school band, and my sister and I played the clarinet. It was not something I enjoyed. I just didn't take to it. We didn't really dance or put on plays or anything as a family. We played other types of games. We were out in the yard playing tag and Red Light Green Light and that sort of thing. I loved to read. We had a swimming pool and swam a lot in the summer.

When I was in college, there would be one or two people living in the dorms who would have guitars, and people would get together and sing along with the people playing, and that was a really nice connection and something I loved. Not singing well was just a feeling I had. No one ever told me I couldn't. In a big group, I felt okay, but if asked to sing along, I wouldn't do it. There is a whole language around music that I don't understand.

Marie, IT professional:

My Dad had a regular job but joined every band possible—The National Guard, The American Legion, and more. When he retired to Florida, he even joined a band there. Music was a big deal to him. So growing up, all my brothers and sisters had to play an instrument. The mechanics were fine for me, but I don't think I have that heart piece of it. I could read the music and get the mechanics of singing. But I cannot recognize a song. If the radio is playing a song, I am the worst person! You know the game Name That Tune? Some people can name it within seconds. I can name it ten seconds before it's over! In high school, I played the flute in the band and sang in the chorus but didn't keep it up in college. The artistic piece of it just doesn't exist for me. I have five siblings, and four of them are very musical and have that artsy thing. You'd think that people from the same family would share that, but no. I do love dancing and got into swing music. Not just swing from the 40s and 50s. Even the modern stuff—I love Jazz and Motown. I love so many different kinds of music.

There are many intriguing elements of how an unmusical identity began to form for these people, yet each of them did have some parts of their lives that sounded *quite* musical to me.

The point here is not that they should have all stuck to playing an instrument or that they could have learned how to sing in tune with encouragement (though they could have), but that they are each defining their musicality according to quite a narrow lens, based on a single aspect of musicianship that they each felt they lacked. Or a belief that one is born talented or not, and they were not.

These narrow definitions and beliefs about musicality pervade our society and are often passed down from family to family through subtle hints or cruel jokes—*You couldn't carry a tune in a bucket!*

I agree that you are more likely to feel musical if you come from a family of musicians, not solely because of some genetic predisposition, but because you are more likely to witness the hard work, the doubt, the judgment, and the boredom as just part of the game.

You are also more likely to feel like a musical person if you have a community of musical peers by your side because you are surrounded by people who also understand the struggle and can cheer you on.

Having that surrounding family or peer group also means that you are more likely to be offered options and encounter more access points. "The guitar isn't your thing? Try a trombone!" Or, "You aren't singing in tune? Let's get through puberty and then try some vocal lessons." Or maybe even, "Let's experiment together in the garage and see what sounds good together."

Here's a suggestion: You can't change your childhood or go back and surround yourself with supportive peers and teachers. But it's not too late to call yourself musical. And it's certainly not too late to influence others around you. Notice how you talk about your musicality and what subtle messages you are passing on to your children and others around you. What is it that you are carrying around in that proverbial bucket? What kind of bucket will you pass on to your kids?

Saying "I can't sing" carries the assumption that one can or can't. It erases the possibility of learning or improvement. Instead, try saying, "I wasn't ever taught to sing on pitch," or "I carry a full bucket of beautiful tunes that I'm not comfortable sharing yet." Or maybe singing simply isn't the way that you engage with music, and that's okay. Maybe you are more of a dancer or a passionate listener. Or maybe you will experiment now, just to find out what feels right to you! Start humming or join a song circle where singing in tune doesn't matter, and maybe you will open your mouth, and it will just feel good.

"Hector Sings Too Loud!"

I recently went on a guided hike up Mt. Agamenticus in Maine. The hikers moved in and out of conversation with each other, enjoying nature and getting to know each other.

I started chatting with Fred, a very friendly man in his 70s, who asked me what I do. As soon as I mentioned that I'm a music teacher, Fred said, "I love music, but I'm completely tone deaf!"

I asked him to tell me more—who told him that? How did he come to that conclusion?

"Well, I had this music teacher in elementary school who tested each of us on our ability to match pitches with the piano. When it was my turn, she tried several different pitches and then declared that I was tone deaf. She said, 'Don't you know that you can't distinguish one note from another?'" *Didn't she know that she, as a music teacher, could be teaching him to do just that?*

Hector entered my first-grade music classroom at age six, with wide, dark eyes, excited to participate. It seemed, at first, that he could not sing on pitch. Last year, when he was in kindergarten, I noticed that his singing was off-pitch and very loud, but since those qualities describe many kindergarten students, I did not address it. Rutkowski's (2018) extensive work with young singers shows us that before the age of seven, many kids who may not fully understand how to sing will self-adjust when they experience enough singing around them and have enough practice engaging in singing opportunities. I wanted to wait to see whether he would self-adjust or whether the leap to first grade would make a difference.

It did not. Instead, he sang glaringly louder and didn't seem to notice that his classmates were giving him the side eye. I spoke to the class about "blending" and encouraged them to listen carefully to the voices around them and adjust. Most of the class did this beautifully, which unfortunately made Hector's loud and off-key singing all the more obvious. On the way out of music that day, soft-spoken and socially sensitive Izzy (also not her real name) leaned in and whispered to me, "Hector sings too loud!"

I knew I had to do something to help Hector before he was made to feel terrible. Before anyone else's evaluative words would leave him feeling unmusical, possibly for the rest of his life. I could easily imagine that this would be the moment, in generations past, when a music teacher would sweetly say, "Honey, I think you should just mouth the words..." But music teachers (hopefully) know better than that these days. Those of us who have studied vocal pedagogy have learned many tricks, and I was anxious but eager to try to help Hector.

When someone sings off-key, there could be several factors in play. My first step was to approach his first-grade homeroom teacher to ask about his hearing, since it is the first major link to being able to sing in tune. Was it possible that Hector was singing so loudly because he was hard of hearing? Was he generally very loud in class? The answers were no, and no. Very often, children do sing in tune within a certain range, but simply don't yet have the skills to sing at higher registers (Rutkowski, 2018). Or, there might be a disconnect between what someone hears and what someone produces with their voice.

There is also an interesting phenomenon that often happens with singing where someone might be able to sing in tune by themselves, but if they stand next to someone or try to sing along with a recording, their brain subconsciously sends their voice to a different pitch to be able to hear themselves sing. To work on this in a group setting, a music teacher needs to ask students to cup their hands over their ears while singing so that the singers' brains can focus on their inner hearing, distinguishing their voice from those around them. Interestingly, this did seem to help the class as a whole, but Hector still needed help. It was time to "Woo" him and "Loo" him!

For our next music class, I told the students that we were going to play some games with our voices and then teach them all some tricks that singers use to help make their singing voices get better. I asked students to turn to someone next to them and say, "Hello, my name is..." in a baby voice, a mouse voice, a robot voice, a whisper voice, and an angry voice. Then we yawned and scooped our voices from very low to very high and back again like sirens.

I explained that our voices can make many different sounds and that our vocal cords move differently depending on how we use our voices. For low or commanding voices that live in our chests, our vocal cords clash together rather harshly. But for yawns and high open sounds, our vocal cords gently flap against each other. I asked them to hum with a "yawn position" in their throats and feel their lips vibrating. We *yawned* our voices from high to low a few more times, and then we tried singing some five-note descending scales on the syllable "loo."

Lastly, I asked my first graders to sing their entire concert song using the syllable "loo" instead of words. I walked around the room and excitedly noticed that Hector was singing perfectly in tune!

Here's a tip: the reason why singing "loo" rather than words increases the likelihood of singing in tune has to do with where language is stored in our brains. Though our brains process speech in the same left-hemisphere section that we use for singing, the circuits for each of these functions overlap and do not work in the same way. The moment someone tries to sing a song with words, the speech-processing area of our brain can hijack us into producing more speech-like sounds, which (for English speakers) are produced at a much lower register, with stronger vocal-cord collision. When we eliminate words from the equation, our brains can focus on producing a higher pitch, employing the more gentle, flapping motion of our vocal cords.

Interestingly, certain languages, like French, are naturally higher-pitched and cause the vocal cords to move in that same gentle motion of a singer. As an undergraduate student, I remember my vocal pedagogy professor, Mary Goetze, questioning whether French speakers do, in fact, have a better track record of singing in tune, but I have yet to read a study that confirms this.

What I can confirm is that after just one group voice lesson, Hector became a proficient singer. I didn't ever need to single him out! When I finally asked the class to sing their song with words, Hector had made the switch, blending well and singing in tune. In just one lesson, he went from what some would call "bad" to "good."

Some people do seem more naturally disposed to singing beautifully in tune, but others can easily learn. No one needs to feel like a bad singer who should mouth the words, and I do believe it is a music teacher's job to believe every student can sing, encourage off-key singers to try a few tricks, and work with students to improve their sound. Almost everything is learnable. Rutkowski (2018), who has worked with thousands of young singers, states that everyone can learn to use their singing voice. Can we imagine a scenario where someone who struggles with math or reading is told, "Oh well! I guess you're not born with that talent?"

Professional opera singer and voice teacher at Baylor University, Kimberly Monzón, confirms that singing lessons can help adult singers improve their voices as well, even after just a few lessons. When I spoke with her about writing this book, she told me that she has often had students of varying ages who wanted to sing but couldn't match pitch. Within one to three months of lessons, they could do it. They could expand their range and technique and get much better. This shouldn't feel surprising, but for many people, it is because we continue to think of singing as an innate talent, not a buildable skill.

She said, "Everyone connects with music somehow. Music can *always* be encouraged!"

As we walked up Mt. Agamenticus, I told Fred a little bit about Hector and about the fact that a "tone deaf" label doesn't have to be fixed. Fred stopped suddenly along the sun-speckled path and emitted a big sigh.

"Well, that's quite a relief," he said.

"What Is that Terrible Noise?"

Beth, a chemical engineer, is a unique case. She is a joyous and exuberant singer who even feels a deep calling to be a singer, yet she describes her voice as intolerable to others. Her deep connection to specific songs and to celebrating her connection to others through song is what propels her to keep singing despite being hushed and some rather harsh criticism. She is perhaps the only person I interviewed who understood that being musical is more about a feeling than a specific skill, and that being "in tune" is less important than tuning into yourself:

> It's the reality that I can or will sing, but it might be horrible, and people will have to tolerate it. What I loved as a child was singing a bunch of Jewish songs. I was in the school choir, and I knew I was never going to be the star. I tried out for the musical in grade eight, and I remember practicing for it. It was an inside feeling/understanding that I shouldn't try out for other things. My singing can be joyous, but it's not going to be in a musical. There is a place for joyous singing. My sister and I now love belting out on the phone together. We just embrace the "la la las" and the awfulness. I also can't dance. My daughter loves it when I sing and dance because she sees a big smile on my face.
>
> During the Covid-19 pandemic, they had something online with singing. My sister and I were on the couch, belting it out, having such a good time, and they wanted us to unmute ourselves and we were like, "No!" One of the perks of the pandemic was that we could rock out together and not offend anyone else. The pandemic brought some joyous freedom to singing because we could sing and not have an effect on anyone.
>
> My husband and I were in a kayak, and there were friends from college. I was in the kayak singing up a storm, and my friend Gary said, "What is that horrible high-pitched noise?" He wasn't trying to be mean. He honestly didn't know what the sound was. My friend Ellen said, "Oh, that's Beth singing."
>
> The only sadness around all of this is that if I have a song stuck in my head, I wish I could sing it and have people recognize what it is. What I feel sad about is the lack of being able to communicate through song. But I've never held back in front of my kids, husband, and sister. I love singing "Happy Birthday" for people, but for some friends, a birthday gift for them is me *not* singing. But those are people who love me anyway. My dream isn't to be in a chorus or be the next Taylor Swift.

"In Tune" According to Whom?

When adults tell me that they aren't musical, I ask them to tell me about what makes them feel that way—who told them, or how did they come to that conclusion? For most of these adults, their perceived inability to sing "in tune" is the number one reason for identifying as unmusical. I say *perceived* inability, and I put "in tune" in quotes, because I want to reiterate how very subjective and cultural these definitions are!

As an undergraduate student at the Indiana University School of Music in Bloomington, IN, I was a member of the International Vocal Ensemble. This was a unique and non-traditional choir pioneered by Dr. Mary Goetze, then a professor of music education at the university. Having devoted extensive research and a large portion of her career to vocal pedagogy (teaching kids how to sing), Dr. Goetze loved to tell the story about how she woke up in the middle of the night with a vision: Classical Western music was not the only kind of music that a top music school should engage with. She wanted future music teachers to learn music outside of the Western Classical tradition.

While many choirs at the time sang songs from various cultures, the norm in the mid-1990s was to bring these songs into a classical *Belle Canto* style of singing, designating that style to be superior, and, in effect, erasing the vocal style and traditions of non-Western cultures. Dr. Goetze wanted us to learn music in the way it would traditionally be taught and learn to sing using each culture's unique vocal style. To do this, she invited guest teachers, or what she called "Culture Bearers," to visit our choir and teach us songs. Some of these teachers were already employed at the university, others she drew in from our local community, and still others were colleagues of Dr. Goetze's from other universities.

We learned to sing Shape Note songs from Appalachia, which used scooping notes (not so fixed on one pitch) with a nasal quality. We learned Gospel songs where we dug deep into our souls to feel "in tune" with our spiritual core. We learned Jamaican mountain songs that allowed us to play with different harmonies, deciding in the moment what notes felt right to land on. We learned to sing in a Zimbabwean style, with a much faster vocal vibrato than we were used to. Singing in a Ghanaian style meant that we would need to thicken our tones to sound more "chesty" and rich. We learned one West African song where the expected intonation was ever so slightly wider than what classical musicians call a "Major Fifth" leap, moving from *do* to what felt like a sharp *so* on the music scale.

A Mongolian teacher tried to expose our ears to some of the microtones in a traditional Mongolian scale, which is divided into many tones that most of us classically trained musicians couldn't even hear!

Though I haven't studied it myself, my Indian colleagues and friends tell me that Carnatic Indian music scales (also known as rāgas) each have their own note system. One of the most common ones, called the Mēḷakarta, has 72 seven-note combinations. The lower and upper notes are fixed, but the ones in between can fluctuate and are open to multiple variants.

Most of the music from these vocal traditions cannot even be written properly within the five lines and four spaces of our limited European notation system! To try to do so would be to compromise and, some would say, colonize those songs.

How are most people in *our* culture measuring their singing intonation (ability to be in tune), and why is it such a significant marker of musical ability in our minds? To help me answer these questions, I traveled back to Indiana in the summer of 2024 to meet with Mary Goetze. Little did I know she would soon pass away. We sat in a cafe eating veggie burgers and sweet potato fries in what would be our last conversation. This is what she told me:

> Singing is the first thing that people hear, so it's easy to want to evaluate it or measure it early on. In America, we really had a culture of singing. Everyone sang everywhere—in churches and places of worship, in schools, at festivals, etc. In the 20s and 30s, there was no TV or even much radio, and so the singing was all live. Everyone participated, so if you sang off-key, your voice would really stick out. And at that time, it was believed that tunefulness could not be taught. Teachers would group children, dividing them into "singers" and "non-singers" by calling them "Song Birds" or "Crows." These euphemisms didn't fool the kids. I made it my mission to show that anyone can learn how to sing in tune. I even taught my cat to sing! I would hold out a piece of food and sing to my cat until she meowed at the same pitch, and then I would drop the food. I was very persistent. Eventually, she could do it. I used to tell people, "If I can teach my cat to sing, I can teach anyone!"

The misconception that someone is a singer or not a singer by nature has taken many, many years to correct. Many adults, like Fred, were told by music teachers that they are tone deaf, can't sing, or should just mouth the words. Thankfully, music teachers these days seem to at least be aware that singing is a learnable skill. But this pedagogical knowledge hasn't yet made its way into mainstream culture.

When people measure their ability to sing in tune these days, they are often judging themselves or being judged by how well they can match the pitch of a singer on the radio (or whatever platform they are streaming music from). This is problematic for several reasons. For one, the singer might simply have a higher, lower, or wider range than you. Maybe you can keep the pitch just when they sing in their middle range, but you veer off pitch on the lower or higher notes, for example. Every person has an ideal range for their vocal cords that makes it easier to naturally hit certain notes. My daughter, for example, has a gorgeous low register, but her vocal structure makes it hard for her to hit higher notes without professional training.

Another problem with matching pitch to a radio singer (or to a group of singers around you) is the phenomenon discussed above, where we can't properly hear ourselves against the backdrop of other singers, and subconsciously go off-key to hear our voice.

I know what some of you are thinking: *My voice sounds awful no matter what!* Or, *Even my children tell me I can't sing well!* For you, I have two questions: 1) Have you ever tried to take voice lessons? My guess is that if this were a skill that you felt strongly about developing, you would vastly improve with lessons. 2) How else are you musical? If you are judging your entire musical capacity on your ability to stay in tune, doesn't that seem rather limiting? Do you love dancing? Do you listen euphorically? Do you feel good when your favorite song is playing? How can you recognize your other musical connections as being just as worthy?

Singing is vulnerable. We care about our singing ability because we want to join in when our friends sing "Happy Birthday." We want to feel the powerful, energetic connectedness that comes with singing together in houses of worship, or with friends at a party, or even with our children. We want to be a part of this without feeling embarrassed or judged. But let's please recognize that it is learnable, teachable, and *not* the only measure of being musical.

From That Moment On: Stories from Queens

For several years, I worked as an adjunct faculty member at the Aaron Copland School of Music at Queens College. I taught a required undergraduate course for elementary school majors to learn ways of integrating music into their homeroom classes.

Most students came into my room claiming not to be "musical." As I mentioned in the introduction of this book, my first assignment for them was to write a "Musical Autobiography." This was an assignment I myself had been given by Lori Custodero as a graduate student at Teachers College. Custordero believes strongly in the power of autobiographical writing to uncover new truths about one's musical childhood. Over her years teaching at Teachers College, she has collected, reflected on, and analyzed hundreds upon hundreds of these autobiographical stories (Custodero, 2024). Yet her students were all musicians, earning advanced degrees in music education. My students were undergraduate education majors, most of whom claimed to be "unmusical."

The assignment, which I modified from Custodero's model, was this: In under ten pages, write about significant musical memories and events that shaped your lives from birth to the present.

Despite their claims that they didn't know much about music or didn't come from musical families, almost all of my students described a childhood rich with musical memories—parents or grandparents who sang to them, danced with them, and celebrated life events with music. Here are just a few examples:

> —Since my parents always listened to music, I was used to listening to them as they sang along, so I started to do the same. I specifically remember joining my mother in her singing and dancing around the house, which probably serves as an explanation for my current love of dancing. Clearly, my musical education started at home, under the

influence of my parents.

—There were these family gatherings where our Greek music was played, and we all gathered to dance. The songs being played from within my family's house or at special events will never be separated from my heart. Music brought back memories of happiness, sadness, the birth of someone, or the death of another.

—My family is Spanish, and we love to listen to merengue, bachata, and salsa, so when I was young, I already knew how to dance to many of those songs by observing how everyone else in my family danced to the songs. My all-time favorite has to be a salsa song that I got hooked on, and that was also one of the most played songs when I took salsa lessons. Music is something that has helped me so much in life. Music lyrics, and the emotions that you feel—for example, the guitar when they play it really loud and really low, they show different emotions within that song. I love meaningful songs that I can really relate to. Depending on my emotions, I pick different types of songs that calm me down and make me realize many things, and make me feel grateful for many things in my life. Instead of thinking of my problems as negative, music teaches me to learn from life and do something better than I think I can.

—When I was little, my favorite song for my mom to sing to me was "You Are My Sunshine." Even to this day, when I hear it, I still remember sitting on my mom's lap, having her rock me back and forth, and her singing that song.

—My mother cooked and cleaned all while dancing to French music and Michael Jackson. The Michael Jackson music had me dancing along and re-enacting skits from his records. My imagination ran wild; it was fun and endless.

Wouldn't you agree that these families are indeed musical? Yet these students felt that they came from unmusical families simply because there were no professional or performing musicians in their homes. When they began to understand that "musical" could mean any number of ways of experiencing or engaging in music, they began to smile and relax. When they wrote about being unmusical themselves, they often described a major turning point that caused them to stop playing an instrument or drop out of chorus or just "mouth the words."

Looking at the specifics of when, why, and how these turning points happened for these students, it was clear that many of these negative turning point moments happened in school, with the blow of judgment usually delivered by a music teacher.

These turning points were not unique to my Queens College students. Research shows that most positive or negative musical feedback comes from our school music programs. These experiences have a direct impact on how we perceive our musical skills and abilities as adults (Richards, 1999).

Carlos Abril, who is a widely known scholar in music education, reports that the majority of general music teachers continue to attribute "talent," rather than effort, to students' musical success (2007). The idea that someone is born to sing or play an instrument is keenly felt by students. This is why a negative judgment or rejection at an audition, or even a harsh evaluative statement from an "expert," can cause someone to turn away from the hope of being "musical."

Where and when do these assessments take place? Students often encounter auditions for the first time in middle school. The emotional impact of auditioning for choir, band, or orchestra can directly lead to ongoing anxiety and negative thoughts about ability. While we would like to believe that adolescents are ready to handle the judgment that comes with the audition experience, the reality is that being negatively judged can have a lasting effect. Lamont (2017) surveyed 1800 school children ages five to sixteen to learn more about their beliefs and definitions about musicality, talent, and ability. 48% of these students considered themselves "non-musicians" even though they participated in school music programs.

While younger students called themselves "musical" if they were simply learning an instrument, older students in that study spoke more about talent and training on a specific instrument, usually in connection with their participation in school band, chorus, or orchestra programs. Richards explains that once someone believes that they are not musical, it is incredibly difficult to change their mindset. Conversely, getting the lead in a school musical, getting accepted into a show choir or concert band, can be a highlight for other students who might feel their musical identity strengthened by such an acceptance.

However, whether we receive positive or negative feedback on our artistry, the very act of being musically assessed places judgment strongly on our subconscious shoulders in a way that we cannot let go of (Richards, 2007).

11 — The Classical Musician

Vignette: Congratulations! Now You Are Bad!

I couldn't believe it. Being accepted into the Indiana University Jacobs School of Music was surprising and scary for me because it is considered to be one of the best music schools in America, alongside Juilliard, Eastman, and the Curtis Institute.

According to the judges who had heard my audition, I was not quite good enough to make it in as a performance major, which meant I was not allowed to request one of the top violin teachers. They assigned me to a violin teacher visiting from Russia, whose name I will respectfully omit. I was told that I could re-audition the following year if I wanted to. For now, I would be in the Bachelor of Science in Music program.

It is still a sore point for me that only performance majors can select top teachers. Are we, music education majors or "science of music" majors, truly less important than performers? Aren't we the ones who help create the very audiences needed to support the careers of performers?

My new Russian violin teacher was a small man with thick black glasses and thin black hair, slightly balding at the top. Week after week, he would deliver harsh commentary on my playing: "You're not good enough to play anything more than a scale yet." "You are holding your bow wrong. We will need to start from the beginning." "You're not ready for *vibrato* yet. Just play open strings for now."

I was made to play only scales and finger exercises because he felt I was not ready for anything else. Finally, one day, after playing my scales for him, he gave me a big smile. I had never seen him smile before, and I giddily awaited some type of compliment or maybe even permission to play a piece of music. Instead, he said, "My congratulations. Much improved. Before, you were horrible. Now you are bad."

I have given what we call "classical music" its own chapter in this book because entering into and succeeding in that world is different from most other types of music around the world. Not to say that other traditions and genres don't also have extremely high levels of skill, requiring many hours of practice and physical dexterity, but there is a certain grit and gruel of competitiveness that comes with being trained in this Western-European art form that sets it apart. And let's face it: the music produced by classical musicians continues to be regarded as the highest form of music by much of the world. Why else would our school music programs continue to be structured around chorus, band, and orchestra? The top music conservatories in the world are those that teach Western music theory, ear-training, opera, and orchestral instruments.

I remember accompanying my friend Jennifer to her bassoon audition at the Juilliard School in New York City. Considered to be the most famous and prestigious music school in the world, thousands of hopefuls travel from all over to play for one of the master teachers, hoping to be accepted into their studio.

As a budding violinist myself, I remember looking over the violin pieces required to audition and realizing that I was not even skilled enough to put together the audition repertoire, let alone to surpass the hundreds of other violinists who would fly in from Tokyo, Hong Kong, Russia, France, and beyond to have a chance to get in.

As I waited with Jennifer to be called up, we traded stories that we had heard about music competitions at Juilliard—someone slipping razor blades between the piano keys of their rival, for example. Whether these legends were true or not, the tense atmosphere of the Juilliard lobby certainly was. I witnessed a violinist's finger physically shaking as she pushed the elevator button after being called for her turn to go up.

I am keenly aware of the irony, or perhaps hypocrisy, of placing classical music in its own chapter within a book

that seeks to even the playing field on what it means to be a musical person.

Yet I felt that classical music must be discussed separately, precisely because it is not what I consider to be normal everyday music that everyone can connect with. While anyone can enjoy it, to hone the skills of performing classical music, one must be privileged enough to have access to these pricey instruments, have access to teachers who can teach the language and theory of note-reading, and be willing to be put through a physical and emotional rigor of the highest degree.

I have placed classical music here in its own section because I want to stress the point that this music and its gatekeepers *want to maintain a superior separateness.* They want to impress us and have us respect the immense amount of work that goes into learning these instruments at a high level. The very system of auditions is designed to weed out and keep out anyone who can't keep up. Audiences who pay money to hear the finest orchestras and operas expect perfection—expect to be transported to the apex of listening pleasure. Silent, passive listening to those who are placed before us on a grand stage is an expected part of this cultural experience.

Unlike the folk musician, who might come out on stage and talk to us about their lives or connect with us about the state of the world, a classical musician enters from backstage and barely glances at the audience. We are meant to see the classical musician as otherworldly, as they share some godly or angelic gift of sound with us. I write this with all the love in my heart for what classical music is and with a very deep and personal understanding of what classical musicians go through to get anywhere.

What I would like you to realize, as you read the following stories, is this: just because you couldn't make your way around a clarinet or didn't get into the choir in high school, does not mean you are not musical! And this very particular way of being musical is dependent on so very many variables being in place at the right time.

Yo-Yo Ma: Having the Constitution to Succeed Professionally

Yo-Yo Ma, human being and cellist:

I think everyone experiences many turning points in their lives. We make micro-decisions every single day, and each micro-decision is a fork in the road. Maybe you like light, and you go towards that. Or you like loud noises, and that's what you go for. You make choices based on a combination of instinct, thought, and feeling. And you never know which tiny choices will have the biggest impact, like a rivulet that turns into a stream or a brook or a great riverway.

I think it was Howard Gardner in his discussion of musical intelligence who said that a loving first teacher is incredibly important. A loving teacher inspires love of their subject. While examining what makes "talented" kids excel later on, Howard Gardner found that having a parent who is also dedicated to the subject, not necessarily as a professional, is very impactful, because that parent will sacrifice to find a really fabulous teacher to teach their child. This is what happened with me.

But what is important to remember is that a love or talent for music does not necessarily lead to a successful career in music. A lot of musician parents say, "Don't go into music—it's too hard!" And it's true. Many musicians are incredibly talented but choose not to become professionals because they realize that the job isn't just playing music. As with any profession, it gets messy, political, and hierarchical. Some very talented people can't or don't want to navigate the performance world and prefer to engage with music for their personal gratification rather than as a career.

When it comes to identity, if you're musical and decide to play the flute, then your identity becomes "I'm a flutist." The famous cellist Pablo Casals thought of himself as a human being first, a musician second, and a cellist third. I have held onto this like a lifesaver. People say, "He's a cellist." But that is just part of me. Maybe not even most of me. A lot of me is invested in that thing, and it becomes my known identity. But I think a lot more about people and music than about just the cello. For me, this micro-decision not to define myself as "a cellist" was an important turning point.

Where does judgment fit in? I think the idea of success is

a fallacy. It's so different for everyone. How soon does someone start talking? What does that mean? It's the same thing with music. The ways that we engage with and interpret music develop differently for different people. Being adept at playing an instrument is just one way that people can express their musicality.

Yo-Yo understands what many of us need to hear: having a career as a professional musician does not mean that you are a better musician than those who pursue other careers. It just means that you had the right set of circumstances and support networks, and that you have chosen to navigate this rather competitive arena. We heard a similar sentiment earlier from *American Idol* singer Melissa Karger: To "make it," you need good marketing, perseverance, and good connections.

Measuring musicality solely according to who "makes it" is quite limiting. As we have seen in Part Two, musicality develops in all of us from infancy in myriad ways. How we gravitate towards or away from specific types of music, as well as the people who nurture or squelch that inner musicality, are what shape our musical identity. The choices we make—what we do with that identity, or how we engage with our musical preferences are limitless if we remain open to different possibilities.

"It's Just What We Do:"

Kate Kayaian, cellist:

My mom used to sing "You Are My Sunshine" and rock me to sleep in a chair. We had family friends whose kids played instruments (violin, piano, and cello). I listened to them play a lot, and when I was about four and a half, my mom encouraged me to pick an instrument. I had a crush on a boy who played the cello, so I chose the cello too!

In middle school, every Wednesday night, we would have weekly cello workshops with piano. I was often nervous but also inspired. These performances were just for us cello students. One day, the pianist said to my mom, "Kate has never played an unmusical note in her life." I didn't know exactly what this meant, but I knew that it felt good. It made me feel musically special somehow. I knew I would show up and play, and that I was doing okay at it. Later on, in high school, I spent every Saturday from 8 AM to 8 PM all day at the music conservatory. I got to be with my friends there all day. We took classes together, had breaks together, and everything. It would sometimes get a bit competitive, but it was really fun. There were several times when I wanted to quit, but I would have missed my friends too much!

The community and social aspect of playing was very strong. I remember one incident where someone in my cello group won the Fishoff competition. It was a really big deal. The runners up were my friends who were pianists, and they made a big stink about it: "What were the judges thinking?! Is this a joke?" And those students' parents did nothing to apologize. It haunts me to this day because it was handled so poorly and showed me the dark side of classical music. Musicians work so closely together and grow up in each other's worlds, so we need to be more accepting and kind to each other.

It wasn't until much later, in my adult years, that I realized how ego-based music performing could be. Chasing the carrot. Nickel and dime. Selling tickets, dealing with promoting events, social media, etc. But I loved interacting with audiences and actually playing the music. During the Covid pandemic, I took a real sabbatical and realized I wanted to be home more, to garden, or coach others rather than perform. Now I rarely perform unless it's something truly exciting for me. For me, there really was no "turning point" when it came to becoming a musician. It was just a natural progression of growing up around incredible musicians. It was one natural step to the next. It would have been against the grain not to become a performing musician! It was casual. *This is what we do.*

What is a "musical" person? Anyone who can connect with and express themselves through music. Someone can feel a deep connection to music without being a professional musician. They can still be musical.

Kate mentions how "ego-based" performing can be. Perhaps this is what Yo-Yo Ma meant by saying not everyone has the constitution to succeed professionally. Kate did have the constitution, but eventually chose to engage with music in a more relaxed way.

High Heels, Short Dress, and a "Toxic" Mistake

Katherine Needleman is the principal oboist for the Baltimore Symphony Orchestra. She writes regular blog-style essays that give her followers an honest and sometimes humorous window into the life of a performing musician. I was particularly enthralled by this entry, which she posted on Facebook on August 7, 2024, about a small chamber music concert she and her colleagues arranged. Mistakes, mishaps, clothing choices, and lack of time to practice made for several heart-pounding, stressful moments on stage. I am including her full blog entry here to demonstrate how even a top-notch professional musician with a successful career can make devastating mistakes, feel horribly embarrassed, and negatively judge themselves. Yet Katherine understands that this comes with the territory and is not a sign of her musical ability. Her post also illuminates just how much thought and preparation might go into a single public performance:

> For this oboe quartet program, I practiced and prepared as well as I knew how and had a good reed and some spares. I had a really nice rehearsal with my group two days before the show. We were supposed to have another rehearsal the day before, but that got canceled because someone got really sick. That threw things into quite a disarray, because as a quartet program and especially with the repertoire we had chosen, one cannot simply substitute a sight-reading player at the last moment. It would have never worked, especially because we have a history of working together, some of the music is very difficult, and we've played many of these pieces together before. So, we worried about a plan B, and changing repertoire, and I arranged another quartet at the last minute to try to fill some of the voids in the program if we'd had to use a substitute. The two days before the concert, when our long rehearsals were scheduled, I also performed and traveled for eight hours each day for my regular work services. I was thinking a lot of thoughts about mental endurance, physical endurance, and self-preservation.
>
> In the end, we canceled the day-before rehearsal because our player was running a 102° fever. Instead, we decided to get to the performance venue early to do a touch-

up/triage/best-we-can rehearsal in place of the long rehearsal the day before. The sick player drove separately. The three well people had a super fun drive. But I was driving the three well people, and there was a detour that the GPS hadn't accounted for. We arrived forty-five minutes later than planned, and the rehearsal had to be really short. You could tell everyone was trying to be calm, but maybe not actually feeling so calm.

We hit all the hardest parts and beginnings of the difficult repertoire. Our last piece was "Toxic" by Britney Spears. It was one I screwed up in our initial run in the rehearsal, misreading a repeat in the score. The day before the show, during the time we were supposed to be rehearsing but weren't, I decided it would be better to play from the part, so I put that in my iPad and carefully marked the repeat (incorrectly). We had one minute before the audience was allowed into the hall. One of my colleagues said, "Should we rehearse 'Toxic'?" And I said, "No, that's the easiest one. Let's just have fun, and it will be fine." You know where this is going. We went onstage for the concert. The audience was packed and enthusiastic, and when we spoke to them, they laughed. It was really nice and warm and lovely. It was also warm onstage—quite warm.

I made the choice to wear a dress with slits, which I found quite uncomfortable sitting down in because I was showing the audience more leg than I wanted. I always tell students to practice in their concert attire at least once, but I did not follow my own rule. I also wore an absolutely ridiculous pair of heels because I figured I'd be sitting for most of the show and it wouldn't matter. But by the time I sat down in the quite low chair in big-ass heels (and I am NOT tall), I looked like Michael Phelps sitting in a nursery school chair. And two of my colleagues had doubled up their chairs between the quick triage rehearsal and the concert. So I was thinking about how short, and yet how tall, and ridiculous I looked. I was grateful for the pair of teenage, tight running shorts my daughter had lent me, which were under my dress. The audience was sitting quite below me, especially the front rows, and you know, I was worried about giving them more of a show than they had bargained for. I was thinking again how grateful I was for those tiny teenage black running shorts, and also I was thinking about Yuja Wang [pianist]. Does she wear anything under her outfits? I was thinking about how I will never wear this dress while sitting again. I was also thinking about how

I will never wear heels that high ever again. I was thinking about how I promised myself in 2013 that I'd never wear a strapless dress again (something I have stuck to) and how I'd never wear heels on stage again (something I haven't.) "Self, will you ever learn?" I asked several times. This is all while I was playing the Mozart oboe quartet in front of countless members of the public.

You always want to feel good about your start of a performance, but it was quite hot and dry onstage for the Mozart, our first piece—no excuse, of course. I was riding a bit high in pitch and wasn't enjoying trying to fix that, making a big fish face. The acoustic was also very dry, more so than the rehearsal, and I wasn't enjoying that. Especially with my distraction about the discomfort of my attire, it was not my best performance. It was also not my worst. Life goes on. Then we played this Piazzolla duo we arranged for oboe and cello. I was really suffering with my pitch at this point. The awesome thing about high temperatures is that wind instruments go high and string instruments go low. That was kind of my sole focus at this moment, that and trying not to fall over standing in my stupid heels. I was thinking about drugs. I should've maybe taken propranolol[13], but haven't for months, and was enjoying riding that wave. I know it's a drug I'll probably never go fully without.

The next piece was my favorite—one I didn't play, a duo by Jessica Meyer for violin and viola. I ran backstage and chilled out (literally) in the air conditioning. My pitch was dramatically improved for the rest of the show. Then we played my piece. I spoke before, and my reed was totally dried out, and one of my low attacks at the beginning was suboptimal, but that kind of freed me up to not worry about anything. Perhaps it was a blessing in disguise. I was also happy to have lowered the temperature of my oboe by about 15 degrees, and not to be struggling with pitch, finally. I was able to focus appropriately for the first time. The audience seemed to like it, or at least pretended to. My high F# at the end was better than I've ever played it, but I lost a bit of the end of my low A# at the end. It's always one or the other, it seems, on the oboe. What a petulant child that thing is. I hope to gain full control of it before I die.

Then we played this Samuel Coleridge-Taylor piece I

---

[13] A beta-blocker drug that some people use to help with performance anxiety.

arranged for oboe quartet for the occasion. It's something I suggested for the concert, thinking it would take me an hour to arrange, but it took me more like 50 hours. It was one of those things that did not go easily from piano to strings. Sometimes these things go very quickly and easily, and sometimes, it's a wreck. My string-player colleagues were super helpful in educating me about what would not work, and I am really grateful to them. The best parts of my arrangement ended up being the parts that I basically had to re-compose for a general effect rather than make a direct transcription. For all my stupidity, I at least know you have to trust good instrumentalists when they tell you something. Despite lots of haranguing over the end, which is soft and basically recomposed, the audience loved it. They made a collective little sigh—very sweet—four bars before the end, where the oboe finishes a long diminuendo on low C (my best instrumental achievement of the evening) at the same time the cello arpeggiates up to a ridiculously high C (the oboe's "normal" high C) and after the violin reaches up to her highest C (the one which should never be played on an oboe but is sometimes.) The audience even started clapping after the cello made his soft high C, obscuring the final two chords. It was a lovely moment. Bringing Coleridge-Taylor's piece, which is basically never played in its original form nor commercially recorded so far as I can tell, to the public and having them get off on it made all the labor of the arrangement worth it, that one moment where they all sighed at the end.

The arrangement isn't one I'm quite ready to make available to the public yet. It could benefit from a few more tweaks and better engraving, but I was really grateful for all the rests I put in for the oboist. It will make a nice addition to any heavy quartet recital once I get it all ready, especially because it is not hugely taxing for the oboist but is a charming affair. I also get a D-plus for one of the low attacks at the beginning of this one after introducing the piece to the audience and letting my reed dry out again. Maybe next time I can talk with the reed in my mouth, but that will be pretty inelegant.

Now came the most memorable part of the evening: Britney Spears' "Toxic" for oboe quartet. We played an arrangement we bought from the internet. We added a bunch of percussive elements in the cello and some slides for everybody, and thought it would be fine. It was certainly the easiest piece by a long shot on the program—or so I thought after our rehearsal. When we only had one minute before the doors opened to the public, I was the one who said it would be fine. But I was the one who made 47 seconds feel like 15 minutes in the concert. I had incorrectly marked the repeat in my part. "Self, always play from the part you will use for the concert at least once," I have told myself many times. But I ignored my own advice this evening. We started. I was thinking, wow, this is the weakest thing we've done all night. I felt awkward and not cool enough. I should be feeling like I'm a sexy young woman pushing a beverage cart through an airplane, but instead I feel like an old person showing too much leg and maybe tiny running shorts to the audience, unable to find a suitable position in her chair, and obsessing over touching my skirt or not. I was praying, as I often do, to the God of I-Hope-This-Isn't-As-Bad-As-It-Feels-To-Me,-To-My-Shitty-Internal-Dialogue.

One minute and fifty-one seconds into the performance of the piece, which had up to that moment been a professional affair (and also the whole performance so far had been, too), I took a repeat back to the beginning, while the rest of my (professional and correct) colleagues only went back twenty-four bars. I was playing the leading voice, and one bar into it, I realized something was majorly off. Of course, like a total asshole, I assumed it wasn't me. One bar later, which felt, of course, like five minutes later, I realized it was indeed me. I was flipping my pages back and forth with my crazy high heel on my foot pedal, trying to figure out WTF I had done. I needed the score but didn't have it. By this point, other people were jumping around. They all thought some people had taken the repeat and some hadn't (in reality, we all took the repeat, but I went to the wrong place.) Okay, I'll just keep playing the main tune and making shit up and looking like I know what I'm doing. Then I'll try to figure out where my colleagues are and then join them. But I had forced them all off the rails to different places. I also didn't realize what specifically my error was until backstage after the concert, because I had marked it wrong. It was one of those slow-motion train wreck things. We played a bunch of random eighth notes with accents. I played some trills to the dominant. The cello had an unplanned solo bar. I played the main instrumental tune like sixty-nine times, gesturing like a maniac, but we couldn't get back on because no one knew where to go.

The last time I was a part of something like that as a professional was the Beethoven Coriolan Overture about 15 years ago, where the conductor mis-cued after a G.P. [Grand Pause] and half the orchestra went with him and half didn't, and everyone stepped on each other's toes for half a page trying to get back on. I still cringe thinking of it. But this time, I caused it. One colleague, without an instrument in their mouth, whispered quietly to another, "Where are we?" But of course, there was no answer but an imperceptible shrug. Somehow, praise Dog, we did a bunch of gesturing and played the tune over a couple times, and all ended on a low C, well, all of us except for one who was on a D. (For you non-musicians, a major second doesn't typically generate a feeling of great finality.) It went from I-Hope-This-Isn't-As-Bad-As-It-Feels-To-Me,-To-My-Shitty-Internal-Dialogue to Oh-God-Joe-Biden-Is-On-The-Debate-Stage in two seconds. It was an elementary school mistake with embarrassing implications. I apologized to my colleagues immediately backstage. I took 100% responsibility. They were all worked up and apologizing. I told them not to because I had screwed it all up, AND I had said, "Oh no, we don't need to rehearse this in one minute because it's easy." I had prioritized being in the right mental and endurance space over re-touching the "Toxic" to devastating effect.

On the drive home, we listened to an iPhone recording of the train wreck. We clocked how many seconds (forty-seven) it actually lasted. We cringed and laughed listening to it on the car speaker. It's all that we could do. I apologized, again, for being the Toxic Agent. They were more mortified than I was, and I felt bad about that, especially because I was the manufacturer of the disaster. My main teacher used to say that once you embarrass yourself enough on stage, you don't get nervous about it anymore. I think perhaps I am coming close to this wonderful point in my life. I was pleased that no one died, and I didn't fall over at any point. I was more upset about my pitch earlier and the detachment from the Mozart in the program. I was more upset that I hadn't followed my own advice. I was very pleased that I was able to smile and walk offstage afterwards without falling.

The audience was super lovely after. There was a nice reception. People asked about my oboe reeds and why I touch them and mess around with them when I play. I got the comment I receive very often at least three times last night, that I look much taller onstage than in real life. I said, yeah, it's because I was wearing some ridiculous shoes. One audience member told me she appreciated that I wore them. I'm sorry, but I won't be wearing them again.

How did you feel reading Katherine's account of her concert? I, for one, felt the incredible anxiety, exhaustion, embarrassment, and detail-driven mindset that musicians find themselves facing during so many performances. Having spent a lot of time with classical musicians before, during, and after performances, I can tell you that even when you, as an audience member, think you're listening to a seemingly flawless and relaxed performance on stage, these musicians often come off stage ruminating on all the mess-ups and flaws. In the classical world, perfectionism runs rampant, the stakes feel high, and musicians often practice their instruments for hours each day just to prepare for one performance.

Deb Wilfond, who you may recall, wasn't allowed to play the cello because it wouldn't fit on the public bus, talks about what this felt like for her, attending a prestigious high school music program in the UK:

> At age fourteen, I went to the Royal College of Music every Saturday. I had to practice about four hours a day. It was amazing to learn an art form and study recordings and theory, but there was so much criticism. I loved playing but hated performing because I had developed such stage fright. My teacher said, "If you don't perform, what's the point?" She was very old-school and imposing. There was a mentality that you should play until your fingers bled. It was abusive and unhealthy. It was really sad because I did love music and had a passion for it.

This "play until your fingers bled" perfectionist mentality was and is not all that unusual in the classical music world. I faced this myself as a young aspiring violinist at Indiana University. I thought that playing through pain was normal. The red marks under my chin and the permanent creases on my left fingers from pressing down on the strings seemed par for the course. It was only when the pain overtook both of my hands, and I could no longer play, that I began to realize where I should have recognized my limits.

The seriousness of learning to play an orchestral instrument (versus folk/rock instruments) was keenly felt by Joe Deninzon, who is the violinist/rhythm guitarist with the touring rock band Kansas. He's also the lead singer and electric violinist of Stratospheerius, and a professor of performance and composition at New Jersey City University's Multi-Style Strings program. Joe was born in Russia in a family deeply immersed in classical music, but quickly discovered a love for rock. He has spent his life and career straddling these two musical worlds. When I asked him to tell me about the differences between the classical music world and the rock or jazz worlds, this is what he said:

When I moved to New York, I attended the Manhattan School of Music and went into their gig office looking for any work I could get. I was hired to play Italian Tarantella music with a singer/percussionist named Alessandra Belloni. I had a background in jazz & improvisation, but was unfamiliar with Italian folk music. Alessandra loved to host jam sessions after her performances. Anyone was welcome to hit a drum or make a noise, whether they were professional musicians or not. My wife, Yulia, is a violinist with the New York Philharmonic. One time, we hosted a backyard BBQ with her colleagues and invited Alessandra to join us. Alessandra wanted to start a jam session with these accomplished musicians and started passing out tambourines, but everyone just froze like deer in headlights. I was observing this phenomenon with fascination and thought, "These guys are afraid to make a sound in public without it being perfect. They have a visceral fear of being judged or making mistakes." This is the result of years of being conditioned to approach music that way.

I've inhabited both the jazz, classical, and rock worlds. People in each world are wired very differently. As a person who teaches improvisation, when I'm working with classically trained musicians, we try to get back to thinking like a child. When you're a baby, you cry or sing without caring whether you sound good. You have to make mistakes and sound awful to become a better improviser. It's a journey of self-acceptance and overcoming personal fear and insecurity. Improvisation celebrates imperfections and sees them as opportunities, whereas classical training strives for perfection at all times, which is not natural. Rock is basically folk music. Hip hop is folk music. The people who invented it were not trained musicians. They were playing from the heart and making a cathartic noise to express themselves. It's not even with the intent of becoming a professional artist or making money. There is a certain philosophy in classical music that you're not mature enough to have an opinion until you're an adult. Classical musicians can feel like their whole musical life depends on an expert's (teacher's) opinion.

My audition at Indiana University when I was eighteen was a very intimidating experience. I was playing in front of a jury of legendary teachers and performers who all came from a very traditional classical background. I had long hair, and they knew I was going to major in jazz. They automatically assumed I was not a serious musician, and I was berated at the audition. I'd heard that some of those teachers wouldn't even accept you in their studios if they found out you played other genres outside of classical music. In what other fields would you be shunned for wanting to diversify and make yourself more employable?

In this day and age, when it's so hard to make a living as a strictly classical musician, I just think it's a backward way of thinking. It's changed a lot in the past twenty years, but that tunnel-vision mentality still exists in many conservatories. For me, once I saw the spectrum of what was possible, I never went back. When you improvise, you develop a different part of your brain. Research has proven that it translates into other things you do, both in music and in life. It develops creativity and the ability to think on your feet and find new ways to solve problems. While it builds discipline, technique, and musicality, my personal experiences have led me to conclude that classical training should only be *part* of the equation. I grew up in a household of classical musicians and married one. I have a deep love for classical music. It's more the narrow-minded mentality of some of its musicians and teachers that turns me off.

Top-Level Technique

Here, again, is Carol McGonnell, professional clarinet player, talking about the unhealthy work mentality of many classical musicians. Like Joe, Carol compares this type of perfectionistic training to the more casual and community-based playing that exists in the folk music world. Carol grew up and currently resides in Ireland, and I could sense her joy when she spoke of the freedom and lack of judgment involved in playing music together in an Irish pub:

> The majority of musicians at the top of their game are very consumed with intonation, tone, playing correctly, historically correctly, and making sure they have the accepted interpretation. All of this is BS. Even at the top level, you find that there. Of course, that's impressive to hear technique and people want to hear them play, but…I sometimes play with the top-level people and sometimes with people all the way down the line. Just because people have massive shiny careers doesn't mean they're tapped in or connected to themselves or to what I would see as an essential part of making music and communicating and being part of this thing that's much bigger than technique. Sometimes playing with people far down on the talent scale can be just as satisfying as playing with top-notch, shiny people if they're communicative and attentive.
>
> The reality of classical music is that there has to be a very high level of technique. That's just how it has to be. But to acquire that level of technique so often beats musicality out of people. Or the kinds of people who can sit for hours and hours—those individuals with that attention span, and maybe those kinds of people aren't as creative and are worker bees, and maybe not as creative. It breaks my heart.
>
> In Irish pubs or fiddlers like Martin Hayes—he's one of the most spectacular musicians on the planet. He has a miraculous technique, but you feel that his technique was built for the purpose of being able to express [Irish fiddle music]. Technique was never built just for technique as an end goal. You just join in and sit in, and people start to build their own abilities just by playing together and through exposure. The end goal is to be together and communicate together, and play together. Not to be the greatest.

Music Conservatories Versus Rock-N-Roll

I asked Joe Deninzon, the violinist and rock rhythm guitarist, to tell me more about his background in Russian-style classical violin training. Part of me wanted to better understand my own traumatic experience taking lessons with my Russian violin teacher, who said, "My congratulations, now you are bad." As with ballet, some of the greatest, most famous classical musicians of all time were Russian-born and trained, and I wanted to learn more about how that style of teaching worked:

I was born in St. Petersburg in the Soviet Union. I grew up in a classical house, taught by my father, who was a very traditional classical musician. He's my best friend, and he supports everything I do, but I rebelled against him a lot. He could be very tough and rigid when he was teaching. There's a really deep tradition of classical music in Russia. Very conservative and very strict. My father went to a music school for gifted kids in St. Petersburg. It's very hard to get accepted, and you have to re-audition each year to stay in. So you start when you're age six and you're basically trained to become a professional musician. In Russia, there's a legacy of classical music tracing back many generations. So many legendary composers: Tchaikovsky and Mussorgsky. Shostokovitch and Prokofiev! And virtuosos that came from Russia, like Heifitz and Oistrach. Also, a great tradition of Pedagogues.

From a cultural standpoint, Western popular music was banned in the Soviet Union. Jazz was forbidden for a long time. Rock was forbidden as late as the 90s! My wife Yulia had bootlegged tapes of Bon Jovi, Scorpions, and Deep Purple. Buying rock records and tapes on the black market was an act of rebellion. That music was not sold in stores. Maybe in the States there were conservative people who hated rock music, but that was just a circle of people. In Russia, it was the government and all the institutions. That's not to say people didn't crave it. My grandfather was a huge fan of Duke Ellington. Swing jazz was popular in the 40s, but it was listened to in secret. Duke Ellington would tour the Soviet Union in the 60s or 70s. So there were pockets of it, but still, rock and metal music was not sold in stores up through the 80s. It was forbidden. So it was decades and decades of that classical tradition.

We moved to Cleveland when I was four years old, and the initial thing that drew me away from classical music was entering kindergarten in the public school system. I didn't speak English very well. Classical music was not considered "cool." The violin was not considered cool. I was an outcast. I had a huge desire to fit in and be accepted by the other kids. It was the early 80s. I would turn on the TV and watch MTV and listen to the radio and say, "What is this amazing music?!" Rock and pop music had so much power and connected with a wider group of people in such a visceral way. And I was a bit of a ham who loved to perform in front of an audience. This was not what my parents were listening to. I embarked on two parallel roads. I studied classical repertoire since age five, going to CIM (the Cleveland Institute of Music), but I loved pop and rock music, and later discovered jazz. I was always writing songs and singing.

The first instrument I learned to improvise on was the electric bass. Then I learned guitar and found a local mentor who taught me how to play jazz. I just never saw those two worlds together. I was leading two lives. One day, I would play in the Cleveland Youth Orchestra. The next day, I was writing songs and playing guitar and bass in bar bands. That world excited me. That Pandora's box was opened to me when I was very young. But I also needed to work on my violin technique, and I needed the discipline of practice. My violin teachers would question why I did that other stuff and tell me, "That's not real music—why don't you just focus and play serious music?" I would ignore them. I was kind of always looking from the outside at the whole ridiculous classical institution, amused and refusing to play the game.

In Cleveland, we had a local celebrity named Michael Stanley. His band broke local arena attendance records, but was not well known outside of Ohio. He was also a big local TV and radio personality. His twin daughters attended my high school, and he saw me play violin at a talent show when I was sixteen. He invited me to play in his band. Up until that point, I had never played any form of music outside of classical on the violin. I was playing rock on my guitar and knew how to improvise, but I had never even considered translating that language to the violin. When I played with the Michael Stanley Band, playing rock-n-roll on the violin came naturally to me because it was just a matter of translating the language of the notes from the bass and guitar to the violin. It was a watershed moment for me. Shortly after that, I discovered Jean-Luc Ponty, Jerry Goodman, Stéphane Grappelli, and all these great jazz and rock violin players. I realized. Wow! This is something I can do pretty well that not a lot of people know how to do. This might be a path I should pursue. My dad was quietly guiding me. I wanted to go to the Berklee College of Music, but he wanted me to go to Indiana University because it was more traditional, in hopes that maybe I would eventually follow in his footsteps. It didn't happen that way, but then he realized that I had to follow my own path. I'm grateful that I always had a good support system from my parents, even though they came from a traditional background. I realized a lot of people don't, especially coming from a traditional Russian background.

Sometimes, in defense of that kind of teaching, you need some tough love. You need some bluntness. But don't tell somebody that they'll never be a musician. You have no right to do that. That kind of thing upsets me. Or the idea that a career in music has to fit a narrow criteria. There are a million ways to make a living as a musician now. I think a lot of the older teachers just maybe are not aware of all the opportunities. It's outside of their wheelhouse.

Joe pauses his story here to get up and show me his shiny black seven-string electric violin with an edgy, angular bottom.

Some people say it's not a real violin. But the electric violin is not trying to be a traditional violin. It is its own instrument and requires a different skill set and alternative techniques. There's definitely a learning curve and an art to playing this instrument.

After reading about the lives of classical musicians and considering this beautiful but restricted world, do you have a new understanding of why it is problematic that our school music programs have focused almost entirely and exclusively on this type of music? So many students leave their school years believing that they aren't good musicians and aren't musical simply because the type of music that most schools have focused on is too perfect, too rigorous, and too demanding.

While a number of schools in America have begun to include

other types of music education (Balinese *gamelan* orchestras, "garage band" programs, hip-hop, or Jamaican steel drum ensembles), Western classical music still dominates. Even at the elementary school level, music teachers are expected to prepare their young students to read classical music notation and understand its elements. While it's true that this type of music education might open doors for children who want to walk through that world eventually, it shouldn't be the be-all and end-all of musical learning. And, perhaps most importantly, children need to learn that there are numerous pathways into being musical. Not just through Western-European classical music.

12 — Listening as Musicianship

Vignette: Catherine's Piece

I was sitting in the audience in a small theater at the Chigiana Academy of Music in Siena, Italy. I was just sixteen years old. It was the final concert for the twelve students who attended the one-month masterclass. I was number thirteen in this group—not accepted, but allowed to participate as an "observer." My violin, in its brown velvet-lined case, was squeezed between my knees as Catherine walked onto the stage in a dark green dress. Her long curly blond hair was pinned up elegantly as she raised her violin to her shoulder. She was about to play the Franck *Sonata for Violin and Piano* (1822).

I had come to know her playing and the most challenging spots of the piece, as day after day I observed the master teacher drilling, admonishing, explaining, encouraging, and once even slamming his fist on the piano in frustration. My heart was pounding with anticipation, not only because I felt the intensity of this moment for her, but because I had fallen in love with this piece of music. The perfect caramel sweetness of the slow movement, that pulled my heart out with its tenderness; the rumbling deep river of the last movement, both angry, soaring, and rich with pleasure.

Catherine's playing had me on the edge of my seat. Her cheeks were flushed as her body swayed and jolted. Everything inside me felt like I was dancing with her. When the last movement came, with its furious, deep low notes, some hairs on her bow snapped free as it chopped and dug into the strings. Her hair began to come loose from its neat pins—spilling across her face and flying into the air. As her bow reached the final chords and lifted off the violin into a roar of applause, I could barely speak. I had been transported into the depths of my own heart and then spat out again into the theater as people began to gather their bags to leave.

At age twenty-one, I finally stepped out onto the stage to play this same Franck sonata for my senior recital at the Indiana University School of Music. It would be my first and last time playing this piece for an audience. I wore a green dress in honor of Catherine. I tucked my short brown curls behind my ears as the piano began its introduction. My focus didn't waver as I made my way through each note, phrase, and movement of this piece that took me over a year to learn. When my bow drew across the last chords of the piece, I looked out into the audience at my friends and family—were they moved the way I once was?

For the previous two years, the pain in my hands had been so great, I had nearly lost hope that I would be able to tackle such a challenging piece. As you may remember from Chapter 3, I had to stop playing the violin entirely for a semester, during which time I joined a choir and took voice lessons to stay in music school. But little by little, I worked my way back to playing because something inside me needed to play this piece. I had spent months staring at the knotholes in the wood of my practice room walls as I slowly repeated finger patterns and slides, and worked through how to bow or articulate each phrase so that I could express the way that I felt it inside. I took many breaks, stretching and applying cooling packs to my fingers so that the pain remained manageable.

Did the audience feel what I wanted them to feel that day? Could the audience possibly know how *I* felt? I wanted to graduate as a "violinist" even though the near-constant pain in my fingers, wrists, and forearms told me that I would likely never become a professional. I had already given up that dream. I was already, at that point, trying to redefine what it meant to be a "musician" when one can't physically play. As I packed my violin into its familiar brown velvet-lined case, something inside me knew that I would not pick it up again for a very long time, and probably would never play again the way I had just played.

At age forty-two, I found myself driving through my Boston neighborhood on a Saturday afternoon in October. I was listening to the radio, reflecting on my week of teaching—exploring the spooky sound of the gong with kindergarten students and using a minor chord on the xylophones to accompany a pumpkin song with first graders.

I was suddenly jolted from my thoughts as the opening bars of that same Franck Sonata filled my car. It had been over twenty years since I had played the violin, and I couldn't help the tears that spilled down my cheeks as a familiar narrative played through my mind: *I was once a "violinist." I was once good enough to play this piece. Look at me now, teaching Halloween songs!* And then I must remind myself: *No, Sara. You are still a musician, and you are making music every day with students. You don't need to perform to be a musician. Your heart can still be passionately filled by music. You are a Listener–Musician. When you listened to Catherine, you were feeling much more than when you played the Franck yourself!*

When I listened to Catherine play, I was a listening musician. When I listened to the radio, I was being my full musical self, overcome with emotion.

Yet if even I, the author of a book about redefining musicality, can feel the heartbreak of not feeling like a "real" musician because I don't play an instrument or perform on stage, how difficult will it be to sway your minds to the possibility that one can be "musical" in so many different ways?

At age forty-nine, I recently sat down with my former professor, Dr. Lori Custodero. After catching up on life and telling her about this book, she asked me, "Sara—how are you defining being a musician *for yourself* at this point in your life?"

After a long pause, I said, "I am being a musician and my most musical self when I'm creating music with the children I teach." I don't think I even realized until that moment that this was completely true!

Sensuality and Cell Phones at the Boston Symphony

I was sitting about twelve rows back in the orchestra section of

Symphony Hall, leafing through the program to the cacophonic sounds of the Boston Symphony Orchestra members warming up on stage.

This concert was a treat for my son on his sixteenth birthday. He had been enjoying piano lessons, and tonight he would hear the famous "Rach 3." This piece, Rachmaninoff's *Piano Concerto No. 3* (1909), is said to be one of the most technically difficult pieces for piano, and I prepared my son by sending him a recording and explaining that it was written during the height of the romantic era of classical music.

As we each read through our programs, I spotted the soloist's name in the program: Yunchan Lim. At the age of eighteen, he became the youngest pianist ever to win gold at the Van Cliburn International Piano Competition in 2022. Based on this information alone, I was expecting to hear a young technical wizard who would impress us all with his dexterity and speed. I was not expecting to hear one of the most moving performances of my life, but that is exactly what transpired.

The conductor stepped on stage, the orchestra tuned, and Yunchan approached the piano as the audience coughed, shuffled, and came to a hush. Three rows ahead of me to the left, a man was scrolling through his phone, which, I hoped, was on silent mode.

From the moment his hands touched the keys, I was transfixed. He was pulling honey straight from the piano like magic. As he continued to play, my heart was filled with a kind of euphoric longing that I can only describe as being in love, being timeless, being in beauty, being truly in myself. In those forty minutes, I did not need anything else in the entire world. There was no other world. My insides were dancing as tears filled my eyes.

Did my son feel any of this? I glanced over at him, and he was listening intently. I glanced three rows up and saw the man who continued to scroll through his phone. A woman was sleeping to my right. Yet for me, I was healed and held within what felt like a brilliant embrace of sound, which felt as if my entire life was being cradled before me.

Later that evening, I couldn't help but think about the man scrolling on his cell phone. Maybe he was there on a dare and had never been to a concert in his life. Maybe he was the runner-up in the Van Cliburn competition and was feeling resentful of this younger star. Maybe his wife or partner was in the hospital, and he wanted to be available for her. We cannot know where his mind and heart were that evening. We don't need to know, and I don't need to judge him. How we respond to or connect with music depends on so many factors—from our previous experiences, understanding of particular sound patterns, and familiarity with the piece, to family life, stress or hunger levels, deadlines, and exhaustion.

I am not a superior listener to that man. I was simply in the right place and time within myself to be open to feeling what I felt. I was being and feeling my full musical self that evening as a listener, but I wasn't simply listening. I couldn't help but feel that I was an active participant in the concert experience.

Can I Be Only a Listening Musician?

When I was a young aspiring violinist in high school, I was accepted in the New York Youth Symphony, a group that rehearsed and performed in Carnegie Hall. Just before our first concert of the season, I remember standing on that gorgeous and famously perfect stage after the dress rehearsal, and looking out at the sea of thousands of empty red velvet seats. My feet were standing where so many very famous musicians' feet had stood. Soon the hall would be filled with hundreds, if not thousands of people, but at that moment, I was relatively alone with the adrenaline-induced beating of my heart. I made a silent promise to myself that day: *I will never be just an audience member. I will always pursue being on this side of the velvet curtain—the stage side.*"

Several years later, when my hand injuries made it impossible to perform on the violin, I was doing just that. I mourned my identity as a performer, holding back tears (and sometimes not holding back tears) at so many concerts. At parties with fellow performing musicians, I would often get the question, "So, are you a musician too?"

After answering "yes," the follow-up question was one I always dreaded.

"What do you play?"

Sometimes I would tell the story of how I could no longer play the violin, but I hated this sad line of conversation because it didn't allow for what I *was* doing. Sometimes, if I was feeling annoyed, I would simply say, "I don't."

At some point, I decided that at the risk of sounding obnoxious, my best answer would be, "I play CDs!" This last response would usually get a confused look or a laugh, but I do think it was the most true to what I wanted to be seen as: a musician who loved to listen.

Over the years, something else began to happen: I began to understand that the experience of being a listening musician is no less than a performing one. The magic is quieter and happens on the inside. If I am receptive and tuned in to what is happening on stage, I can feel the music zing through me in much the same way that it did while playing. Perhaps even more so, since I didn't have to keep time, keep an eye on a conductor, or focus on the correct fingering or bowing in the score.

No one claps for me when the music is done. No one brings me flowers or comes over to me after a concert to congratulate me on my fine listening experience, but I have truly come to believe that one can be just a listening musician, even if one never had the chance to be on the "other side" of the curtain.

Emergent research by Beatriz Ilari, Professor of Music Teaching & Learning at the USC Thornton School of Music, confirms that musical listening can be a true form of musicianship. She explains that listening to music is not just being in attendance or completing a task, but that it requires agency, intention, and direct involvement (Ilari, 2025).

In a personal conversation with me, she relayed how most people in Western culture focus on music as a performative act—something done as a presentation for others. She suggested that I take a look at Thomas Turino's work to dig deeper.

Turino is an ethnomusicologist interested in exploring how music can help build communities and sustain our humanity in a capitalist world. He writes about the importance of engaging in alternative ways of music making that focus more on the social and spiritual benefits, rather than on something that can be marketed or purchased. This, he explains, is how indigenous people tend to approach music.

Inspired by what he experienced among the Shona people of Zimbabwe and indigenous Peruvians, he offers a "Four Fields

Framework" (2009) as a way of thinking about music as a social resource: Participatory Performance, Presentational Performance, High-fidelity Recording, and Studio Art Recording.

In "Participatory" music, there are no boundaries between performers and audience—everyone takes part, participating by clapping, dancing, or engaging socially together. The point is community connection and joy—not performance. But Turino says that Participatory music can also be a silent engagement— just listening to others as in a concert setting. It seems clear that Turino believes listening to be an active form of musicianship!

The second field of music making that Turino describes is what he calls "Presentational Performance"—when one person or group of people prepares music to show others.

The third field is "High Fidelity Recording," or recordings of live performances intended to preserve the performance. The artistry of *making* the recording and the process of preserving a performance with finely-tuned sound technology, he argues, is a form of music making in itself.

The fourth field, "Studio Audio Art," involves the creation and manipulation of sound with synthesizers, technology, and other electronic acoustic tools. In this last field, the creator is in complete control and does not need to depend on or interact with other performers. It is at the opposite end of the spectrum from Participatory music making.

Why does this matter? Turino explains that in our competitive and capitalist culture, the focus on Presentational Performance far outweighs other fields of music making. He suggests that to return to a more natural, joyful, and sustainable way of making music, we should give more weight to Participatory music making.

He writes, "Participatory performance is unpredictable, and sometimes messy— surprises and things unfolding in the moment, according to the abilities, needs, and desires of participants, tend to be at a maximum" (Turino, 2009, p. 107). This means that perfectionism and judgment are minimized and that mistakes and imperfections are welcomed. Furthermore, Participatory music making (such as group Salsa dancing, singing circles, drum circles, jam sessions, or call-and-response singing) "...provides potential spaces for experiencing, and developing, alternative cultural habits and values right in one's own hometown" (p. 107).

Let's develop and explore alternative cultural habits! And you can do that right where you are, in your hometown, without any formal training or shame. Participate! Attend a sing-along concert, find a drum circle, or go to a family contra dance session. Make mistakes! Let your voice explore new sounds. And yes, you *can* be just a listening musician!

The Armchair Musician

I was delighted when Neel Shah, Professor at Harvard Medical School, and the parent of one of my students, described himself as an Armchair Musician. For him, listening to music, actively taking it all in, and analyzing its structure was one of his favorite ways of being musical:

I didn't necessarily grow up in a very musical household, meaning my parents are not musicians—they don't play instruments. My parents are Indian immigrants. Their music was more about connection back home and nostalgia—60s and 70s Bollywood film tracks. It was about being connected to films and a certain era of growing up. Their reason for listening to it was homesickness. Many of the songs were sad, and it sounded like wailing music. We had a record player in the 80s, and the only pop record we had was the first Madonna album. I don't think they liked me listening to Madonna very much, which made me like it even more because it was transgressive.

My parents didn't grow up with a lot of resources, so they thought it would be great for me to play sports and learn music. I was in a Yamaha group class. It was the 80s, and synthesizers were a big thing, so I got interested in orchestration because I could push a lot of buttons on the keyboard. I loved that you could create lots of different noises and do a lot of different things. Back then, MIDI systems were new. I had a floppy disc that I could plug in to record and layer and track, and it unlocked a whole other level of creativity. And then, around the time I was fourteen, I picked up a guitar because everybody did. Guitar was unlocking for me because I just think guitars are so much easier to noodle with. I took to the guitar really fast. I was in a high school garage band, and so I learned to play everyone else's instruments too. I would mess around on the drum kit... There was a skateboarding scene on the Jersey Shore, and we'd play shows. Then I went to India, and I became very interested in Indian classical music because it was so different and felt connected to my parent's music. I brought a lot of that back with me. Sometime in high school, I brought in Indian drums. And then we moved from being a punk band to a band that had no market, I was told. It was like an acoustic twelve-string guitar, a violin, an upright bass, and acoustic drums like bongos, congas, and djembes!

We learned how to harmonize by ourselves and played up and down the Jersey shore. We made an album that we made in some kid's basement by looping and tracking. We had a 4-track at some point. And then we went to college and went in different directions. In college, I had some temporary bands. And then I went to medical school, and playing music went away for like a decade and a half. We were living in small spaces, so it was hard to make any sound, and I think I was just exhausted. It wasn't until the pandemic that I realized I'm an adult and can buy my own toys!

I think of myself as an armchair musician because I'm literally in an armchair and my favorite way to enjoy music is by deconstructing it—paying attention to the chords and harmonies, etc. Because nobody ever hears a good bass player unless they're really showy, but that can make the entire song. My childhood gave me a deep appreciation for the creative process of music, and now I have these friends that I pass music back and forth with. Another quirky thing about me is that I think everything should have a soundtrack. For example, there was a recurring meeting at work once that I hated, so I would always assign it to "Cherub Rock" by the Smashing Pumpkins (1993). It would just get me through it because I would giggle to myself. I could imagine myself sitting through an absurd scene in a movie. It's also a good cocktail party trick. Like, once I get to know someone, I just like to assign them a theme song. I've done this my entire life. It's really weird, but it brings me joy.

Neel begins his story by saying, "I didn't necessarily grow up in a very musical household." I hope that by this point in the book, when you hear someone saying, "I didn't grow up in a musical household," that you pause to question what they mean and whether it's true.

What I also find intriguing about Neel's story is that he understands that you don't have to be a performing musician to be a musical person. The idea of an Armchair Musician seems to describe someone knowledgeable about music or strongly connected to music from the comfort of their home or office. The reality is that unless you are a professional performing musician, we are all probably Armchair Musicians in one way or another.

The fact that Neel did experience being in a band and performing is probably what allows him to continue to feel musical about himself, even though he no longer performs. Yet it's much harder for those of us who have never played or performed on any instrument to call ourselves musical simply because we love listening to music. Perhaps the idea of an Armchair Musician, or Car Musician, or Shower Musician, etc., can open pathways in our minds towards feeling musical in our own quirky and comfortable way.

The Audience Is the Music

In their documentary film, *It's Only Life After All* (Multitude Films, 2023), Amy Ray and Emily Saliers of the Indigo Girls speak a lot about the energy and motivation they get from their audiences. It feeds their spirits and reaffirms their faith in the power of community and the feeling of commonality.

Amy said it like this: "I'm talking about synchronicity and critical mass. People feel the same response to that song at the same time, and you're just having that sense that you're being held by something."

When asked about how powerfully their music seems to affect their audiences, Emily said, "Music is such a mysterious force. It's so physical. It's so in our bodies. I know what it's like to have music save you at a particular time. But I never feel like, 'Oh, I can write a song that can change someone's life.' It's never, *never* that. Music is so powerful, isn't it? And your life is hooked into our journey, and we met on that journey, and that is awesome."

The feeling that their fans are on a musical journey with them signifies a strong relationship between these two performers and the people who follow them. At their concerts, they seem to especially enjoy it when the spotlights are turned onto the audience, so that they can feel and see them singing right along with them. Looking back on how the audience receives, shares, and supports their musical journey, Amy adds:

> The context of your song affects [the audience] too. The people that mentored us, the other people that are listening at the same time, the person sending their friend a mixtape, and them sharing that song. The sharing of that made it more powerful. And that happened a lot with our music. Our music wasn't just listened to by one person in a vacuum. And so you feel the embrace of more than just us. It feels better when you know there are actually people [out there].

Folk guitarist and singer Dar Williams (2021) describes it similarly, like this:

> When I go to a concert, two things are happening. I am taking in the lyrics and music. I am also taking in the collective experience that we are all having: the performer, the stage crew, the house manager, the promoter, and the audience. We are all participating in an event with the express purpose of experiencing our lives poetically. Art in general reminds me that there are things we call meaningful. Time is an impersonal force, and life itself can feel airy and insubstantial, but when I hear a song that I love, something catches me and holds me the way gravity holds us to the ground.

For folk musician Peter Mulvey, the audience's role in a performance is more than a collective feeling. He interacts and jokes with his audience quite a bit while performing, similar to the way a stand-up comedian might. When I asked him about the performer-audience connection, he described it to me like this:

> The audience is the only place where the music happens. When we say "music," what we really mean is the interior experience of each person who is listening to some sounds. The music couldn't possibly be just within the sounds, because what would it be for? If you put on a record in a soundproof room and close the door, there isn't music happening in that room! There is the song and the performer

(or recording), but the communal experience is that third thing. You really need the audience. I know a jazz musician who got schooled by one of the greatest mentors who asked him, "When you're playing in an ensemble, what is the most useful thing you can do?" My friend answered, commonsensically, "listening." It's the fundamental part. You won't add anything good to the ensemble unless you begin by listening. Then [the mentor] asked, "What does the audience do for the entirety of the show? They listen. So, who is the best musician in the room?" It's the audience. They are the ones making the most music in the room.

Music is the experience of sound hitting consciousness and your reaction in that field of consciousness to that sound. So I make some music when I'm playing, and I've played thousands of shows, and I've learned to walk outside of my own mind and stop thinking and stop intending. I am letting go of thinking and intending. I try to live at the edge. It's difficult to describe… but I can say it's simply to get out of [my] own way. On my best days, I'm still probably about 60% "busy" (producing/thinking) and 40% being an audience member. But the audience can achieve 60 or 70% presence. It's hard to listen. It's a meditative thing. You'll have an emotional reaction to the music, and then you'll have a thought about what that means to you, and then you'll follow that thought, and you're out of the moment. Then you have to return to it. Going to concerts makes you a better person! You know, the great empires did a lot of conquering. I wish they had sat in song circles more. We would have come a lot further.

Peter's words about the music happening within the audience and between the audience and the performer make me think that when we say "making music," it isn't necessarily about producing it, but can also be about what is being made inside yourself. Perhaps this is why, when we walk out of a concert, we sometimes glow with an inner feeling of belonging, being understood, and vibrancy. Something internally musical was being made from within us.

Collective Musical Joy

I recently listened to Esther Perel and Brené Brown, two of the most listened to influencers on personal and relational growth of our time, talk about staying "tethered" to our humanness in the face of social media and Artificial Intelligence (AI). Brené's podcast, "Unlocking Us," is described as featuring "Conversations that unlock the deeply human part of who we are, so that we can live, love, parent, and lead with a whole heart." This particular episode, "Esther Perel on New AI—Artificial Intimacy," invites listeners to consider how increasingly disconnected we are from real, human lived experiences.

What she observes is a profound human longing for connection and community. At a time of unprecedented freedom, people are also living with unprecedented doubt and uncertainty. As systems and technologies grow larger and more powerful, people increasingly seek what is genuinely nurturing. She quips that the real meaning of AI should be "artificial intimacy."

In-person relationships, she says, are often difficult, tense, messy, and require a lot of constant care. People make bids for connection which are often missed, creating a sense of loneliness. At the same time, the intimate everyday moments that tend to go viral online, such as a funny cat video, cause us to miss moments of true connection (such as your actual cat's activities).

Esther and Brené spoke a bit more about how the events in our lives feel like they don't matter unless we can share them with others through our social media platforms. Esther mentioned her recent conversation with Trevor Noah, whom she'd met with two days earlier. Trevor questioned whether people are capable of having moments where they are actually *in the moment*, rather focused on what is sellable or replicable. Could people feel fully present at a concert, for example, without seeing it through their phones, recording it?

I reflected on the fact that people in our time take photos of their food before eating, as if the food won't be special without sharing it with others who aren't in the room, maybe at the expense of the person or people actually sitting in the room dining with us. I thought about the irony of seeking nourishment through the "sharing" of our food, rather than the actual experience of eating the food. I thought again about how the arts nourish us and create community through shared experience.

And then, finally, Brené mentioned music. She spoke about the 2024 Austin City Limits (ACL) music festival, where she asked David Grohl (former drummer for Nirvana, current lead singer and guitar player of Foo Fighters) to do something special. Brené had been learning about the idea of "Collective Effervescence" that French sociologist Emile Durkheim introduced in the early 1900s to explain the commonality that forms during large social gatherings and human rituals.

In the podcast, Brené explained that when it was first being studied as a phenomenon, it appeared some type of magic was at play. She said, "They saw it always in community, often at church where people came together and left individual affect or emotion to join collective emotion. And so I've been really interested in this idea of collective effervescence, especially as it pertains to music."

In that moment of listening to their conversation, I realized that Brené and Esther did not need me to call them and explain the power of music to connect us. They clearly understood this, as experts on human connection and society. Peacemakers understand this. Creators of protest march chants understand this. Composers of national anthems know this. You, I am sure, already understand this as well, and have probably experienced it several times already in your life, hopefully in its most positive life-affirming form.

At the risk of stating the obvious here, and in light of the many stories, anecdotes, and personal vignettes already shared here, I will simply ask you to recognize one thing: your inner musicality is what allows you to connect powerfully to others through the music that feels most centering to *you*.

13 — Reclaiming Our Musical Selves

Vignette: Maraca Magic

In the year 2000, I was a master's student at Teachers College, Columbia University, taking a class with Lori Custodero called "Young Children's Musical Development." On one particular day, about midway through the semester, our group of about fifteen students entered the classroom to find it transformed. The desks were pushed to the sides, and music instruments of all kinds were everywhere. Xylophones, drums, wood blocks, castanets, and more had been strategically placed in different areas of the room. There were dancing scarves and puppets, musical books, and plastic microphones in small baskets, placed enticingly in various corners.

Our professor's instructions were, "Play for as long as you want to. When you're satisfied, have a seat." We shyly began to wander the room, trying out some of the instruments, all of us feeling a bit self-conscious and uncertain where to start.

Little by little, our playful sides began to come out. Someone was dancing with a blue translucent scarf to the sound of another student improvising on the wooden tone blocks. Another student took a plastic microphone and began singing playfully. Were we supposed to act like kids or like ourselves?

I spotted a basket of small child-sized colorful maracas on the piano, and took one in each hand. I gave a few shakes and was about to put them back when something inside of me said, "This feels kind of nice!" I kept shaking, letting my eyes close, and allowing the sensation to course through my body. I felt myself begin to move into some kind of dancing rhythm, my arms stretching outward, while my feet took on some light steps. The feeling of those shakers changed as I kept going. They became angry and forceful, then slow and intentional. I held them close to my ears at times, and then high above my head. I wove my rhythms in and out of the other melodies and sounds that spilled forth around me. I shook, and shook, and shook until a wide smile spread across my face. *Ahhhhh. This is what a child must feel when they are free to just play!*

I couldn't believe how two small and seemingly simple maracas could give me such a diverse array of pleasurable sensations. Something about this experience changed my view of musical playfulness and reminded me about Picasso's famous words: "It took me four years to paint like Raphael, but a lifetime to paint like a child.[14]"

Letting go of what music is supposed to sound like, or how we think we are expected to sound like while making music, might be nearly impossible. Some of us can say we "play" a musical instrument, but how playful is that playing? If you ever find yourself with an opportunity to simply play as a child might on any instrument, whether it's a trumpet or triangle, why not just see what happens?

What Does It Mean to Be a Musical Person?

My colleague Sue Cook tells me that in Botswana, where she lived for several years, music is something that everyone gets involved in—a regular part of life for everyone, much as I described traditional cultures in Chapter 1. This is how music has functioned since the beginning of human existence. Let's keep that in mind!

So what does it mean to be a "musical" person? I have posed this question to hundreds of people over ten-plus years as I collected stories for this book. I asked children, teenagers, adults who called themselves "not musical," adults who involve themselves in music on the side, as well as professional musicians.

And now I want to show you just how incredible these

---

[14] This quote is widely attributed to Picasso, though I was not able to find an original source.

definitions are, and what we can understand about musicality by asking this seemingly simple question.

So-called "Unmusical" People Defining Musicality

People who called themselves unmusical answered this question quite differently from anyone else! I have intentionally left names off of these quotes because I feel that when read together, the collective power of these words carries the most weight. I also want to preserve confidentiality here, as the picture I want to paint for you with these quotes might feel somewhat discomfitting to those who spoke the words. I encourage you to read these responses carefully—can you spot the same themes that I have? Or perhaps you will notice something entirely new! Here is what they said:

> —Finding some level of commitment to bettering yourself at it. You have to like it and have some affinity to it. We are a culture of being the best at something or needing to excel at something. You need to be driven, or you can get crushed.

> —Someone who I imagine plays music a lot or has an active relationship with playing music a lot.

> —Musical people just pick it up and understand notes and rhythms. Yes, you can learn it. Anyone can dedicate themselves and get better. Like I can work hard at becoming a black belt in martial arts, but with music, some people are just born with it.

> —I would say that a musical person doesn't necessarily have to be the best singer or best performer or best instrument player—but they have a grasp of melody and what makes great music, and most importantly, a passion for music.

> —You could have the mechanics of playing, but there's also an artistic piece of it and the HEART piece of it—where you feel the music. I never had that on the instruments I tried: flute, clarinet. But dancing? Yeah, I love dancing!

—A musician would not be a word I would describe myself as. Although I enjoy listening to music, singing, and dancing, I cannot see myself composing a piece of music. When I think of a musician, I think of a composer or someone who actually makes their own music.

—I always knew music wasn't really my thing. I used to sing along with Barry Manilow on the radio and loved it, but I just couldn't sing in tune. I wasn't good at it.

—Somebody who has some sort of talent that is part of who they are. Something that's a skill for them. Music is just not one of my skills. I think of a musical person as being a performer—someone who is good at it and has the skills to make it a part of their life.

—Someone who has a good ear for music and be able to play instruments and sing, and carry a tune probably.

—Being able to feel the music and the rhythm. Being able to sing or play an instrument.

—Somebody who has a good singing voice or who is good at playing an instrument.

—Being able to carry a tune or do something pleasing and not jarring to people's ears. I don't have any natural talent.

Do you see what I see? People who call themselves "Unmusical" are using these types of words to describe someone who *is* "Musical" in their minds:

- Born with it

- Natural

- Talent

- Can pick it up quickly

- Specific instrumental skills

- Passion

- Drive

- Good at performing

- Can carry a tune

Let's pick these words apart! As the debate about "natural talent" continues (see Chapter 9), I want us to question what "IT" is. What is the "it" of having musical talent? Does it mean that you can sing in tune?

We have already learned that being "in tune" means different things in different cultures, and that singing on pitch is a highly learnable skill. Does it mean being able to understand or feel rhythm and beat? Well, in that case, all babies with the ability to hear are born with a sense of rhythm and beat, beginning with the sound of their mother's heartbeat in the womb.

As we learned in Chapter 5, responding to the pulse of music through body movements comes naturally, but is often unlearned in modern Westernized cultures, as babies mature into children. And if researchers say that some people are just born more musical than others, I question how those researchers are defining musicality! Is it according to an ability to produce Western-European style music on a highly performative level? I am fairly certain that those researchers are not studying the musicality of folk guitar players, of indigenous or shamanic healers, or of audience members who sway and weep with musical pleasure while listening to a performance that moves them.

The people I spoke with who said, "I'm not musical" also spoke about passion, drive, and artistry. There are two different ways we could think about these areas of musicality. First of all, if no one ever encouraged you to pursue and practice music, or if you never had opportunities to try out different instruments to find a good fit for your heart and body, it would be difficult to develop a passion or drive to keep doing it.

We have also seen in this book that to feel good (let alone passionate) about playing an instrument or singing, each human needs the right combination of opportunity, supportive guidance, and a community of peers or family who help them to understand that mistakes are just a part of the process. Artistic musical expression can exist in a young child's unfiltered, unabashed songs, drumming, or dancing. And it can be honed and developed throughout one's life if we have the right set of circumstances.

But let's look at musical passion, drive, and artistry another way. What music are you passionate about? Heavy Metal? Rap? Celtic reels? What kind of music makes you feel as if you want to jump out of your seat and dance across your living room? What kind makes your eyes well up with tears? In other words, you likely already have a passion for some type of music inside you that can be released when you come in contact with it. Yo-Yo Ma spoke about this earlier when he described the way different people are drawn towards doing what is enjoyable to them. Do you have a "drive" to connect with that music? To listen to that music when the mood strikes you? I would wager that unless you belong to that small percentage of people who physically don't like or can't tolerate any music, the drive that moves you is strong.

Artistry can mean different things to different people. I know that when I hear a performance that is dull, it is often because the performer isn't able to communicate well during that show. Maybe they are exhausted, dealing with bad circumstances (like Katherine in Chapter 11, who was more focused on her too-short dress and high heels), or just not feeling it within themselves as they stand on stage that night. A computer-generated performance of a piece I know and love will never move me in the way a human performance can, with its imperfections, vulnerability, and mostly its human connectivity. I hear artistry in musical mistakes, in brief moments where someone is trying to communicate something within themselves. I hear artistry in the music that children invent as they play with the sound of their voices or with a cluster of keys on a piano.

Rather than thinking of ourselves as musically artistic or not, maybe we can acknowledge that we all have artistic moments when we can express something beautiful (in whatever form or shape that takes), and moments when we are less expressively available to connect in that way. I think that when you read what professional musicians say about musicality or artistry, you'll actually feel a sense of relief! Perhaps we can all begin to move away from the binary of "having it" or not, and give ourselves some grace.

Responses from Professional Musicians

It is important to carefully read through how professional musicians and self-identifying musical people define musicality. Each of these definitions carries an important message about connection, resiliency, opportunity, and following an inner feeling. Some also mention letting go of ego; many mention that musicality is a basic human trait that anyone can access. Collectively, we can see that these responses carry very different feelings and are much more open-ended and inclusive. We can also see that these definitions resonate more with how music operated in traditional, ancient, and pre-modern societies. I have included the names of the individual musicians here because they each have a wide following and were eager to share their personal view :

Kate Kayaian, cellist:

> Anyone who is able to connect with and express themselves through music. You can feel a deep connection to music without being a professional musician. You can still be musical. With students, the musical ones are those who can drop the walls down and really connect with music.

Laure Marshall, violinist:

> To hear music and it moves your soul, and you want to keep that feeling going. You want to keep interacting with that feeling—with that musical moment.

Courtney Kaiser-Sandler, singer-songwriter:

> Everyone can make music. Music is accessible to everyone, and kids should all believe that they can write songs, invent

songs, and be musical. But not everyone needs to become a professional musician and share their music with the world.

Lauren Cregor, singer-songwriter:

Music is vital for people's lives. It is a lifesaver for people. For some people [who are more musical], it is like a life force that rushes into their very core. Music is important to everyone, but not everyone allows the music to come inside them and transform them!

Kimberly Monzón, opera singer:

With my singing students, the musical ones can more readily take cues and bring the words of the music to life in a more organic way. They can translate the emotion within the music to be able to come out through their instrument—their voice. They have a deep connection to the music. Everyone connects with music somehow. Music can always be encouraged!

Suzy Perelman, Broadway violinist:

Somebody who feels the need to express themselves through some sort of performing art. It could be a child, a homeless person—anyone. The general public sees "musical" as someone who is good at playing an instrument. We musicians define "good" in terms of technique, but everyone can be musical. Anyone can get to some level of competency. Maybe it's less natural for some and more for others, but you can still do it.

Rebecca Hartka, cellist:

There is an aliveness to it. Skill can always be learned, but connectedness is everything.

Brian Karzan, singer:

You connect emotionally to the sounds and tones. It's an emotional feeling in response to music. You don't even have to play an instrument to be musical.

Carol McGonnel, clarinetist:

To be alive. To me, music is like a means to an end. Here we are on this planet and it's a total miracle that we're here in the first place and we get to experience what it is to be alive and to be human and whatever way it is that you can have that fullest experience as a human on earth, vibrating with the forces around us. Once you're feeling that—for me, it's music. Our entire experience as humans is vibration. It's how we connect with each other. Our feelings, our healing, our energy. It's all vibration. So music is a very direct connection to all that.

Mickey Katz, cellist:

Someone who is interested in music! Everyone has some interest or some connection. If you think about recognizing musicality in children, it's usually more about the ease of getting something—learning something musical quickly. If you're talking about adult performers, it's more about their ability to connect with music in a way that connects with the audience and with themselves. If there is an emotional or communicative disconnect, it doesn't work. It's like a circuit between the instrument (or voice), the self, and the audience. These three things need to be connected to be successful and "musical." And then it's also about the context and the goal. Yes, you can have musicians casually just playing together, and this happens all around the world. In jazz music, for example, people could just come together and improvise and play. But there are also masters who devote their lives to it. An Indian tabla player devotes his life to that too—he lives and breathes that music. There is a lifetime devotion. And it's this way for a lot of different kinds of music or art around the world. You can have anyone trying it and doing it, enjoying it and you can have specialists.

Peter Erskine, jazz and Latin percussionist:

A person who listens to or pays attention to the song that's inside of them. Everyone is musical, just as everyone is dramatic. We understand stories and music and literature, and drama on stage.

John Fitzgerald, drum circle facilitator:

> It's a rhythm river and we're all wet. If someone's struggling or getting stuck, there are ways to reconnect them. Musicians don't make music. People do. Some people have mastered an instrument or a technique. But people make music. Period. At every point in our lives, in whatever way we have. Music is a legacy of the human race, and traditional music making for most of our time has been done through a relationship with somebody who already plays. It's not about learning notes. Music is not notes; that is a map. Music is the territory itself, and it brings all these benefits: social, emotional, and physiological. Without that sense of place and social bonding, how much value is your intellectual musical knowledge? The term "musician" connotes somebody who has practiced to reach some level of proficiency. However, "Music Makers" is more egalitarian. It does not hold the baggage of musicianship. We're all music makers. My sense is that when somebody says, "Everyone is a musician," we feel, "No, that's not true." But when they say, "Everybody's a music maker," it's like, "Oh! Maybe!"

Melissa Karger, jazz singer:

> Somebody who wakes up wanting to listen to music. Anyone touched by music is musical. It's not limiting. As much as music has timing, I also think it's a way for people to detach. It's their therapy.

Joe Deninzon, rock and jazz violinist:

> It's someone whose heart is in connecting with people. Connecting with the audience and sharing an experience. Transcending our mundane lives. Telling a story with what you're playing. Making yourself vulnerable and making mistakes. Someone says, "All you need is three chords and the truth." I agree and disagree. You could have three chords and the truth, or you could have a thousand chords and the truth. But the one fundamental is the truth. Good music is honest music, no matter how complex or simple it is. People feel that honesty and know if it's contrived or overintellectualized, or corporatized. If something is sincere, people will feel it. If it comes from you, how can it be bad? It's your story.

Matt Goldstein, song-circle leader:

> Everything is music at a sort of cellular level. The nature of matter is that it is both physical form and vibrational energy. Everything is vibrating with a tone. Everything is appearing to us in time, in cycles. Time and time again in the natural world, we see that everything functions on rhythms and seasons. Everything is kind of in harmony and in rhythm. Nature is music, and music is our nature. I really believe everything and everyone is musical. I don't think there's such a thing as an unmusical person. There are various levels of musical fluency, like any language. Like I know four words in Arabic and I know 200 words in French, and I'm pretty fluent in English. There are many dialects of music. I'm not so fluent in Carnatic music, for example, and I might have an experience of showing up to that space and feeling "less-than," but with training or practice or exposure, I could be.

These quotes represent less than half of the professional musicians whom I interviewed, yet these are the types of definitions that I heard repeatedly when I asked them what it means to be a musical person. Despite their diverse backgrounds, perspectives, and the different types of music that these musicians engage with, there are several common threads here that I find fascinating! Laure Marshall, Brian Karzan, Joe Deninzon, and Kate Kayaian each describe the **deep and soulful connection** that musical people feel. Similarly, Lauren Cregor, Kimberly Monzón, and Rebecca Hartka talk about how musical people **"let music in"** and express it honestly. The idea that **everyone is musical** came up over and over again. Courtney Kaiser-Sandler, Suzy Perelman, Mickey Katz, and Matt Goldstein all mentioned that musicality is **not exclusive** to professional or highly trained musicians. Anyone can make, appreciate, or engage with music.

Many professional musicians also mentioned the **communicative** aspect of music—the ability to tell a story or create a **shared experience** between the performer(s) and audience. Carol McGonnel, Matt Goldstein, and John Fitzgerald explained that musical people understand that music making is not just an activity but a state of being—a way of **experiencing the world fully and authentically.**

Many of these professional musicians thoughtfully made a distinction between technical skill (which can be learned) and musicality, which is more about **connection and expression**.

Lastly, Matt Goldstein, Melissa Karger, Carol McGonnel, and Lauren Cregor all touched on themes of **vitality, energy, and healing**.

When we put these themes together, here is what we see: professional musicians define musicality as:

- Emotional Connection

- Universality

- A way of being

- Communication and expression

- Vitality, energy, and healing

Are these aspects of musical engagement not something that each of us already possesses? We all feel a deep emotional connection to the music we select, play, or share with others. We use these emotional connections to communicate our feelings, express our thoughts, and allow ourselves to heal, giving us vitality and energy. For all of us, music can be a "way of being" in the world if we allow ourselves to be open to broader definitions of what musical connection and engagement look like. I'm talking about the music we interact with and that is embedded in our daily lives and rituals.

Professional musicians understand that music is universally something we can all do. They believe everyone can be musical, yet people who call themselves unmusical think that only a few possess that "talent."

This is a big deal! It means that we might only need to expand and diversify our definitions of musicality to be able to call ourselves musical!

Responses from Teenagers

Thirty-six teenagers (ages fourteen to nineteen) from various US states, as well as Canada and Australia, responded to an online survey asking them to consider their own musicality and to provide a definition of what it means to be a musical person in their own words. Interestingly, many teens who did not consider themselves to be musical or who were unsure about whether they could call themselves musical did, at some point, take music lessons, participate in school ensembles, and feel comfortable singing in groups.

Teens who consider themselves musical defined a "musical person" like this:

—I think being a musical person means you love and enjoy playing or singing.

—To have a musical ear: being able to hear things in music and listen to music in a different/special way from others.

—I think a musical person means that you can catch onto group songs easily and have a musical ear (be able to replicate and maybe even harmonize with songs).

—Have some knowledge and experience (feel the beat).

—Love music and play a lot.

—To have an appreciation for music and also be able to make music of some kind.

—To like music and to be a singer is to have tone and pitch to recognize where you are on the scale.

—If you play an instrument well, then you most likely have good internal rhythm and or melody, which is what makes you good at your instrument, along with drive and passion.

—Someone who enjoys playing and/or listening to music.

—If you like music, singing/playing instruments, and stuff.

—I think being a 'Musical' person means to enjoy contributing to creating your own music, whether that means singing a song by someone else, playing instruments, or writing your own pieces.

—Being able to make music in some way, shape, or form.

—To know about different types of music and to make music.

—I think it means that you like music and appreciate it.

—To really appreciate every bit of musical performances and be able to recognize the attributes of music.

—Someone who likes to listen to music and enjoys learning about it.

—I think being a "musical" person means that you are connected with music and that it stirs up emotions in you, whether you play and sing every day and it's the biggest part of your identity, or you just find joy in listening to music. Of course, many musical people will have lots of musical knowledge, like how to play instruments, read music, count rhythm, etc., but I guess it's more about the connection than the knowledge.

—Having a strong interest in music and feeling very motivated about it.

Teenagers who do not consider themselves musical defined a "musical person" like this:

—Someone who is talented with music or who is good with singing and playing instruments.

—Someone who is good at and/or who likes playing music or singing.

—To be good at musical skills, like identifying notes or playing an instrument.

—Someone who is musically talented and enjoys

playing/making music.

—To be musically talented? Or to have an interest in music in general.

—You're musically gifted, can sing, and love music.

—Being involved with singing or playing an instrument.

—Someone who can properly appreciate music and who enjoys singing/playing.

—Someone who can play an instrument or sing.

—To like and be involved in music.

—Someone who is interested in or spends time making, learning, practicing, or analyzing music.

—Someone who just enjoys music and is passionate about something musical like an instrument, songwriting, or singing.

—Play an instrument, sing, be in musicals, more than just listening to music.

—Giving yourself some organized time for a musical instrument or to sing.

A significant number of teens simply answered "I don't know" when it came to identifying themselves as musical, as well as what it means to be a musical person. When I condense these responses into categories and separate the self-described "musical" from self-described "unmusical" responses from teens, here is what I see.

There is a notable overlap here: the enjoyment and appreciation of music seem to be clear indicators of musicality in both groups. These teenagers realized that a musical person is someone who understands musical concepts and relates to music. Yet I now wonder what first came to mind for them when they thought about music itself! Knowing that I am a music teacher writing a book about musicality, did they think that *my* focus was mainly on classical music? Did they subconsciously or even consciously link school music programs, which highlight chorus, band, and orchestra, with being good at "music" or with their enjoyment of "music?"

I have never met or heard of a teenager (though I'm sure a few exist) who didn't immerse themselves in some type of music, sharing playlists with friends, screeching with excitement when a new song by their favorite artist is released, or finding the "perfect" song to match their ever shifting mood. If this isn't musical enjoyment, I don't know what is. Wouldn't all teens say that they enjoy or appreciate music? Yet clearly, many of the teens who answered my survey and who felt they were not musical defined music according to an ability to enjoy and devote oneself to it. I can't help but think that these teens were thinking of music only in terms of what a school music program offers:

—I hated orchestra, and couldn't seem to get a good sound out of the clarinet, so I must not enjoy or understand music.

—I am not musical. My friend plays the clarinet really well and loves practicing it. She made it into our school's elite marching band. She is musical.

The fact that there was quite a bit of overlap in their answers, and that many of them simply answered "I don't know," indicates that their identities are still malleable at this point in their lives. This makes sense! The teenage years are famous for the shaping of identity and uncertainty with the question, "Who am I?"

Responses from Children

As I began speaking with children about their feelings and ideas about musicality, I first wanted to know what kinds of musical experiences have a big influence on them. Here is a small collection of responses from the children I spoke with:

Ryan, grade 6:

My dad taught me "Imagine" by John Lennon (1971). I practiced the chords and played it at our Christmas party. I felt so good about it—just the fact that I could do that. I could choose something that is actually easy to learn and sounds really good. To me, it felt really good. It started something musical in me. People were clapping and laughing, "Good job, Ryan!" My dad inspired me. We have a whole music room downstairs with lots of instruments. Sometimes it would distract me and I would forget to do my homework. I could play with my dad for hours.

Lila, grade 5:

When I saw Taylor Swift on the Eras tour, it was the best thing I've ever done. It was so hard to get tickets. My mom had made a promise to succeed. It meant the world to my mom. She was on the phone for nine hours. When she finally got them I was screaming and couldn't fall asleep. The pure joy and the buzz around it made me so happy. It was pouring rain. Even though it felt like I was in a shower, it was the best thing I've ever done. It connects all the Swifties together. I'm really not that good at singing, but nobody cares because you love her and you're just screaming!

Calvin, grade 5

I transfer to another universe where I have no worries and where I feel everything is under control. Usually, that's in the car on my way to school or sports. It really makes me feel like life is good and there's a straight path ahead. It triggers something in my brain. I really like pop music to get me ready and pumped up before sports. I guess I like music where it's slow and low. I make musical choices based on different moods. It transfers me into a world where everything is in reach.

After I had had a number of these conversations, I realized I needed to know more about how their definitions of musicality were developing. I chose to refrain from asking children whether they considered themselves to be musical because I wanted to believe that their definitions of musicality were not yet solidified and because I did not want to force their thinking and their musical development into binary terms. I wanted to simply understand what they think a musical person is:

Maya, grade 3:

> Everybody could be a musical person. It doesn't have to be something you practice. It could just be for fun. Music can be natural or something you come upon as a hobby, or something taught to you. It can be a part of everybody. I love doing music. It's a natural feeling for me.

Ani, grade 4:

> A musical person is somebody who really loves to create music. It doesn't have to be a song or a specific piece. It can kind of be whatever feels like music to you. I like creating music. I have a lot of fun doing it.

Sam, grade 3:

> A musical person is someone whose job it is to let out their feelings through songs. Anyone can do it if they have the guts to. Strong emotions can make you want to do that. Like Taylor Swift has super strong feelings.

George, grade 2:

> My songs usually come from my dreams. Like my song "Toxic Crocodiles." I had a dream about a toxic crocodile! A musical person? You have to go on with the beat with whatever piece you're working on, and you have to focus, and most importantly, you have to have fun.

Enid, kindergarten:

> Everyone can be musical if they want to be.

Ari, kindergarten:

> A musical person is someone who loves to sing and let out their voice and make it beautiful. Everyone could like doing it if they want to.

Bella, kindergarten:

> A musical person means you can express your heart. Instead of talking, you can show your heart with songs.

Franco, kindergarten:

> A musical person means fun, harmony, and peace. They are making peace, and it's just inside themselves.

Sara, grade 4:

> Everyone has a little music in them. Music can make a person feel so overwhelmingly happy or sad. It can describe what a person is going through. It can make you laugh.

Dami, grade 4:

> For me, it's about emotions. If someone has strong emotions when they hear music, they can be considered a musical person. People should know that music is like a story. It's poetry, and I think you can get lost in it. It can make you cry or feel so overjoyed.

Graham, grade 4:

> You're a musical person if you listen to music or like to sing a lot. I consider my mom musical because she's always singing. It's nonstop, and listening to music too. You don't have to play an instrument to be musical. Music can change your mood, like if you're sad and listen to a happy song, you can get happy again. If you're feeling sad, go to your phone, put on some music, and then you usually feel better.

Children's understanding of musicality is profound and perhaps most similar to the way mature professional musicians talk about music. It's about connection to family and friends, self-expression, and being transported to a special place.

What can we conclude from all of these definitions? It seems to me that children define musicality in such open and inclusive terms, and teenagers aren't quite sure where their musicality lies or what it means, but they likely tie their musicality strongly to school music experiences. By the time adulthood is reached, there is a clear sense of being either musical or unmusical.

Somewhere between elementary school and high school, musical identity begins to take shape and solidify.

This is a critical time when we develop our musical identities based on our experiences, rejections, acceptances, and enjoyment. These years can also involve more formal music participation, either with music lessons or in school ensembles, as well as realizations and roadblocks. Relationships with peers and teachers who might cut us down or raise our confidence also significantly help shape our musical dispositions. In short, "The musical self [is] constructed through the intersection of dispositions, opportunities, and environmental support systems" (Custodero, 2024, p. 63).

As a society, if we are going to try to reclaim our birthright as musical beings, we need to focus strongly on how to keep children (of all ages) musically engaged and open-minded in the face of roadblocks, lack of opportunities, and teachers or family members who might leave children feeling dejected and incapable.

Do you remember the "Subway singer" that I wrote about in the introduction to this book? Her resilience during a moment of harsh musical judgment was remarkable. We can't truly know what was happening for her in that single moment, but we can acknowledge that for some people, sometime between childhood and adulthood, a single moment of judgment or criticism of their musical ability can change the course of their perceived ability for the rest of their lives.

It bears repeating that these harsh judgments that lead so many to feel "unmusical" usually happen at school, given in the context of playing an instrument in band or orchestra, or singing off-key in chorus. It is time to knock that triangle of perfectionistic Western classical "goodness" off its track.

It is time to add more pathways and perspectives to the way music shapes us and is shaped by us. How can we, as a society, legitimize the music that is all around us? That we engage in outside of the dominant arena of orchestra-band-chorus? How can we recognize and celebrate the music that children already have inside them?

Music for Children or Music by Children??

If you search the internet for "children's music," you will find hundreds of songs made by adults to educate, entertain, and soothe kids. *Sesame Street*, Ms. Rachel, and Raffi alone offer enough songs to cover any long-distance road trip with your little one buckled in the back and bopping along. Most of these songs have simple melodies, an upbeat tempo, and someone singing in a silly or sugar-sweet voice.

Do babies and children actually prefer these songs? While they might love singing along to "Down by the Bay" (Raffi, 1976) and "Baby Shark," (Pinkfong, 2016) I have not seen evidence that these types of songs are preferable to rock, jazz, country, folk music, or any other type of music that babies or children encounter. When parents model their excitement and preference for a certain type of music, children usually wind up loving what their parents love. While there is a common belief that children have an easier time singing along with songs that have a simple melody and a limited range of notes, it is simply not true. In fact, young children can hear subtleties in the music that we adults may not even be attuned to! What's to stop a five-year-old from learning an Indian raga, a Bulgarian village song, or a song by Michael Jackson?

The psychologist Jerome Bruner explained that anyone can learn anything at any stage of life: "We begin with the hypothesis that any subject can be taught effectively in some intellectually honest form to any child at any stage of development." (1960, p. 33).

It has more to do with *how* something is learned than what. When a parent sings "Itsy Bitsy Spider" to an infant, they are usually holding a direct gaze with a wide smile on their face. They use their hands to show what is happening in the story along with the beat of the song. They repeat it over and over so that the baby learns to expect the descending trickle of fingers with the words "down came the rain" or the brush of a hand on their belly when they hear the word "washed." It is enjoyable because of the bonding effect of sharing a predictable music experience.

But if you were to sing a Billy Joel song like this, it would likely have the same effect. The fact is that the music that babies *do* prefer above all else is the sound of their primary caregiver singing to them, even when it's out of tune. This bears repeating:

Your baby thinks your singing is the best kind of music there is in the world, no matter what kind of singer you are! This is because you are tuned in to *each other*.

The Radio Project

I believe deeply in children's ability to create meaningful music and use the musicality they are born with to express themselves. As a music teacher, I have long felt that the music that children create on their own, without teacher instruction, should be a core part of my curriculum.

At the start of my teaching career, I began setting up "Free time" sessions every few months in my music room, where children could simply play with the instruments that I made available. It was noisy, chaotic, and incredible!

This playful way of learning music often seems at odds with the way "real" music lessons work, but over time, I became confident that the experience helps children to grow their musicality in profound ways.

I saw a young boy, who had been struggling to keep a steady beat during formal instruction time, play his drum with the most solid beat anyone could have asked for. Another group of young children discussed how to listen to each other while playing together, so they could sense how to get quieter and slower, bringing their piece to an end with mature finesse!

Given that the focus of these sessions was instrumental, I wondered if I could I do something similar for singing play. I thought about how children naturally create songs throughout their day, and introduced what I called "The Radio" (Zur, 2024).

Second graders having "Free Time" to arrange their own musical ideas in a band.

The joyful performance of their piece had everyone in the class enthralled!

I began by standing outside on my elementary school's playground during first-grade recess with a microphone and a sign that read, "Sing for the Radio!" As students approached the mic, I explained that I wanted to collect songs for my new Radio project. The only rule that I set for them was that their song had to be created by them—it couldn't be something copied, heard, or learned elsewhere.

Within minutes, students were lined up to sing, and friends were calling out to each other to join in. Some children sang spontaneously on the spot. Others pranced off to the swingset or play structure with friends to create something together, giving me a shout when they were ready. I repeated this with kindergarten and second grade students, and visited the beginner (preschool) classrooms as well.

Whenever possible, I began saving the last five to seven minutes of each class for "Radio Time," in case any of my students wanted to sing a song. While many students were initially too shy to sing in front of others, I consistently had two to five children per class who stood up to sing into the mic. The more students did this, the more popular the Radio became. More and more friends joined together to make songs, and soon many more students wanted to sing.

Over the next few years, I experimented with how to introduce the Radio to students, how to best capture their songs, and how to make time in my curriculum to allow students to listen to each other's songs.

I felt that something rather important was happening here and realized that I wanted to find a way for students to hear each other's inventions. I met with someone on our tech team to design a "Listening Station," which was built out of wood in our school's makerspace. I placed an iPad inside the console and set it up with headphones in the entryway of our school.

My plan was for young children and their families to have an opportunity to listen as they entered the building at the beginning of each day. Friends called each other over to share their favorite songs, and some songs like "A Chicken Does Not Violate the Laws of Physics," were so catchy that they could be heard being repeated throughout the school, even among the older students who had not taken part in the project. I began to see the Radio not only as a way to capture the songs that children wanted to share, but as a potential means of building community and fostering social connections within our school.

The "Radio" Listening Station

I kept this project going throughout the Covid pandemic, allowing children to privately record or send in their songs. A few songs were even sent from home. The following year, during Back to School Night, I secretly hoped that with this new project in place, the discussion of "real instruments" would move to the background and I could begin to relay the values of community and spontaneity in the music curriculum. While several parents seemed generally excited by the idea that their children might create a song for the Radio, I was surprised at how many of them commented about how "cute" (there's that word again) it would be. They didn't seem to recognize that these songs could be deeply meaningful, poetic, moving, or important to the children who created them. These young children were just getting to know their musical selves.

Music education researcher Margaret S. Barrett explains that when children have the agency to create their own music, they are also shaping their own musical culture (2006). As children develop their musical identities and define their place in the world, they are being authentic—a far cry from something "cute." Other parents wanted to know if this project allowed me to discover any students with "actual talent." And there we were—back to the Western, seemingly prized notion of "talent!"

I realized then that my definition of musicality was quite different from the norm. I would need to explain the importance of music as a tool for processing feelings and connecting with others—talent had nothing to do with it.

Playfully Playing Music

Playing an instrument does not always have to be a serious endeavor. The image of a pianist in a small, isolated room practicing for eight hours a day is often not very playful. We imagine that musical learning is a long and rigorous road because, for classical musicians, it often is.

You may recall the story told by Chris Serkin in Chapter 7, where he described his grandmother's approach to piano playing: the piano was a serious instrument, not for "noodling" on.

Similarly, Joe Deninzon was only taken seriously by his music teachers when he played the classical violin, not his electric rock violin. Classical music is seen as the pinnacle of artistic excellence. We might call it "playing" an instrument, but there is very little *playing* or playfulness involved. Classical teachers don't usually teach improvisation, which is reserved for jazz or folk styles of music, and much more playful!

The idea of what it means to practice an instrument is a cultural construct that takes on different meanings in different languages. A quick search on ChatGPT elicited some interesting examples.

The French word for practice, *répétition*, for example, means to repeat something over and over again. This feels very different from the Spanish word *ensayer*, or the Italian word *provare*, both of which translate to trying out. The Mandarin word used for practicing is 练 (*liàn*) to train or drill. In Japanese, the word *Keiko* (稽古) is a combination of two words: *kai* means to think or reflect, and *ko* means ancient.

According to ChatGPT, the idea of learning to play an instrument in Japanese culture is not mere repetition, but learning reflectively through tradition. What are your cultural traditions and meanings when it comes to the word "practice"? Practice can mean so very many different things! We can practice kindness, or practice awareness. Practice can also connote a career, as in "She practices medicine." So, what does practice mean to you?

If you are someone who didn't pass an orchestra or band audition, or who just couldn't keep up with the hours of practice needed to maintain technical skills on an instrument, I think it is quite challenging to ever see that particular instrument in a playful light. Given my history of violin playing, friends and family have asked me repeatedly over the years, "Do you ever feel like picking it up again just for fun?" I have tried to pick it up again, but it never feels fun. Each time I try to re-establish a relationship with the violin, I unzip the case, remove the velvet cloth that covers it, and remove it from its case. I attach the neck support to its back and bring it to my chin to tune it up. I try very hard to just "play." I draw my bow across the strings and try to just feel the vibrations and let my fingers make some notes, but nothing about it feels playful; there are only memories of intense hours of playing and the physical pain that my body seems to conjure up after only a few moments. The emotional and physical baggage feels too heavy to play with, and I lay it to rest again within minutes.

In my music classroom, I have a piano, but I am not a pianist by any means. My skills are such that I can sometimes plunk out a few chords to accompany a basic children's song. But one day, in between classes, I sat down and just *played.* I pressed my fingers into the notes just to see what they would sound like, as if I were a child. Slowly. A few notes at a time. I listened and adjusted the notes, taking time to figure out what sounded good to my ears in the same way a painter might put color on a canvas just to see what looks satisfying and interesting.

When I "practice" this way, I am not necessarily working on skills, though they may develop as a result of continued exploration. But I am enjoying the feeling of what the piano can be and what I can express on it. I am fully present and at play.

When I mentioned my realization in Chapter 10 that my most creative and playful musicality comes alive through my teaching, this is what I mean. It is the playfulness, lack of perfection-seeking, and the reinforcement of community through shared music-making that feels most musical to me. This happens when, for example, I am dancing with kindergarten students and I use their interesting movements to bring our dance to a new level, or when I sing out passionately with my first-grade students.

I fully understand that for performing musicians, honing top-level technique might feel most musical, but for the rest of us, can we allow ourselves to adopt a more playful and curious approach to our music-making?

Can we all try some playfulness on an instrument? Maybe one that we have no painful history with? Can we try drumming, humming, or strumming with curiosity, in search of delight? Play outside in the garden. Play with your eyes closed. Get into character and put on a ball gown to have a pretend singing competition with friends. Gel your hair back and put on some sunglasses, grab a hair brush or spatula "microphone" and make your kids laugh as you sing your favorite song.

There are many ways that we can get back to being playful with ourselves as we try out different music sounds and instruments. I simply love Custodero's (2024) statement that

"**What is important is not necessarily** *learning how to play music* **but rather,** *how to become music.*"

It's not just about making sound; It's about "understanding the essence of life."(p.130)

Killing the "Spider" with a Harmonica Solo

Candace Bertotti teaches "Arts of Communication" at Harvard University's Kennedy School. She is also the President and founder of Candid Communications, an organization geared towards helping individuals and teams improve their public speaking and communication skills. She is highly sought after across the globe for her expertise "...in negotiation, interpersonal communication, influence, crisis communication, and conflict resolution."[15]

What has Candace always really wanted to do? Play in a blues band! Her story about killing the "spider" is one that so very many of us can relate to on so many different levels:

> When I was in my 20s, I really wanted to learn to play the harmonica, and so I took a week off from my federal government job and went to blues camp in West Virginia. And basically, you go into the woods and you have teachers who teach you and you get into circles and you just jam. I would always be so eager, and I would go into these circles, but always freeze up. I didn't know how to just jam—just play.

Candace stopped telling her story to play me a clip of harmonica music on her phone of her teacher playing. She said, "That's it! That's my teacher. That's what I wanted to sound like!"

> He's not playing from a script. It's so amazing. That was my goal. And every night I'd go into the woods and just watch, and I'd be full of anxiety, but I just didn't want to play the

---

[15] Candid Communications, About Candace Bertotti, https://candacebertotti.com/about/ Retrieved June 30, 2025.

wrong notes. Then I took another week off and flew to California to the Legends of Blues harmonica conference. It was basically just a bunch of old dudes and me. Lee Oscar was there, if you've ever seen Lee Oscar Harmonicas, and I just wanted to free myself up and play. I spent the weekend just observing and trying to take it in, but I could not play. And after a while of just being so frozen, of being so worried about playing the wrong note whenever I would play in front of people, I just put my harmonicas on a shelf. And they literally stayed there for almost 30 years.

Later on in my twenties, I tried banjo, but I would get so angry and frustrated that I couldn't get it. I had this teacher who said, "I've taught thousands and thousands of students. Not just hundreds, but thousands, and out of all my students, I don't know what to do with you." Right after that, I would start getting this pain in my shoulder every time I would go to pick it up, and I haven't picked it up since.

So one day not too long ago, I was in choir practice and we were playing a song called "Don't Dream It's Over," and there's this beautiful organ solo in the song, and we weren't doing that. So I said to the choir director, "That would be a great harmonica solo!"

And she said, "You're right! Do you know anybody?"

And I was like "Oh crap!" but I was like, "I'll try it."

So I practiced these 30 notes that are on the recording that I found on YouTube over and over and over again. These exact notes, trying to get them in the right place on the harmonica and trying to figure out the right way to play them—over and over and over. So we got to practice, and I was practicing with the choir, and my throat totally closed up. I couldn't get a note out. So I think, "Okay, I'm going to go home and practice it even more." So I went home and practiced and practiced and practiced these thirty notes. Over and over and over again. We got to the actual day of the performance, and I was soooo nervous. And I tried all these different techniques, like *breathe deeply* and *think of how you'll be successful,* and I got the irony because I teach people at Harvard how to get in front of people and not be nervous and none of my own techniques worked. And I tried everything like pinching myself and trying to count the fingertips in my fingers, smelling the air. Nothing worked. Then the minister got up and read this poem by Nikki Giovanni (1997):

Allowables

I killed a spider
Not a murderous brown recluse
Nor even a black widow
And if the truth were told this
Was only a small
Sort of papery spider
Who should have run
When I picked up the book
But she didn't
And she scared me
And I smashed her

I don't think
I'm allowed

To kill something

Because I am

Frightened

And I just started bawling and crying. And I was sitting in the front row, and people were handing me tissues. And I was crying because I realized that I had killed my voice of playing harmonica for almost thirty years, because I was afraid of playing the wrong damn note. And then I thought of all the other times in my life when I have killed my voice because I'm afraid of not saying the right thing or not being perfect. I had even turned down an offer to be a keynote speaker because it would make me too anxious. And I just cried *so* hard. But I still had to do this damn solo. So he finished up his sermon, and I got up there, and I was just shaking. I got to the mic, and my solo came. It started off fine—I had practiced so much, but I lost the thread and played some wrong notes, and I was out there on my own. I luckily got it back by the end, and I could finish on the note I wanted to. And it was okay. And I rarely have an emotional experience, and I really wanted to feel that, so I ran out before the service was even over and I just stood behind a doorway and ugly cried for about 15 minutes. Just letting it all out. I kept telling myself, "Candace, it was okay. It was okay." And then this voice crept in that said, "Candace, it was *just* okay. *Just* okay. How dare you spend so many hours practicing, and it was just okay? What a waste!"

And I just kept crying and finally found Greg, my partner, and I said to him, "I know I f-d it up. I know it was just okay. I know I'm going to go out there and everyone's going to tell me it was great, but it wasn't! And I'll have to pretend and be gracious...I don't want to deal with all that BS!"

Greg was like, "Candace, you've got it all wrong. For the first time, you finally went off script, and you just played and that was the most beautiful part. It was the off-script notes where it really resonated,"

I agreed to go back to the congregation. Most people had left by then. I was picking up my things, and this guy whom I did not know was talking to some people, and he excused himself from that group and literally ran across the church. "Your playing!" he said. "The sermon was great; the music was great. But your playing took my spirituality to a different level."

And I totally just started ugly crying again because I guess it doesn't have to be perfect. And sometimes, not being perfect is actually what speaks to people. It's not just in playing harmonica. It's being vulnerable and doing something hard, and exposing yourself. That is what really connects us. And I feel like I'm so scripted! I have to be perfect and do it just right. And it's those moments when I put myself out there where I've had the most growth. But it's so hard to do. I think I've been taught to suppress my emotions, which is why I didn't stifle my crying when I felt it. So that's the spider I'm killing now.

We Are All Singers

I may have a "breathy" voice, whatever that means (see Chapter 11). You may sing off-key in certain registers or not be able to match your voice to a song on the radio. We may get stared at or told we're tone deaf. Maybe you are one of those people whose voice cracked while singing solo in front of your whole school, and couldn't bear to try singing in front of others again. Or maybe you *did* try again—you persisted, took a few lessons to improve, and you generally love singing! I dare to guess that deep down we all love singing because, since the beginning of human existence, singing has been a joyful, connective, communicative, joyful, and essential part of being human.

We all love singing, whether alone in the car, at a karaoke bar, to the baby in our arms, or to the children we raise. We don't need to be professional singers to call ourselves singers. Go ahead and say it: "I am a singer."

If this is the first time you have said this about yourself, what does that feel like? Is there a part of you that can believe it's true?

Heather Baker, a singing teacher from the UK, gave a TEDx Talk in Norwich in June 2019 called "Chase the Joy—And Sing!" She describes singing as an inherently joyful activity, which uplifts the person who is singing and often has a similar effect on those who are listening. She refers to research which has shown that singing can slow the heart rate, strengthen immune response, lower levels of cortisol associated with stress, and stimulate the release of dopamine and oxytocin—chemicals linked to pleasure and connection. Yet, singing is often treated as something only meant for people who are naturally talented or highly trained. Heather questions why people deny themselves something so rewarding simply because they are not experts. She likens it to exercise—you wouldn't avoid going to the gym because you can't lift the heaviest weights.

Heather urges people to care less about performance and more about participation. If singing were only for professionals, it would be impossible for anyone to ever become one. She reminds us that mastering anything takes time. If discouragement sets in after only a few early attempts, the hours it takes to develop mastery will never accumulate. The difference between those who become skilled and those who do not is usually just a matter of persistence.

Heather relays a childhood memory of singing in her choir, which she loved. When the opportunity came to perform a solo she was happy to volunteer. She practiced as much as she could and felt confident before the show. When the moment came, however, she felt her voice shaking. She sang off pitch and her confidence plummeted. She lacked the technical skill and wherewithal to make a comeback in the moment. Afterwards, Heather was no longer encouraged to sing solos-- she was led to conclude that she simply wasn't good.

Something inside Heather—an inner knowledge of how much joy singing brought her, made her refuse to let that one negative experience take that away. She continued singing, and, over time, that commitment led her down the path to where she is today—a professional singer and singing coach!

There are many professional, accomplished singers who, at some point, were told they weren't very good:

- Fred Astaire was judged as not being able to sing or act, but could dance a little.

- Elvis got a C in music at school. His teachers said he had no aptitude for singing.

- Shakira wasn't allowed in her school choir because her vibrato was deemed too strong. Now she's a multi-platinum performing artist known for her unique vibrato.

Heather Baker:

They chased their joy rather than listen to opinions. Our talent mindset (good or not) rules. It goes against the growth mindset that we're constantly being told we should use in our everyday lives. This mindset is very highlighted by the popularity of the TV talent shows that people love to watch. On *X-Factor*, they show you the best of the best and people on the far opposite end of the scale. They don't show you the 99.9% that land somewhere in between because that's too everyday and mundane to show what normal people are like.

X-Factor isn't real life. It's just TV. Real-life singing isn't standing up in front of Simon Cowell. Real-life singing is singing in the car, shower, cheering on a sports team, drunken karaoke, or crowding around your child singing "Happy Birthday." Real-life singing is joyful, and we should be taking each and every opportunity to do more of it.

No Wrong Notes in a Song Circle

You may remember Courtney Kaiser-Sandler talking about pop music. She said, "Everyone can make music. Music is accessible to everyone, and kids should all believe that they can write songs, invent songs, and be musical. But not everyone needs to become a professional musician." Folk Guitarist Peter Mulvey shares a similar sentiment to this. Speaking of guitar playing, as well as singing, he says:

> Does everyone have to be the absolute pinnacle at this? Could we all just do music? I like that folk music is democratic. Fungible. Pluralistic. I love a song circle. I don't care if someone in a song swap is not as great a singer as the person next to him. I used to play for my nieces and nephews' classes, and now I play for my son's preschool, and I think it's best if we sing *with* kids and never stop. There's always something they can sing. We can sing *with* rather than *for* people.

This is the idea of the "Song Circle," which I experienced myself on a frigidly cold evening in December 2024, which felt like a beacon of musical light in the world to me. That night, people of all ages, backgrounds, and experiences filed into a community center in Jamaica Plain, Massachusetts, hung up their jackets, and had their tickets scanned as they headed upstairs.

About 120 total strangers were led by Matt Goldstein, founder of the Gaia Music Collective, where vocal improvisation is at the heart of the experience. It began with some call-and-response echoing. Matt held up one finger for direct echoing and three fingers to suggest that people echo in harmony. There were gentle angelic notes, low guttural sounds, nasally whines, and percussive tones. Matt added percussive body rhythms, which we all began to do, and then we walked around the room interacting with others around us through our movements.

We stood in small groups and got to know each other a little bit, which helped shed some barriers and build our communal experience.

Soon after, Matt brought us to a communal hum in three-part harmony, which grew louder and softer and changed pitch according to his hand gestures. He brought us down to a very quiet hum, and as we sat on the floor in a large circle, he explained how we would play with our voices, with our eyes closed, listening and contributing to the song we would create together: "With each breath you take, let a new note come out. It doesn't have to fit anywhere or be in harmony. There are no wrong notes."

No wrong notes. What if everything you sing is simply what feels right? This is the stuff of pre-modern song circles of our ancestors, wherein people come together, sing, dance, and tune in to each other, fortifying relationships and healing ourselves. Modern "Song Circles" like this bring us back to a time when it was okay to just show up and sing. I could even quip that the modern Song Circles bring us Full Circle back to our roots. Community, connectedness, and an almost animalistic way of expressing oneself.

When our two hours were over, I wanted to hug each person in the room. We felt connected and somehow held by each other, just for being allowed to express our own individual voices in the presence of others, and then being guided to blend our voices as one. Song circles like these are gaining in popularity. I encourage you to find out whether one exists in or near your community and go try it out!

Several months later, I had the chance to speak with Matt about this experience. My first question was about his statement, "There are no wrong notes." I wanted to know if this is really true and where judgment lies in a song circle experience. This is what he said:

There are many ways to make music—music as performance. Music as experience. Music as ceremony, as therapy, as communication. And sometimes it doesn't fall into any of those buckets. There are some instances where we're meant to sing notes written on the page or correct notes, but in so many other settings, music is lifestyle or being with your own body or community, it's not nearly as important as how it feels in our body. Oftentimes, being "in tune" and being in rhythm are important in that we can fall into rhythm, into cycle, into harmony with community. With other humans or elements around us. There's a joy in seeking alignment with the music around us, but even in that joy, I'm much more excited by music that has space for grace. Space for mess. Because we're making music because we're human, and to be human is to be messy. To aspire to perfection is foolish. And to aspire to musical perfection, I think, is also a little foolish.

There's so much music that lives inside each of us, between each of us, and around us. The thing that so often gets in the way of tapping into that is judgment. There's often judgment that was passed down to us by someone when we were smaller—a teacher or parent, or you know, from the world we live in. I grew up with *American Idol*, where the marketing is, "Look at all these terrible singers! Let's watch the show so we can watch all these audition failures." I do think that culture is sort of shifting. We're no longer just getting off on people's musical failure as we were in that era, but there's judgment that we carry. When I'm leading improvised singing or any singing, I lead with the center of my facilitation spiraling around how we can free people from judgment, shame, or fear so that the music that's already in them can be released. So that their native abilities can be unlocked, or so that they can start to experiment. Like, "Here is where I can sing it loud and maybe sing it eight different ways in a row so I can find the one that actually feels good in my voice." They need permission to be a little bit messy until they find that place where they can feel really good in their voice.

We play all sorts of games and various activities with ground rules, all with the intention of acknowledging the judgment and trying to cast it out. I say, "This is a judgment-free space."

But a friend of mine was like, "That was hard for me to hear because I have judgment of myself in my own head, and then I feel like I'm doing it wrong if that judgment shows up." (Judgment of the self for judging oneself!) It's maybe impossible for it to be judgment-free, but we can try to not give judgment the center of the floor. We're going to put something braver and bolder, and freer on the soapbox.

I also asked Matt whether he ever encounters singers who can't seem to be able to blend in or who stand out in a way that indicates that they aren't feeling the flow of the group. What happens then? Does this happen often?

Very, very rarely. What I have encountered is a few people who are neurodivergent who experience hearing or singing differently. I respond to that sometimes by giving them an even bigger "yes and..." You know we're here in the circle and someone's clapping to a beat and it's not quite the beat that the rest of us are in, and some other people start to get a little nervous. Sometimes I might smile and gesture to that person or even invite them into the circle and give them a little clapping solo and kind of celebrate the joy of it, because oftentimes it's coming from joy and excitement. Or if someone is singing out of tune sometimes, rather than fear it or push it away, I go right up next to them and I sing with them and make eye contact. I sing the part over and over with them, mirroring and connecting with them, and there is a sort of mirror neuron magnetism that can bring them closer to it.

Every Monday, I lead a singing group with around 60 people, and oftentimes I'll sing something and they'll sing it back, and I'll hear maybe three of them where their notes are not corresponding with what the rest are echoing back, and it's fine. In a large mass community, it's less exposed. We can carry each other. It's harder if it's just around four people, and then you're very exposed. It can be unsettling and destabilizing because other folks need to provide more vocal strength to hold the music together. But it all sort of works out. With just fifteen to twenty people, it's more fragile, though.

The last question I had for Matt was about the healing aspect of song circles:

Music has this power, and it's known to many of us. From a solo perspective, it stimulates the vagus nerves, which is a cluster that generates cell repair and that's healing from a biological level. There's something about singing in unison in time together. Collective Effervescence. A group of people expressing in rhythm and in time together. You see it in nature—ant colonies, bird flocks. There's something innate in our nature that wants to align. Our heartbeats align when we're singing or stomping in rhythm. But there is this biological and spiritual aspect of healing. The act of being— singing is so personal as an instrument. There's a separation when you play an oboe or a piano between the instrument and the player. With singing, we are the instrument. That can make it feel incredibly vulnerable. It's how we communicate. Our voices are so unique and, again, we're often carrying shame or fear.

So to be with people expressing something together with our voices—to have a community validating us as we sing, saying "Yes! You're here, and I'm going to join you. I'm going to come and harmonize with you. I will add my voice to your voice." There are so many lessons here for how we can organize, uplift each other, validate each other, express ourselves bravely and boldly, and hold space for each other's fullness.

A Letter to Music Teachers

Dear Music Teachers,

You know that I love you and that I am one of you. Like you, I went through a lot of training and schooling to get to where I am. I share your experiences of long days in lonely practice rooms, and know the feeling of the adrenaline rush that comes before stepping on stage in front of hundreds of people. I have been that impatient studio teacher whose student comes to their private lesson not having practiced a bit and whining about how they're not getting to play any "good" pieces. And I have been the classroom teacher, exhausted, stressed, and responsible for the musical learning of the many small bright faces in front of me.

What is the point? Why are we doing this? Really, what is the point of music education?

Several years ago, at a back-to-school night event, the father of one of my students came to chat with me. "So, Sara, tell me about your philosophy of music teaching." Feeling slightly intimidated by his tweed coat and professorial demeanor, I took a big breath as thoughts raced through my mind:

- Should I talk about my dissertation?

- Spew facts about early childhood learning?

- Should I tell him about how music empowers change?

- Maybe I can talk about empathy and emotional development.

- Racial justice? Bridging cultural gaps in understanding?

"Joy," I replied, discarding all of the intellectual banter in my head. "I have a joy-based curriculum."

The father smiled at me and said, "That sounds exactly like what a music class should be!"

This reasoning may be too simple for some, but I do believe it is also comprehensive. Childhood is not easy. As adults, we often look at children as having a carefree existence, but we forget how much anxiety and stress can fill the lives of even the youngest students. So many rules, wishing for more time with parents, sibling rivalry, and having to do what adults demand of them all the time. They must abide by adult-imposed schedules, after-school lessons, and must handle hearing the word "no" a lot.

Music, I believe, should be a place for joy. A way for them to find and express their inner light, letting it shine out for the world to see. A way of feeling, "This is *me*, and this feels good!" Imagine, then, a young student looking forward to music class all week long, only to enter the room and be told:

- Sit quietly and don't touch the instruments.

- Sing in tune.

- Do as I do.

- Repeat this rhythm after me.

- That's not how the dance goes.

- Here is how to hold a triangle.

- Here is how this song should sound.

A joy-based curriculum, on the other hand, means acknowledging the inner musical sparks that children already have inside them—their natural will to create, improvise, contribute, and connect with each other in a musical way. I am not suggesting that music teachers abandon rules or high expectations. But when joy comes first, your directions and requests might look more like this:

- ★ Feel free to play the instrument in front of you until you see the quiet sign.

- ★ Sing in a way that feels good in your body and listen to others around you, appreciating how different our voices can be.

- ★ Show me how you play/chant/move, and we can all come up with new ways to do this.

- ★ Partner up and create rhythms for each other to copy. Each of you can be a leader and a follower.

- ★ That's an interesting dance move you created! Let's decide if it can fit into this dance we're doing, or maybe create a new version afterwards.

- ★ I'm seeing a new/different way to hold the triangle? What does it sound like when you hold it like that? Can you experiment and find a way to hold it that makes it sound best to you?

- ★ We can improvise different ways to sing this song, and then I will show you how the composer intended it to sound. We can decide as a group if we want to add any improv sections or just use the composer's original version.

I fully recognize that there are times when a music teacher needs to be precise, strict, or corrective. I also recognize that intense practice, repetition, and correctness can be part of what makes music joyful both as a performer and as a listener. What I am simply suggesting is that we try as best we can to feature joy and exploration in all of its messiness, curiosity, and wonder so that children's innate musicality can grow and not be shut down. This applies to all music teachers and all music students at any level.

I am reminded of William Cheng's words, "What if the primary purpose of sounding good isn't to do well, but to do good?" (2016, p. 8). Goodness in music teaching means caring for the emotional development and well-being of our students. We hold the power to affect how their musical identities take shape. Let us keep their hearts open and joyful to their unique musical abilities and curiosities so that they don't grow up saying, "I'm not musical," but go out into the world fully believing, "I am musical."

A preschool student experiences the joy of music as it moves through her body in a freestyle dance. (Photo credit: Hannah Garcia)

Rewriting the Score on Musical Abilities

Humans have always been musical, just as birds sing and fish swim. Yet cultural forces have left many of us to feel that musical ability lies outside of the natural human landscape. I have said this before, but it bears repeating: colonialism and elitism have placed Western classical music at the top of the hierarchical pyramid for what is considered "good" music. Pop music, though not considered as serious or important, comes in second. In the minds of our society at large, community music-making, garage bands, impromptu bang-a-can street rhythms, folk music, indigenous fusion bands, or raucous pub songs with fiddles and guitars are not "real" music, even though those types of music are precisely the natural, joyous, human-scale sounds that have existed around the world since the beginning of our existence and which allow anyone to be a part of.

Why have everyday informal musical gatherings disappeared from our culture?

We can blame our busy lives for the breakdown in community and people-centered activities. We can blame technology for eliminating the need to connect with others in daily conversations. Our lives feel fractured rather than connected. We easily access and receive advice, directions, or explanations to our questions from our screens, not people. Some even have romantic partnerships with an AI "being."

The breakdown in human relationships, however big or small, has created an increasing sense of loneliness. This loneliness causes people to turn to drugs and alcohol to try to forget or release the feeling, or to social media for what masquerades as connection and community. The few times a year that we might gather as our ancestors did to sing or dance with family and friends (weddings, holidays, birthdays, etc.) are what Dissenayake calls "fragmentary scraps" that, in her mind, resemble "unintegrated spasmodic movements of a creature that has been mortally injured or taken from its natural life-sustaining element" (2002, p. 201). Instead of being a core piece of who we are and what we humans do, music (and the arts) is removed from our daily lives, relegated to the fringes of entertainment, where we have learned to passively appreciate "talented" people on stages.

Both pop music and classical music have intimidatingly tall gates designed to leave most of us out. They are both largely controlled through competition, financial capacity, and the media. Most people don't pass auditions, can't handle the competition, or simply don't have the family and financial support systems in place that allow them to pursue their music-making dreams. The media, along with many music teachers, orchestra and band conductors, want us to believe that some people have talent and others don't. You're either in or you're out. You have what it takes, or you don't.

It's time to rewrite the score and reclaim our musical birthright!

We can begin by changing our perception of our own musical abilities by telling ourselves a different story from what we've been telling ourselves in the past. We can then begin to speak about musical ability in a generally more open, inclusive, and positive light. We can each make small changes in the way we speak with others, sharing our truest stories and encouraging others to reconsider how they think and speak about musical abilities as well. The more stories we tell, the fuller and richer our tapestry of musical ability becomes.

Here are some suggestions for how we can begin to think differently about our abilities:

Instead of saying, "I can't sing," try saying:

- I never had the chance to take singing lessons.

- No one ever taught me to match pitches.

- I love singing, but I only do it in private.

- I can sing in a limited range but haven't learned to sing high notes, so I go off-key if I'm trying to sing along sometimes.

- I have been told I can't carry a tune, but I haven't tried to improve my skills.

If you notice someone else who sings off-key, assume the same is true for them. This may sound obvious, but if the sound of someone singing is unpleasant to you, simply remove yourself from their presence and avoid rolling your eyes or making critical remarks. You are allowed to dislike the way someone's music-making sounds, but you are not a judge on *American Idol*, and nor should you be. Don't play into that elitist rhetoric, no matter how big the temptation. Even if that person never hears your judgment, others will. Our words can have a big effect on how others feel about their own musicality.

Instead of saying, "I'm not talented," try saying:

- I have less fluency with note-reading (or rhythm, or sound control, etc.) than I would like.

- I never had the chance to figure out which instrument was the best match for my skill set.

- I prefer casual music-making experiences to competitions.

- I didn't seem to have the physical dexterity to play the instrument that I wanted to. Maybe one day I'll try a different instrument.

- I never had a music teacher who inspired or encouraged me to practice as hard as I could have.

- My family didn't offer me the support I needed to keep myself motivated to practice.

- I don't need to be talented to enjoy musical experiences.

Instead of saying, "I'm not musical," try saying:

- I experience music more when I'm dancing than through an instrument or singing.

- I enjoy listening to music. My musicality comes through with the song choices I make or songs I send to others.

- Music connects me to my family. We love dancing together or playing songs in the car together.

- I know exactly what type of music I need to play for each type of emotion or experience that I'm having.

- Music helps get me through my day.

- I'm not a professional musician, but music is an important part of my life.

If you are a professional musician of any kind, the words you use with others hold great power.

You can talk about musical fluency, rather than talent. You can help others understand what you already know deep down inside: Everyone has the capacity to make music and engage with the world through musical experiences. You can help others to see that music is not just about getting a correct fingering or a set of technical skills, but a means of expressive connection that helps ground us and ensures a sense of belonging to a greater whole. In an age when technology has us questioning what it even means to be human, we need to recognize that music can make us feel fully human in a way that nothing else can. Everyone deserves to be their fully human selves.

Acknowledgments

So many incredible people (too numerous to name) shared their stories with me and allowed me to share them with you. I will be forever grateful for their vulnerability, time, and enthusiasm for this project. Tom Holbrook, your expertise in both copy and content editing made the book publication process manageable and enjoyable. I am grateful for your insights and care. Sarah Cole, you generously gave your time and offered your publishing expertise to guide my thinking and advise me on countless details. Furthermore, you oversaw the amazing marketing and publicity work by three of your Emerson graduate students: Izzie Claudio, Ali Dening, and Ella Miller. Tremendous thanks to all four of you! Alexander Camlin, not only was it easy and fun to work with you on the cover art for this book, but you perfectly captured the essence of this project with your creative thinking!

I am also incredibly grateful to the friends who took time to look over my work, have long conversations with me, and offer their feedback, thoughts, and advice: Jacob Appel, Lucinda Berk, Candace Bertotti, Sue Cook, Helena de Bres, Cheryl Freeze, Beth Gallaway, Greg Harris, Claudia Krich, Lisa Moellman, Nina Revis-Bareesi, Marina Strauss, and Indu Viswanathan. A special thank you goes out to Annegret Klaua for connecting me with Sarah Cole, and for handing my personal letter to the Indigo Girls! I am also grateful to the thousands of children who have taught me so much, as well as the many parents in the BB&N community who encouraged me in this work.

Launching this book into publication would not have been possible without financial support from friends and family, including Jeff and Marydale Allen, Serena Allen, Gabrielle Burke, Lori Custodero, Michael Dickel, Kim Greenberg, Orly Halpern, Vivek Jain, Anna Jewel, Airy Krich-Brinton, Cat Livingston, Mel

Rader, Daniel Meller, Zoraya Nambi, Anne Poubeau, Alfredo and Debra Sadun, Rebecca Sadun, Jacob Sife, Laura Stevens, Michael Stevens, Robert Stevens, and Asmira Woodward-Page. Thank you for your generous support and for believing in this work.

To Amitai and Leah, my fantastic children, thank you for your patience and care during my many, many hours of writing and editing, encouraging me with words like, "That's cool," and "Wow" (big words for teenagers). Thank you to my brother Daniel Stevens and my mother, Laura Stevens, for always believing in me. My biggest thanks goes to my partner, Venera Gattonini, whose encouragement ("Just write one more word"), great ideas, endless listening, funny spontaneous songs, dances, and abundant love, I could not have managed without. Thank you!

Resources

Find Community Singing Groups:

- Rise Up Singing: The Rise Up Singing website, <u>riseupsinging.org</u> provides a directory of sing-alongs and song circles, often using their "Rise Up Singing" songbooks. They list groups based on location, so you can find a sing in your area.
- Country Dance & Song Society (CDSS): <u>CCDS.org</u> offers a sing-along and song circle locator on their website.
- Sing Out! Magazine: Sing Out! (<u>singout.org</u>) also maintains a map and directory of community sings. You can find detailed information about specific groups, including their format, location, and contact information.

Find Drum Circles:

- Check your local library, community center, church, or music store for notices.
- Check for local Facebook or Meetup groups
- <u>https://drumcircle.net/</u> lists many local groups across the US

Other Community Music-Making Events and Workshops to Look For:

- Ecstatic Dance events (no judgment and no alcohol—just show up and dance)!
- Attend a Honk instrument parade in your area: http://www.honkrenaissance.net/
- Check on Facebook Events for a fun evening of Salsa dance lessons followed by open Salsa dancing
- Attend a Fiddle Festival such as https://thefiddlefest.com/ where you can listen, learn from master fiddle players, and take part in a fiddle jam session. All levels are welcome!

Text References

Abril, Carlos R. "I Have a Voice but I Just Can't Sing." *Music Education Research*, vol. 9, no. 1, 2007, pp. 1-15.

Asmus, Edward P. "Student Beliefs about the Causes of Success and Failure in Music: A Study of Achievement and Motivation." *Journal of Research in Music Education*, vol. 34, no. 4, 1986, pp. 262-275.

Barrett, Margaret S. "Inventing Songs, Inventing Worlds: The 'Genesis' of Creative Thought and Activity in Young Children's Lives." *International Journal of Early Years Education*, vol. 14, no. 3, Oct. 2006, pp. 201–220.

Bentley, Dana. *Everyday Artists: Inquiry and Creativity in the Early Childhood Classroom*. Teachers College Press, 2013.

Bernstein, Leonard. *The Unanswered Question 1973 1: Musical Phonology*. Uploaded by Norton, 2014, www.youtube.com/watch?v=8fHi36dvTdE. Accessed 20 Feb. 2024.

Borish, N. "Did Neanderthals Make Musical Instruments?" *Carnegie Museum of Natural History*, n.d., carnegiemnh.org/did-neanderthals-make-musical-instruments/. Accessed 26 June 2024.

Bracci, Aria. "What People Who Don't Like Music Might

Tell Us About Social Interaction." *Neuroscience News*, 18 Jan. 2020,neurosciencenews.com/music-anhedonia-social-interaction-15518/#:~:text=AutismFeaturedNeurosciencePsychology,people%20on%20the%20autism%20spectrum. Accessed 21 Feb. 2025.

Brown, Brené, and Esther Perel. "Esther Perel on New AI – Artificial Intimacy." *Unlocking Us*, 20 Mar. 2024, brenebrown.com/podcast/new-ai-artificial-intimacy/. Accessed 23 Feb. 2025.

Campbell, Patricia Shehan. *Songs in Their Heads: Music and Its Meaning in Children's Lives*. 2nd ed., Oxford University Press, 2010.

Candid Communications. "About Candace Bertotti." *Candace Bertotti*, candacebertotti.com/about/. Accessed 30 June 2025.

Carlsson-Paige, Nancy. *Taking Back Childhood: Helping Your Kids Thrive in a Fast-Paced, Media-Saturated, Violence-Filled World*. Hudson Street Press, 2008.

Cheng, William. *Just Vibrations: The Purpose of Sounding Good*. University of Michigan Press, 2016.

Cohen, Cynthia. "Music: A Universal Language?" *Music and Conflict Transformation: Harmonies and Dissonances in Geopolitics*, edited by O. Urbian, I.B. Tauris, 2015.

Cottle, Michelle, Ross Douthat, and Lydia Polgreen. "Can Beyoncé Save Biden?" *The New York Times*, 29 Mar. 2024, www.nytimes.com/2024/03/29/opinion/beyonce-taylor-swift-celebrity-politics.html. Accessed 21 Feb. 2025.

Custodero, Lori A. "The Musical Lives of Young Children: Inviting, Seeking, and Initiating." *Zero to Three*, vol. 23, no. 1, Sept. 2002.

Custodero, Lori A., and Elissa A. Johnson-Green. "Passing the Cultural Torch: Musical Experience and Musical Parenting of Infants." *Journal of Research in Music Education*, vol. 51, no. 2, 2003, pp. 102–114. https://doi.org/10.2307/3345844.

Custodero, Lori A. "Singing Practices in 10 Families with Young Children." *Journal of Research in Music Education*, vol. 54, no. 5, 2006, pp. 37–56.

Custodero, Lori A., C. Cali, and A. Diaz-Donoso. "Music as a Transitional Object and Practice: Children's Spontaneous Musical Behaviors in the Subway." *Research Studies in Music Education*, vol. 38, no. 1, 2016, pp. 55–74.

Custodero, Lori A. *Before We Teach Music: The Resonant Legacies of Childhoods and Children.* Oxford University Press, 2024.

De Quadros, André. & Amrein, Emilie. *Empowering Song: Music Education From the Margins.* Routledge, 2023.

DiFranco, Ani. *No Walls and the Recurring Dream: A Memoir.* Viking, 2019.

Dissanayake, Ellen. *Art and Intimacy: How the Arts Began.* University of Washington Press, 2002.

Farrar, Siobhan. "More Than Melody: Boethius' Music of the Spheres." *Acropolis Library*, 27 Aug. 2017, library.acropolis.org/more-than-melody-boethius-music-of-the-spheres/. Accessed 30 Jan. 2025.

Friesen, Doug, and Laura Menard. "The 'Heart and Soul' of Music Education: Towards Sonic Egalitarianism in Classroom Practice." *Visions of Research in Music Education*, vol. 46, 2024, pp. 59–82.

Gardiner, Martin. "Brazilian Scientists Investigate Beethoven's Cancer-Fighting Properties." *Gizmodo*, 16 Apr. 2011, gizmodo.com/brazilian-scientists-investigate-beethovens-cancer-figh-5792703. Accessed 30 Jan. 2025.

Galtung, Johan. "Peace, Music and the Arts." *Music and Conflict Transformation: Harmonies and Dissonances in Geopolitics*, edited by O. Urbain, I.B. Tauris, 2015, pp. 53-60.

Gifford, Elizabeth. "The Musical Training of Teachers: Old Problems, New Insights and Possible Solutions." *British Journal of Music Education*, vol. 10, no. 1, 1993, pp. 33–46.

Nikki Giovanni. "Allowables." *Love Poems*. William Morrow, 1997, p. 109

Doyle, Glennon, Abby Wambach, and Amanda Doyle, hosts. "How to Turn a Mistake Into Magic with Suleika Jaouad." *We Can Do Hard Things*, 23 May 2024. *Momastery*, https://momastery.com/blog/we-can-do-hard-things-ep-313/. Accessed 20 Feb. 2025.

Ericsson, K. Anders, Ralf T. Krampe, and Clemens Tesch-Römer. "The Role of Deliberate Practice in the Acquisition of Expert Performance." *Psychological Review*, vol. 100, no. 3, 1993, pp. 363–406.

Haas, Malka. "Children in the Junkyard." *Childhood Education*, vol. 73 no. 1 , 2016, pp. 345-350.

Hargreaves, David J., Dorothy Miell, and Raymond A. R. MacDonald. "What Are Musical Identities, and Why Are They Important?" *Musical Identities*, edited by Raymond A. R. MacDonald, David J. Hargreaves, and Dorothy Miell, Oxford University Press, 2002, pp. 1-20.

Harmer, Allison. *Child-Initiated Music Play (ChIMP) in Dens: Reclaiming Play in Playing Music.* Master's thesis, Birmingham City University, 2011.

Hendricks, Karen S., David A. K. Finn, and Cheryl Freeze. "Facilitating Trust and Connection through Musical Presencing: Case Study of a Conflict Transformation Facilitator." *The Oxford Handbook of Care in Music Education*, edited by Karen S. Hendricks, Oxford University Press, 2023, pp. 217–230.

Hutton, J. Christopher, and Elizabeth C. Parker. "Review of Singing and Caring." *The Oxford Handbook of Care in Music Education*, edited by Karen S. Hendricks, Oxford University Press, 2023, pp. 268–279.

Ilari, Beatriz. "Musical Participation Revisited: Lessons for General Music." *Mountain Lake Colloquium*, 19 May 2025, Mountain Lake, Virginia.

It's Only Life After All. Directed by Alexandria Bombach, Multitude Films, 2023, www.itsonlylifeafterall.com/. Documentary.

Kleiner, Lynn. *Kids Make Music, Babies Make Music, Too! Teacher's Guide (Babies - Age 7)*, Alfred Music, 1998.

Kramer, Jonathan D. *The Time of Music: New Meanings, New Temporalities, New Listening Strategies.* Schirmer Books, 1988.

264 Sara Stevens Zur, Ed.D.

Lamont, Alexandra. "Musical Identity, Interest, and Involvement." *Handbook of Musical Identities*, edited by Raymond A. R. MacDonald, David J. Hargreaves, and Dorothy Miell, Oxford University Press, 2017, pp. 176–196. https://doi.org/10.1093/acprof:oso/9780199679485.003.0010.

Langer, Ellen. J. *On becoming an artist: Reinventing yourself through mindful creativity.* Ballantine, 2005.

Laurence, Felicity. "Music and Empathy." *Music and Conflict Transformation: Harmonies and Dissonances in Geopolitics*, edited by Olivier Urbain, I.B. Tauris, 2015, pp. 13-25.

Lippi, Donatella, Domenico R. de Sarsina, and Jean-Paul D'Elios. "Music and Medicine." *Journal of Multidisciplinary Healthcare*, vol. 3, Aug. 2010, pp. 137–141.

Littleton, Danette. *Influence of Play Settings on Preschool Children's Music and Play Behaviors.* PhD dissertation, University of Texas at Austin, 1991.

Littleton, Danette. "Music in the Time of Toddlers." *Zero to Three*, vol. 23, no 1, 2002, pp. 35-40.

Marsh, Kathryn. *The Musical Playground: Global Tradition and Change in Children's Songs and Games.* Oxford University Press, 2009.

Marsh, Kathryn, and Susan Young. "Musical Play." *The Child as Musician: A Handbook of Musical Development.* 2nd ed., edited by Gary McPherson, Oxford University Press, 2016, pp. 462–484.

O'Connor, Karyn. "Tone Deafness (Amusia) and Other Causes of Persistent Pitch Problems." *Singwise*, 2022, https://www.singwise.com/articles/tone-deafness-amusia-and-other-causes-of-persistent-pitch-problems. Accessed 21 Feb. 2025.

Pritchard, Evan. T. *No Word for Time: The Way of the Algonquin People.* Council Oak Books, 2001.

Richards, Carol. "Early Childhood Preservice Teachers' Confidence in Singing," *Journal of Music Teacher Education,* vol. 9, no.1, 1999, pp. 6-17, https://doi.org/10.1177/105708379900900103

Ruddock, Eve E. "Misconceptions Underplay Western Ways of Musicking: A Hermeneutic Investigation." Action, Criticism, and Theory for Music Education, vol. 16, no. 2, Oct. 2017, pp. 39–64.

Rutkowski, Joanne. "Development and Pedagogy of Children's Singing." *Engaging Musical Practices: A Sourcebook for Elementary General Music,* edited by Suzanne L. Burton and Alison M. Reynolds, Rowman & Littlefield, 2018, pp. 33–50.

Sacks, Oliver. *Musicophilia.* Alfred A. Knopf, 2008.

Sarath, Edward W., David E. Myers, and Patricia Shehan Campbell. *Redefining Music Studies in an Age of Change: Creativity, Diversity, and Integration.* Routledge, 2017.

Schei, Bente. "The Vulnerability in Being Heard: Care in the Supervision of Music Students." *The Oxford Handbook of Care in Music Education*, edited by Karen S. Hendricks, Oxford University Press, 2023, pp. 307–317.

Sole, Meryl. "Crib Song: Insights into Functions of Toddlers' Private Spontaneous Singing." *Psychology of*

Music, vol. 45, no. 2, 2017, pp. 172-192.

Solomon, Andrew. "The Longest Night." *Andrew Solomon*, 22 Apr. 2001, https://andrewsolomon.com/articles/the-longest-night/. Accessed 26 June 2024.

Solomon, Susan G. *The American Playground: Revitalizing Community Space.* University of New England Press, 2005.

The Singing Revolution. Directed by James Tusty and Maureen Castle Tusty, 2006. Documentary.

Tolan, Sandy. *Children of the Stone: The Power of Music in a Hard Land.* Bloomsbury, 2015.

Trainor, Laurel. J. "Lullabies and Playsongs: Why We Sing to Children." *Zero to Three*, vol. 23, no. 1, 2002, pp. 31-34.

Trehub, Sandra E., Jessica Becker, and Ian Morley. "Cross-Cultural Perspectives on Music and Musicality." *National Library of Medicine*, 19 Mar. 2015, https://www.ncbi.nlm.nih.gov/pmc/articles/PMC4321137/. Accessed 26 June 2024.

Trevarthen, Colwayn. & Malloch, Stephen. "Musicality and Music Before Three: Human Vitality and Invention Shared With Pride." *Zero to Three*, vol. 23, no. 1, 2002, pp. 8-10.

Turino, Thomas. "Four Fields of Music Making and Sustainable Living," *The World of Music*, vol. 51, no. 1, 2009, pp. 95–117.

Velez, Denise Oliver. "A Mandela Day Celebration of the Music That Helped Topple Apartheid." The Daily Kos, 18

July 2021,
https://www.dailykos.com/stories/2021/7/18/2039368/-A-Mandela-Day-celebration-of-the-music-that-helped-topple-apartheid. Accessed 21 Feb. 2025.

Warner, Andrea. *Rise Up and Sing: Power, Protest, and Activism in Music.* Greystone Books, 2024.

Weiss, George D. and Thiele, Bob. *What a Wonderful World.* Atheneum Books for Young Readers, 1995.

Weingarten, Gene. "The Time When Joshua Bell Went Busking in the Subway, and No-One Noticed." *The Washington Post*, 8 Apr. 2007, www.washingtonpost.com/lifestyle/magazine/pearls-before-breakfast/2014/01/08/8e7f748c-794c-11e3-af7f-13bf0e9965f6_story.html. Accessed 14 Apr. 2025.

Whitehead, Baruch. "We Shall Overcome: The Roles of Music in the US Civil Rights Movement," *Music and Conflict Transformation: Harmonies and Dissonances in Geopolitics,* edited by O. Urbian, I.B. Tauris, 2015, pp. 78-92.

Williams, Dar. *How to Write A Song That Matters.* Hachette, 2022.

Wong, Lisa. *Scales to Scalpels: Doctors Who Practice the Healing Arts of Music and Medicine,* Pegasus, 2013.

Young, Susan. "Seen but Not Heard: Young children, improvised singing and educational practice." *Contemporary Issues in Early Childhood*, vol. 7, no. 3, 2006, pp. 70-280.

Zur, Sara S. *Cultural Perspectives of Experienced Time: An Investigation into Children's Music Making as Manifested in*

Schools and Communities in Three Countries. Ed.D. diss., Columbia University, 2007. *ProQuest Dissertations and Theses Global*, no. 3269132.

Zur, Sara. S. (2007). "Letting Go of Data in Aboriginal Australia: Ethnography on "Rubber Time." *The Qualitative Report*, vol. 12, no. 4, 2007, pp. 583-593. https://doi.org/10.46743/2160-3715/2007.1614

Zur, Sara S. and Johnson-Green, Elissa. "Time to transition: The Connection Between Musical Free Play and School Readiness. *Childhood Education: Infancy Through the Early Years*, vol. 84, no. 5, 2008, pp. 295-300.

Zur, Sara S. "Questioning Universals: Children's Spontaneous Music Making in Israel." Paper presented at the Commission for Early Childhood Music Education, Ede, The Netherlands, 2016.

Zur, Sara S.. "I Got a Song Spark! Recording Young Children's Invented Songs." *Teaching Music*, vol. 31, no. 4, 2024, pp. 28-30.

"30 Takeaways from Futurist Amy Webb's Talk at SXSW." *Silicon Hills News*, 28 Mar. 2024, https://www.siliconhillsnews.com/2024/03/28/30-takeaways-from-futurist-amy-webbs-talk-at-sxsw-2024/.

Music References:

A Great Big World. *Glowing*, Particles, 2022.

Armstrong, Louis. "What a Wonderful World." *Louis and Friends*, Verve Records, 1967. CD.

Avery, Dawn, and Sarah Devol. *Wulankuntewaken*. Tulpe, Okenti Records, 2008.

Bock, Jerry, and Sheldon Harnick. *Fiddler on the Roof*, 1964.

Boublil, Alain, and Claude-Michel Schönberg. "Castle on a Cloud." *Les Misérables*, 1980.

Britten, Benjamin. *War Requiem*, Op. 66, 1961.

DiFranco, Ani. "Both Hands." *Ani DiFranco*, Righteous Babe Records, 1990. CD.

Franck, César. "Sonata for Violin and Piano in A Major." 1822.

Gershwin, George. *Rhapsody in Blue*, 1924.

Glykeria. "Tik Tik Tak." *World Playground: A Musical Adventure for Kids*, Putumayo Kids, 1999.

Lennon, John. "Imagine." *Imagine*, Apple Records, 1971.

Lyle, Graham, and Terry Britten. "What's Love Got to Do With It?" Recorded by Tina Turner for the album *Private Dancer*, 1984.

Mahler, Gustav. *Symphony No. 1, "Titan"*, 1887.

Makeba, Miriam. "Beware Verwoerd (Ndodemnyama)." *An Evening with Belafonte/Makeba*, SONY Records, 1965.

Morillo, Erick. "I Like to Move It." *Madagascar (Original Motion Picture Soundtrack)*, DreamWorks, 2005.

Pachelbel, Johann. "Canon in D, P37." 1680.

Pickett, Bobby "Boris," and The Crypt-Kickers. "Monster Mash." *The Original Monster Mash*, Garpax Records, 1962. LP.

Pinkfong. "Baby Shark." 2016. YouTube, https://www.youtube.com/watch?v=XqZsoesa55w.

Rachmaninoff, Sergei. *Piano Concerto No. 3 in D minor, Op. 30*, 1909.

Ravel, Maurice. *Piano Concerto for the Left Hand in D Major*, 1931.

Rodrigo, Olivia. "Driver's License." *SOUR*, Geffen, Interscope, 2021.

Schumann, Robert. "The Happy Farmer." In *Suzuki Violin School: Volume 1*, revised ed., performed by violin, edited by Shinichi Suzuki, Summy-Birchard, 2007, p. 22.

Schwartz, Stephen, composer and lyricist. "For Good." *Wicked: A New Musical: Original Broadway Cast Recording*, Decca Broadway, 2003.

Strauss II, Johann. *The Blue Danube Waltz, Op. 314*, 1867.

The Smashing Pumpkins. "Cherub Rock." *Siamese Dream*, Virgin Records America, Inc., 1993.

Traditional. "Down by the Bay." Popularized by Raffi, *Singable Songs for the Very Young*, Troubadour Records,

Taylor, James. "Sweet Baby James." *Sweet Baby James*, Warner Bros. Records, 1970. CD

"We Shall Overcome." Songs of the Civil Rights Movement, edited by Various Artists, Folkways Records, 1963.

Williams, Paul, and Kenneth Asher. "The Rainbow Connection." *Jim Henson's The Muppet Movie*, ITC Films, 1979.

www.ingramcontent.com/pod-product-compliance
Lightning Source LLC
Chambersburg PA
CBHW020036110726
47973CB00027B/272/J